Byron's
Politics

By the same author

Editor, Sarah Fielding, *The Adventures of David Simple* (O.U.P., 1969)

Editor, Thomas Otway, *Venice Preserved* (Nebraska U.P., 1969)

Editor, William Congreve, *Love for Love* (Ernest Benn, 1969)

Editor, Joseph Trapp, *Lectures on Poetry* (Scolar, 1973)

Editor, J. M. Synge, *The Playboy of the Western World* (Ernest Benn, 1975)

Christopher Marlowe (Brill, 1981)

Congreve: The Way of the World (Edward Arnold, 1981)

Editor, Joseph Trapp, *The Preface of the Aeneis* (Augustan Reprint Society, 1982)

Editor, John Cam Hobhouse, *A Trifling Mistake* (U.C.C.P., 1984)

Studying Drama (Edward Arnold, 1985)

Byron's Politics

Malcolm Kelsall

Professor of English
University College, Cardiff

THE HARVESTER PRESS · SUSSEX
BARNES & NOBLE BOOKS · NEW JERSEY

First published in Great Britain in 1987 by
THE HARVESTER PRESS LIMITED
Publisher: John Spiers
16 Ship Street, Brighton, Sussex
and in the USA by
BARNES & NOBLE BOOKS
81 Adams Drive, Totowa, New Jersey 07512

© Malcolm Kelsall, 1987

British Library Cataloguing in Publication Data
Kelsall, Malcolm
　　Byron's politics.
　　1. Byron, George Gordon Byron, *Baron*—
　　Criticism and interpretation
　　I. Title
　　821'.7　PR4388
ISBN 0-7108-0692-2

Library of Congress Cataloging-in-Publication Data
Kelsall, M. M. (Malcolm Miles), 1938-
　　Byron's politics.

　　Bibliography: p
　　Includes index.
　　1. Byron, George Gordon Byron, Baron, 1788-1824—
Political and social views.　2. Political poetry, English
—History and criticism.　3. Revolutionary poetry, English
—History and criticism.　I. Title.
PR4392.P64K4　1987　821'.7　86-28847
ISBN 0-389-20715-2

Typeset in 11/12 pt Garamond by Quality Phototypesetting Ltd.,
Bristol

Printed in Great Britain by Biddles Ltd., Guildford and King's Lynn

Contents

Acknowledgements

This book was conceived in Salzburg during the symposium on Byron, Poetry and Politics, in 1980. The annual postgraduate seminars on Romantic Writers and Politics at Cardiff aided the gestation. The labour of writing was made easier by the generous grant of a year's study leave by UCC.

The six essays which follow derive from the lively debates of the Cardiff seminars. The aim is to show Byron's roots in Whig tradition, and how he seeks to adapt that inheritance under the stress of contemporary events. In a short book the argument has been developed of necessity by selective instances, and there are parts of Byron's political life and writings which, therefore, are merely sketched. If the case that is made compels assent, however, then the extension of the same close textual and contextual scrutiny to Byron's work as a whole will produce the same conclusion. My aim has been not to write a large, comprehensive survey, but a cumulative series of essays which form a conceptual whole, and which are conceptually comprehensive.

In the bibliography of my short introduction to Byron in Scribner's *British Writers* series (New York, 1981) I list more fully than is possible here those works which are the fundamental and common heritage of all students of the poet. It has been my good fortune to know many of the recent authors personally. My debt of gratitude to the International Byron Society is immense. Since the notes to this book identify only immediate and major sources of reference, and do not quarry the archaeology of the subject, the names of many friends and colleagues are omitted with regret. For especial acts of courtesy and assistance, however, I thank John Clubbe, Terry Jones and Peter Vassallo.

The staff of the Inter-library Loans Department at UCC, and of the Cardiff Central Reference Library have cheerfully and diligently helped with the many requests I made of them.

Only three volumes of Jerome J. McGann's edition of Byron's *Complete Poetical Works* had appeared when this was written. Steffan and Pratts' edition of *Don Juan* has supplemented this, but the text used here is, of necessity, eclectic.

Cowbridge, 10 December 1985

1

Introduction

On 19 April 1824 Lord Byron died of fever at Missolonghi, and was taken up into the pantheon of those heroes who have given their lives for liberty. When the town was destroyed by the victorious Turks two years later, some claimed that the poet had been killed fighting in its defence. Byron and the town are symbolically present for the Romantic imagination in Delacroix's 'Greece on the Ruins of Missolonghi'. The pathetic hand supine beneath the ruins recalls for the civilised world the artist who died that men might be free; the mourning female figure of Greece suggests analogy with the familiar image of revolutionary France. 'I shall attempt to perform my duty towards this great man', wrote Mavrocordato, for the eyes of the London Greek Committee, 'the eternal gratitude of my country will perhaps be the only true tribute to his memory.'[1] The success of that endeavour may be testified by the sober claim of scholarship 120 years later that 'It was Byron . . . who morally re-armed the defeated and disunited little nation.'[2] For the nineteenth-century liberal and nationalist, Byron, by the splendour of his personal sacrifice, had given the sincerest testimony to the libertarian sentiments so often uttered in his verse:

> Yet, Freedom! Yet thy banner, torn but flying,
> Streams like the thunder-storm *against* the wind;
> Thy trumpet voice, though broken now and dying,
> The loudest still the tempest leaves behind . . .
> (*Childe Harold*, IV. 98)

1

It is a beautiful myth, but it has no part to play in these essays except as testimony to the political importance of Byron's poetry. The simple fact is that Byron, the man, failed at Missolonghi. The real British liberators of Greece were the guns of the fleet at Navarino. Byron also had failed as a Carbonaro in Italy, his revolutionary activity snuffed out before it had begun. His career as a would-be statesman in the House of Lords in London likewise terminated in nullity. The Chartists were to celebrate him as a friend of the people. In practical terms he achieved nothing for reform, and was the determined opponent of the very radical forces who selectively misread his poetry to support their cause. The life of Byron is of no political significance.

The essays that follow are cynical about Byronism—a Romantic phenomenon constructed by revolutionary enthusiasm. But Byron himself learnt to be cynical about politics: to distrust the application of ideology to explain the nature of political events; to recognise the limitations of men or policies to affect the process of history. The ineffectiveness of a life of action does not invalidate political writing, as the example of Machiavelli may indicate. But the development of those ways of writing about events which are called Byronic are the product of failure and frustration. They are also inherently part of a wider movement and experience of thwarted opposition which it is too indefinite to call 'Romantic'. For Byron was the inheritor of the traditions of one of the main political philosophies which has shaped British history: that of the patrician Whigs, the revolutionaries of 1688 to whose order by rank, if not directly by wealth or birth, he belonged. That great tradition was in crisis; so too was the political party that claimed to embody the tradition. The pressures were immense, and the issues of the greatest importance. The 'Byronic' is in part created by the ideology of the Whigs under stress. Byron's writing is also an imaginative attempt both to express the limits, and harness the energy, of Whig experience at that moment in history. It is there that the political significance of the man as writer is to be found.

Let us lay aside the intoxicating myth of Greek liberation and consider a few hydroptic facts. The life of the poet may be briefly reviewed as political context for the verse. Byron was one year old when the Bastille fell. It was an event of which he could have no recollection. The enthusiasm of the 1790s—'bliss was it in that dawn to be alive'—was no part of his experience and finds no reflection in his verse. He came to maturity during the period of post-revolutionary reaction. His life and the war with France are correspondent. If there was a period of youthful enthusiasm—'to be young was very paradise'—it may have found its hero in the First Consul. It is reported anecdotally how he fought for his bust of Napoleon at Harrow.

There would have been no need for such contention in a great Whig household such as Uppark. Its dining room is decorated with the busts of Napoleon, Charles James Fox and the Duke of Bedford. There were many Whig sympathisers for the new force in Europe which shook despots from their thrones, and established liberal constitutions among the freed nations. By 1814–15 little of such hopeful idealism could survive. The fall of the 'Anakim of Anarchy' as he now called him, the 'Pagod', Emperor of France,[3] distressed Byron because a great captain did not conduct himself like a great man. There was no one remaining to whom to dedicate a poetic Eroica. Abroad: the restoration of the *ancien régime;* at home: economic recession and repression: the Luddite riots, Peterloo, the suspension of Habeas Corpus, the Six Acts—these are the events of Byron's mature years. Liberal constitutional movements in the Iberian peninsula, and the Italic, were snuffed out. Had Ibrahim Pasha been given a free hand, the same might have happened in Greece. Byron scarcely survived Castlereagh. 'Toryism' at home and in Europe secured and resumed its power. Shelley wrote in the preface to *The Revolt of Islam* that this was an 'age of despair'. Lord John Russell preferred a term he drew from Hume on the British Constitution: he feared the final 'euthanasia'[4] of free institutions. A later Whig historian offered the word 'stagnation'.[5] The attitude of Marxist historians to the government of Perceval and Liverpool has been unreservedly hostile. Such is the general context in which Byron pursued his unprofitable political life.

A career in politics was the natural aspiration for a young aristocrat who saw his natural talents as oratorical and martial. 'The poet yields to the Orator,' he wrote.[6] The *cursus honorum* began in the usual way: Harrow, Cambridge, the Grand Tour, the House of Lords. At Cambridge he was a member of a Whig club, his fellow members in a small and intimate circle, men like the Duke of Devonshire, Lord Tavistock, John Cam Hobhouse (the future MP for Fox's former constituency, Westminster), Douglas Kinnaird (who also thought of himself as a successor to Fox). Byron hesitated about committing himself to party politics, for like many of his class he prided himself on his independence, but he would never abandon his principles, he wrote.[7] His natural centre of gravity was 'the buff and blue' of Whig tradition, to which, as late as *Don Juan,* he still declared his commitment.[8] By 1812 he was taken up by Holland House and by Lady Oxford. His speeches in the Lords upon the conciliation of industrial unrest, on Catholic emancipation, and on the liberty of the subject to petition for parliamentary reform, are all upon major issues of Whig party politics.

This early political activity needs little further exposition. It has been examined in detail by David Erdman.[9] To Erdman one may add Marchand.[10] The seriousness of Byron's interest is not in doubt. In 1809, before embarking on the Grand Tour, he had attended the Lords seven times in March, April and May. The list of essential reading he drew up included the parliamentary debates from the Whig revolution of 1688 to 1742. On his return to Britain, and to sudden fame as a poet, he attended the Lords twenty-four times between January and July 1812, including all major debates, and also the minor work of committees. He was present at Earl Fitzwilliam's motion concerning Ireland, at the debate on the Orders of Council, at Lord Boringdon's motion for an efficient administration, at Wellington's motion on Roman Catholic claims, even at a debate on the leather tax. He was still a regular attender in the spring and summer of 1813, and was present at Wellesley's motion on the Peninsula Wars, at debates upon the naval administration, the war with America and the treaty with Sweden.

At Holland House, he would have been introduced to the hagiography of the great dead Whig leader Charles James Fox, Lord Holland's uncle and mentor. By way of Lady Oxford, he moved towards the more radical ambience of Sir Francis Burdett and Horne Tooke. Sheridan, Byron's friend, was the familiar acquaintance of the Prince Regent. He visited Leigh Hunt in jail (his future collaborator on the political journal *The Liberal*), imprisoned for libel on the Regent.

At the same time, he turned his talent as a poet to the service of politics. *The Waltz,* published anonymously, flippantly satirised the country as prostituted to Germanic corruption; *The Curse of Minerva* (eight copies published privately) warned of revolution at home; *An Ode to the Framers of the Frame-Bill* published anonymously in the Whig *The Morning Chronicle,* also warned of domestic riot; *The Lines to a Lady Weeping* (anonymously in the same newspaper) criticised the Regent's defection from the Whigs. When the lines were acknowledged at the publication of *The Corsair* (a poem, which by implication, links Turkish tyranny in Greece with British rule in Ireland), the government press turned on Byron with a savagery not to be matched again until his withdrawal from England in 1816. *The Devil's Drive* was too scurrilous politically to print, so too was *Windsor Poetics,* a libel on the Regent.

Such is the evidence for political commitment. It is substantial. 'Ambition was my idol', wrote Byron, reviewing his life in the first canto of *Don Juan,* and by ambition he meant the desire to shine upon the great stage of public affairs, for his own initials N.B. to carry a weight of importance equal perhaps to those of another broken idol, Napoleon Bonaparte. Byron's early years in Parliament have for his politics something of the same significance as Swift's in the last years of Queen Anne. To pursue this biographical survey further, however, would be merely to repeat familiar material.

The word 'Whig' has been introduced into this sketch in place of the usual term of literary criticism, 'Romantic'. Byron, wrote Carl Woodring,[11] was a 'Foxite Whig', but the brevity of Woodring's fine essay precluded definition of the term. What was it to be a Whig lord, and a Whig poet in the second decade of the nineteenth century? The dates, for the party, as for its acolyte, indicate a period when positive liberal hope was difficult to sustain. Of the great Whig figures of the eighteenth century, Fox and the apostate Burke were dead; Sheridan was in a drunken dotage; Erskine, Grey, Mackintosh had declined into the caution of years. The party had dwindled in the 1790s and compromised itself by brief coalition during the war. The allegation of 'apostasy', which Hobhouse bitterly threw at them in the Westminster election of 1819, was common, and Lord John Russell was still writing apologetics as late as 1823. They lost the chance of office in 1812. Throughout Byron's adult life the Whigs were excluded from government. That grouping of the ruling class to which the hostile term 'Tory' was applied, held power as if by hereditary right. To these issues it will be necessary to return in more detail later.

The heroic age of the Whig party was past, or rather the *two* heroic periods of resistance, that of opposition to the Stuarts, and the period from 'Wilkes and Liberty' to Erskine's great defences of consitutional freedom against Pitt in the 1780s and 1790s. To this latter period—so important in *The Vision of Judgment*—Byron looked back through his early familiarity with figures like Erskine himself, Mackintosh and Sheridan. On 6 March 1814, Erskine gave him 'his famous pamphlet, [*On the Causes and Consequences of the War with France* (1797)] with a marginal note and corrections in his handwriting. 'Sent it to be bound superbly, and shall treasure it.' On the 20th he added, 'Any thing in his handwriting will be a treasure, which will gather compound interest from years.' The same day Erskine told him that Mackintosh (an early defender of the Revolution in France), was now writing a history of the English revolution of 1688: 'Undoubtedly it must be a classic, when finished,' Byron commented. On 10 March he dined with Mackintosh and Sheridan, and despised 'my own little prattlement. Much of old times—Horne Tooke—the Trials [of the 1780s–1790s]— evidence of Sheridan, and anecdotes of those times when *I,* alas! was an infant.' He concludes, 'If I had been a man, I would have made an English Lord Edward Fitzgerald', the Irish patriot who died in armed opposition to the Tory government. History was to give him his opportunity at Missolonghi.

The tone of youthful enthusiasm in such utterances is self-evident. If it is 'Romantic', it is on behalf of famous Whig men and issues. The allusions to the heroic age of the late eighteenth century require explanation now for anyone except an historian. We are no longer reared upon the mythology of the Whig interpretation of history. Its foundations were to be the subject of Mackintosh's forthcoming (and uncompleted) 'classic': the Glorious Revolution of 1688—the subject also of Fox's unfinished *A History of the Early Part of the Reign of James the Second,* and the basis of Russell's *History of the English Government and Constitution* (1823). It was in the 1680s that the Whigs emerged as a significant political force, and as the victors in the struggle against the prerogative of the Crown (and the Tories) the party, like many victorious revolutionary movements, laid down its own account of history. From Macaulay to Treveleyan that interpretation was to be dominant—but that is subsequent history. For Mackintosh,

Russell, in opposition, was on the defensive.

Only a sketch can be offered of this Whig tradition to which Byron paid such enthusiastic testimony. But it is necessary if the poet is to be restored to history from the miasma of an indefinable and shifting Romanticism. The inadequacies of the survey which follows are freely acknowledged. To reduce the intricacies of political alignment and personal relationship to a number of broad general principles gives to events an ideological logic which they do not possess. To concentrate only upon Whig discourse runs the risk of yielding to the myth that the Whigs were the only true friends of 'freedom'. Hume, Scott and Southey might readily be brought in on the other side to scotch Whig 'cant political'. But the concern with Whig discourse is not whether it is true or false. It is with attitudes and vocabulary. This was a way of looking at history which Byron inherited; these were the kind of words men he admired used. Our concern, later, will be the way the poet viewed his inheritance.

The record is conditioned further by the need to centre upon concerns relevant to Byron. The emphasis is upon 'arms and the man' because he is the writer of the 'Song for the Luddites' and *Marino Faliero;* whose hero, Don Juan, might have met death as an Anarchasis Cloots in the French Revolution, and who, himself, admired Lord Edward Fitzgerald and conveyed arms for the Carbonari and the Hellenes. The cult of opposition, the rhetoric of resistance, found a potent source of inspiration in the testament of the revolution of 1688. But great swards of Whig political experience are also omitted: economic reform for example. It is not pertinent to this argument that American example was recommended on the grounds of financial good housekeeping! The historian who knows the work of Michael Roberts and Austin Mitchell[12] may justifiably complain that the impressionistic images, and heated passages of Whig discourse which follow, are a long way from the mundane day-to-day frustrations of opposition politicians. They are equally distant from the school of E.P. Thompson. I ask the indulgence of a little patience. There will be place for the other things. This initial survey seeks to go no further than to trace the origins of certain Byronic attitudes, and to explain why a discontented lord in 1812 found temporary home within the party of the Glorious Revolution, and why, until his death, he maintained his loyalty to its traditions.

An image may be more expressive than words. The revolution of 1688 is still written visibly across the face of the English countryside. Its emblems are the great Palladian and neo-Gothic houses of the aristocracy. When Byron chose to show the centre of power in British society in *Don Juan* he invented a political house party in Norman Abbey, a building modelled upon his own Newstead Abbey. The grandeur and the diffusion of these great houses are signs of the spread of power away from the centralised autocracy, which, in Whig opinion, characterised the monarchies of Europe and Toryism. The highest artistic expressions of that culture reside in landscaped parks, in libraries rich in many tongues, in picture and sculpture galleries, even in the very charm of fields enclosed by powerful landlords whose sense of the aesthetic united with a desire for improvement and profit. Culture and politics are related. Charles James Fox's long series of letters to his nephew, Byron's future mentor Lord Holland, characteristically discuss as part of a continuum a nice point of classical grammar, the choice of pictures, the Revolution in France, the latest affairs of the House of Commons. The destiny of birth called the responsible man of classical education to great office (and possibly, great reward) in public service.

The great debates in Parliament manifest a power of principled argument, a richness of eloquence and a depth of culture never surpassed. Nor was this a Venetian oligarchy, it was claimed. There was no golden book in which the names of the great were perpetually inscribed. Instead, a rudimentary democracy took up men like Burke, Sheridan and Moore, and would readily have found a place for the impoverished owner of Newstead Abbey. Private property in the form of 'rotten boroughs' provided immediate entry to high responsibility for the indigent or for young talent. But the possession of property, it was argued, was the guarantee of that educated commitment to the state which distinguished the patriot. The immense wealth, the great power of patronage, the advanced intellectual enquiry of the ruling class have been painted with the sympathetic brilliance of one nurtured in that very tradition, in Lord David Cecil's *The Young Melbourne*. Byron's own portrait in *Don Juan* is more sceptical.

This visible reminder of the wealth and power of the aristocracy to which Lord Byron belonged, is made initially because Whig ideology chose to distinguish itself from Toryism as if there were a fundamental divide between them. Hence Macaulay's famous depiction in the third chapter of his *History* of the ignorant Tory squirearchy and the petty provincial clergy quaintly clinging to exploded notions of passive obedience, Divine Right, and a touching loyalty to the Stuart cause. Addison had used the same strategy more than a century before. But Hobhouse, fighting Westminster in 1819, claimed to see no difference between Whig and Tory. Both were patrician parties of privilege, opposed to reform, engaged in endless parliamentary movement between the 'Ins' and the 'Outs'.[13] Remove the ideological rhetoric which sought to divide Whig from Tory, and one has in reality a self-perpetuating aristocratic oligarchy. Between 1688 and the Reform Act of 1832, British government was aristocratic. That truism, for Lord Byron's politics, is as important as nice enquiry between the policies of the young Pitt and the young Fox (both of whom the poet equally praised after their death), or the determination of how the Grenvillite wing of Grey's Whigs differed, if at all, from the Tories in 1812.

The caveat must be granted. But the concern of this sketch is the *ideal* face of Whig history; the way a patrician party would *wish* to be seen. The historians claimed that the party came into being in an heroic act of aristocratic resistance in defence of the liberties of the people. It was a party born in opposition to the power of the Crown. The great revolutionary achievement was the prevention of the extension of Stuart prerogative in the 1680s which threatened the very basis of the Constitution. As Burnet tells the story, only when the Constitution itself was threatened was recourse to arms justified. This resistance was a fundamental right. But the achievement of the revolutionaries was to restore the rule of law. The Crown took its proper place within the Constitution, subject to the rule of law, and as part of a balance within the state of King, Lords and Commons. Within that balance the historic destiny of the Whig aristocracy was to act as 'friends of the people', and to redress the balance between the extremes; the Crown and the people.

This laconic summary needs fuller exposition to be relevant to Lord Byron. But even in the summary, certain Byronic terms already emerge. 'I was born for opposition,' he wrote.[14] That too was the function of the party: to resist the power of the Crown. The noble poet's opposition to the 'legitimate' crowned heads of

Europe is notably expressed in some of his most fervent verse. That opposition was in defence of 'liberty': *in extremis* it involved the act of armed resistance. The Philhellenes made that choice. They fought as friends of 'the people'. So too in the 1680s would have Algernon Sydney and William, Lord Russell.

Abraham Kriegel, in his examination of Whig ideology in the early nineteenth century,[15] has noted how often the leaders of the party appealed to 'liberty'; indeed, how fervent were the assertions of Brougham, Fox, Grey, Holland, Mackintosh. Fox 'dedicated his life to the defence of liberty,' Mackintosh wrote to Holland. It was a course Burke urged as arising from 'generosity of spirit', which moved in Russell a sense of 'love' and 'ennobled' the career of Fox. 'The nobility of England' were urged in Parliament to lead 'their countrymen in the battles of liberty'. When the memory of a Russell or a Sydney 'shall cease to be an object of respect and veneration,' wrote Fox of the opposition to James II, 'it requires no spirit of prophecy to foretell that English liberty will be fast approaching to its final consummation.'[16] The fear of the party was that such an era might not be far distant.

Fox's *History* of James II defines the position. Its defence of liberty establishes many of the principles of 1688. It tells of the function of the Whigs to defend the 'natural rights' of the people, and at times even 'boldly (perhaps rashly)' to redress the people's grievances and to oppose 'arbitrary tribunals' by appeal to ancient legal and constitutional principles. This was the same 'spirit of liberty which had animated and rendered illustrious the ancient republics' of Athens, Sparta and Rome, and justifies, thus, his interpretation of the Constitution of England as in some measure republican. In the context of his own age, Fox insists on showing that such republicanism was never Jacobinical. On the contrary, the party depended for its success on 'the ancient families and great landed proprietors' who stood in opposition to 'the tools of a king plotting against his people'. He compares with Toryism,

the ministers of a free government acting upon enlarged principles, and with energies which no state that is not in some degree republican can supply. How forcibly must the contemplation of these men . . . teach persons engaged in political life, that a free and popular government is desirable, not only for the public good, but for their own greatness and consideration, for every object of generous ambition.

With feeling, in the tradition of Burnet, he moves pity and admiration for those whose 'unremitting jealousy of the power of the Crown' led to their martyrdom 'out-numbered and discomforted by persecution'. The list extends from the least to the greatest: a young Scottish girl drowned by the evil process of law and servile Ministers; Monmouth 'enamoured of those principles of justice, benevolence, and equality, which form the true creed of the party'; and that 'great man', Argyle, who slept calmly before his execution while a courtier, desirous of 'some vain title, or . . . some increase in wealth', writhed in 'excruciating torture' on his bed. The Whig Fox's 'book of martyrs' draws the moral, 'May the like happy serenity in such dreadful circumstances, and a death equally glorious, be the lot of all whom tyranny, of whatever denomination or description, shall in any age, or in any country, call to expiate their virtues on the scaffold.'[17] From such principles it followed that Whigs (like Byron) were sympathetic to other Foxite martyrs: witness Lord Edward Fitzgerald.

A party founded in opposition to the Crown needed to maintain the idea of Stuart resurgence as an aid to self-definition. In 1715 and 1745 that task was easy. But from an early date any patrician opposition was likely to polarise politics between the adherents of the Crown, who threatened a resurgent Toryism, and those 'patriots' who supported the true interests of the country and the Constitution against the Court. It is a paradox of Whig politics that the language of opposition frequently has a republican ring because opposed to the Crown, and yet, in defending 'the Constitution' insists on the existence of the monarchy as part of the proper 'balance' of the state. The American Revolution is more logical in this respect than the English, with its republican tripartite balance of President, Senate and House of Representatives—an idea in its ultimate origins derived from Aristotle and Polybius. In practice, in the eighteenth century, opposition to the Crown gathers round the heir to the throne—the 'reversionary' interest—as an alternative source of patronage. In Byron's lifetime the Prince Regent for decades served this function, and during the first Regency crisis one finds the Whigs suddenly arguing for an increase in the powers of their man, and the Tories arguing for a limitation of prerogative. In the second crisis, that which involved Byron in 1812, the virulence of the Whig attack on the Regent (witness Byron's verses) is the product of disappointed hope, for the Prince abandoned his former friends. The reversionary interest then gathered round the female members of the family. Byron's *Lines to a Lady Weeping*, and the lament of 'Freedom's Heart' for the Princess Charlotte in *Childe Harold IV* is part of that pattern.

For the *principles* of opposition to the Crown at this time one may turn to Burke's *Thoughts on the Cause of the Present Discontents* (1770):

> The power of the Crown, almost dead and rotten as Prerogative, has grown up anew, with much more strength, and far less odium, under the name of Influence.[18]

By 'Influence', Burke means the award of place and pension by an administration to its adherents, and the use of wealth and power to buy seats and men. As Walpole was claimed to have said, 'All men have their price'. The classic formulation of the issue was John Dunning's, in the motion passed in the House of Commons (1780):

> The power of the Crown has increased, is increasing, and ought to be diminished.

It is a commonplace. In Byron's circle one may find Thomas Moore elaborating upon the issue at length in *Corruption and Intolerance* (1808):

> In the disposal of an immense revenue and the extensive patronage annexed to it, the first foundations of this power of the Crown were laid; the innovation of a standing army at once increased and strengthened it, and the few slight barriers which the Act of Settlement opposed to its progress have all been gradually removed . . . 'till at length this spirit of influence has become the vital principle of the State—an agency, subtle and unseen, which pervades every part of the Constitution, lurks under all its forms and regulates all its movements.

The proof of the effectiveness of that corruption was provided by George III's destruction of Whig power in 1784; it was confirmed by the interference of the Crown in the fall of All the Talents on the Catholic emancipation issue in 1807; it emerged again when the Prince Regent, the declared admirer of Fox, ratted on his friends in 1812. The administration's view, of course, was different. The

Whigs had neither the policies nor the men to make a government which commanded the support of Parliament.

The fundamental opposition to the Crown extended naturally to the interpretation of events in America, whose colonists were in the position of the Whigs of 1688, and then to the early stages of the Revolution in France. Louis XVI's hostility to constitutional government was true to type. So, too, was the interference of the crowned heads of Europe. The partition of Poland, the 'barbaric' Brunswick manifesto, the invasion of France, corrupted the course of revolution. At the end of the long years of war, for Byron's generation of Whigs, the restoration of the Bourbons on the bayonets of the allies, the Congress of 'legitimate' monarchs at Vienna, the suppression of constitutional movements in Spain and Italy, all still testified in gross form to the evil of the unchecked influence of monarchy. For the Whig, the international conspiracy of monarchical governments (the Holy Alliance), was the counterpart to the ubiquitious Jacobinical agitators the Tories everywhere suspected. *The Edinburgh Review* (1818) wrote of the Tories that they

> will yield nothing of the patronage of the Crown; and, until forced, they will lessen none of the people's burdens. They are friendly to large military establishments; patrons of arbitrary power abroad . . . At home, they undervalue the rights of the people, and carelessly treat the most sacred points of the constitution . . . (LIX. 204-5)

The expression 'until forced' may serve to introduce that fundamental principle of opposition to the Crown in the defence of freedom: the famous 'right of resistance': 'I will not submit to arbitrary power, while there remains any alternative to vindicate my freedom', declared Fox on 23 November 1795, speaking on the repressive Treason and Sedition Bills. It was a measure he had described on 17 November as introduced by a Jacobite administration intent upon cutting up the Bill of Rights and threatening the very basis of the Constitution. The allusion to 1688 was clear. He warned the government 'that resistance, in certain circumstances, was impossible to be avoided'. His opponents accused him of raising anarchy. But it was the Tories who provoked by oppression. In a choice of dangers a man might need to forfeit life and property. He admitted, as a member of the

Legislature this was not a 'direct and practical maxim', but he trusted that 'the people of England would not tamely surrender their indisputable and hereditary right, whatever inclination an arbitrary minister or a supercilious prelate might betray, to wrest them out of their possession'. 'If the constitution were threatened it would, indeed, be a case of extremity alone which could justify resistance, and the only question would be, whether that resistance was prudent.'[19]

The speech of 23 November was notorious. Southey recalled it as late as January 1817 in his *Quarterly Review* essay on 'The Rise and Progress of Popular Disaffection':

> Resistance, according to the memorable declaration of Mr. Fox, must always be considered by such men as a question of prudence; they are held to their allegiance by a cable of which one weak strand is uncut—when the first gale commences it will part. (XXXII, 518)

In 1819, at the time of Peterloo, Hobhouse referred again to the same speech, and for asking what prevented the people marching on Parliament, was despatched to Newgate.[20] The Tories would deny Fox any prevarication. Resistance—that 'most holy of duties' in La Fayette's phrase—is hedged about by Fox with 'certain circumstances', if 'prudent', if provoked in 'the people' (not Fox) by the Tories. It is a 'general principle' he was defending, he said, and by 3 December forced on to the defensive, he excused himself by arguing that he had not *recommended* resistance, either active or passive, but if other persons were determined upon resistance, it was passive he would recommend.

This is hot rhetoric, followed by cold. But the events of 1688 had been carried through by force of arms, even though the constitutional fiction was that James had abdicated. The familiar Whig toast, 'Our Sovereign, the People', sounded revolutionary, even on the lips of the Duke of Norfolk. The cause of 'Wilkes and Liberty' had been sustained by tumultuary demonstration on the streets of London. 'The principle of resistance', wrote Byron's mentor Lord Holland, is that 'to which our Constitution owes its stability, if not its origin, and on the acknowledgement of which all free Governments whatever must ultimately depend.'[21]

In fact, the right of resistance was written into that very Constitution, in so far as Blackstone's *Commentaries* express an entity more often evoked than precisely defined. In his chapter 'On the Absolute Rights of Individuals' he lists personal security, personal liberty (as represented by Habeas Corpus), the right of property, and as the safeguard of these rights the existence of Parliament, the limitation of prerogative, the courts of justice, the right to petition, and ultimately the right to bear arms, 'a public allowance under due restrictions of the natural right of resistance and self-preservation'. De Lolme in his more popular account of the Constitution cites the same principle.

Attacking the government over Peterloo on 29 August 1819, *The Examiner* appealed to Blackstone and De Lolme, reminding the Tories of the *last* appeal of the people 'to the right of having and using arms for self-preservation and defence'. If Byron's fellow journalist Hunt is not a witness of sufficient weight, one might turn instead to the sober legal authority of the great Whig champion of the people, Erskine, in the Constructive Treason trials. He defended the Dean of St Asaph from the charge of seditious libel. The Dean had promulgated the revolutionary doctrines of Sir William Jones, among which was the right of the free citizen to preserve that freedom by keeping a 'strong firelock in the corner of his bedroom'. Erskine appealed to revolution's Bill of Rights itself. He went further. In a typically dramatic gesture, he asked if the Court would proceed against him as advocate—'So say I' was the challenge the Whig threw down to the government.

That kind of Whig rhetoric, in its kinetic energy, is very far from the philosophy of Locke from which it may ultimately derive. To the Tories it seemed too readily to provoke the violence of the mob. In Hume's great history the Whigs are attacked as popular demagogues, infatuating and corrupting the people by courting their favour, pandering to their folly and rage, encouraging calumny, provoking violence, and tampering with the record of history itself. After the outbreak of the French Revolution this charge became of greater urgency, and the disintegration of the party as a political force will be considered more fully in this context. But seen from an ideal position, Erskine's appeal to arms, within the framework of the law, is expressive of the best traditions of the party. The purpose of resistance was to defend the law: the fundamental rights of the ancient Constitution of the realm. These rights were enshrined in certain documents: Magna Carta, the 'palladium' of the British Constitution (as Erskine called it);

Habeas Corpus—which Byron wrote in *Beppo* that he loved as a freeborn Englishman; the Bill of Rights. Certain major historical events made these issues dramatically clear; Hampden's refusal of the illegal demand of ship money; the acquittal of the seven Bishops under James's tyranny. They had exercised their fundamental right of petitioning the Crown. Tyranny had arbitrarily sought to imprison them. The uncorrupted British law had released them and the applause of a supportive people heralded their triumph in the streets of London. To come closer to Byron's age, one might instance too General Washington—'before whom all borrowed greatness sinks into insignificance',[22] as Fox said; Grattan, helping to form the armed Irish volunteers, in order to secure for Ireland her own free Parliament; Erskine, his coach drawn in triumph by the people through the streets of London, having secured in the Courts of Law Thomas Hardy's right to petition for parliamentary reform. On that coach Erskine later inscribed the motto 'Trial by Jury' as testimony to his success (and Fox's) in securing freedom of speech through the law.

It is a sign of a great shift of opinion that whereas all students of the 1790s will read Paine, few now turn to Erskine. But the great speeches at the trials of the Dean of St Asaph, Frost, Hardy, Stockdale, represent one of the high water marks of Whig idealism. They combine the most penetrating and astute understanding of the process of law, with a passionate expression of the principles of freedom. It is heartening to consider Erskine in triumph, before turning from this summary of principles to the crisis of the party under the pressure of events which threatened to overwhelm it. At one time the 'beauties' of Erskine were anthologised. Perhaps the most famous passage of all was that upon the oppressed Indian in the defence of Stockdale. Its Byronic quality needs no emphasis.

'The same being who gave you a country on the other side of the waters . . . gave ours to us; and by this title we will defend it', said the warrior, throwing down his tomahawk upon the ground, and raising the war-sound of his nation.—These are the feelings of subjugated men all round the globe; and depend upon it, nothing but fear will control where it is vain to look for affection.[23]

The great peroration in the same trial is equally stirring. It merits extended quotation, for it is the voice of an age in which Byron wished he had been a man. In isolation it sounds 'Romantic'. In context, it is the justification in general terms of the principles of liberty on which Erskine's detailed legal argument had been based. The specific issue, in fact, was Stockdale's right to publish John Logan's *A Review of the Principal Charges Against Warren Hastings.* The Byronic sentiments are those of a future Lord Chancellor and member of the Greek Committee.

> It is the nature of every thing that is great and useful, both in the animate and inanimate world, to be wild and irregular—and we must be contented to take them with the alloys which belong to them, or live without them. Genius breaks from the fetters of criticism, but its wanderings are sanctioned by its majesty and wisdom, when it advances in its path;—subject it to the critic, and you tame it into dulness.—Mighty rivers break down their banks in the winter, sweeping away to death the flocks which are fattened on the soil that they fertilize in the summer; the few may be saved by embankments from drowning, but the flock must perish for hunger.—Tempests occasionally shake our dwellings and dissipate our commerce; but they scourge before them the lazy elements, which without them would stagnate into pestilence.—In like manner, Liberty herself, the last and best gift of God to his creatures, must be taken just as she is;—you might pare her down into bashful regularity, and shape her into a perfect model of severe scrupulous law, but she would then be Liberty no longer; and you must be content to die under the lash of this inexorable justice which you had exchanged for the banners of Freedom.[24]

One may understand why Byron wished that he had been a man at such a time. But even as Erskine secured his triumphs in the courts, the party to which he belonged was disintegrating. He himself, as his legal career came to fruition later, was to be particularly singled out as an apostate. Byron's commitment to Whig principle was to be an ultimate guarantee of failure and frustration. Whig discourse must be related more closely to specific historic events to perceive what went wrong.

*   *   *

On 2 June 1780 the Duke of Richmond had planned to bring in a motion for parliamentary reform. His argument was for universal suffrage and annual parliaments. As the Whig historian Lecky tells the story, 'no serious discussion was possible. Pale, bruised, and agitated, with their wigs torn off, their hair dishevelled, their clothes torn and bespattered with mud, the peers of England sat listening to the frantic yells of the multitude who already thronged the lobbies.'[25] Lord Mansfield, seventy-six years old, and the Bishop of Lincoln barely escaped with their lives. Mansfield's house was looted later, and his great law library destroyed. The issue on which the violence unfolded was not the Duke of Richmond's Bill, but opposition to proposed measures of Roman Catholic relief. Until the night of 7 June, substantial areas of London were in the hands of an uncontested mob which looted, burnt and drank itself into directionless violence.

The French Revolution is so much more important than the Gordon riots that their parallel significance may be missed. The Whigs, as champions of liberty, chose to describe themselves as 'the friends of the people'. It was part of the 'entailed inheritance' of the aristocracy (Burke's phrase) and the proper duty of 'men of education and property' (Holland's words).[26] But a drunken mob had no nicety of distinction between the chivalrous sense of honour of their Whig guardians, and the encroaching prerogative of the Crown. Nothing may more simply illustrate the divide between 'the people' and their 'friends' than the conduct at this time of John Wilkes (a crucial figure in *The Vision of Judgment*). No one had more astutely employed the forces of the masses to resist 'tyranny' in his famous defence of the right of the electors of Middlesex to choose him as their Member. He was a champion of the freedom of the press; the enemy of the increasing power of the Crown. Now, armed, he was among the most vigorous and courageous in quelling the very rioters many of whom must earlier have been his supporters. 'You call the people a mob . . .', Byron accused the Tories in 1812, but the distinction is crucial in Whig discourse. At what point does the defence of 'rational liberty' (as Burke called it), by 'the people' degenerate into the excesses of 'the mob'?

No better argument against giving power to 'the people' can be envisaged than the conduct of 'the mob' in 1780. Their mythic image continued to haunt the imagination as late as Dickens's *Barnaby Rudge*. The Terror in France confirmed the danger which faced a state when the mob became institutionalised as the sole arbiter of power. A writer like Paine gave to the Yahoo a tincture of reason. The mob was supplied with arguments for subversion.

Our concern is with the frustration of the Whigs, not with the arguments of 'the Tories'. But if their frustration, and Byron's, is to be understood, it is necessary to eject any subsequent history of democratic 'progress' from our minds, however one might define that progress: the growth of freedom from precedent to precedent; the extension of the franchise; the growth of responsible trade unionism; the diffusion of education—whatever commonplaces seem right in general now, and thus whatever writers *then* who seem to point forward: Paine and Cobbett, Shelley and Wollstonecraft. Instead, one must imagine Parliament in the hands of a mob. There is no police force; law is ineffective; the possession of property is the provocation to plunder. London is burning. One may then appreciate the force of the following passage from a Byronic ambience:

> What prevents the people from walking down to the House and pulling out the members by the ears, and locking up their doors, and flinging the key into the Thames? Is it any majesty which hedges in the members of that assembly? Do we love them? Not at all—we have an instinctive horror at the very abstract idea of a boroughmonger. Do we respect them? Not in the least: Do we regard them as endowed with any superior qualities? On the contrary, individually there is scarcely a poorer creature than your mere member of parliament; though in his corporate capacity the earth furnishes not so absolute a bully.[27]

The writer is Hobhouse, already cited in general as an advocate of the 'right of resistance'. The issue was Peterloo, and he was accusing Erskine of being lukewarm and apostate on the matter. To understand the threat of the passage, and why Hobhouse was imprisoned, one must forget the canonical place Peterloo now occupies in the history of freedom, and recall Gordon and Robespierre.

The matter is described in a way a Whig might call 'alarmist'. But one cannot approach the impact of the French Revolution upon Whig thought without recognising the fear of the violence of 'the people' transformed into 'the mob' in English society (of whose violence, the Gordon riots are merely the most spectacular and influential instance). Lord Sheffield, retrospectively, put the case for those former supporters of freedom who took alarm:

> I am fully convinced that if our Good Old Island had been drawn into the torrent of the new philosophy, Holland, Germany, Spain, etc., would

have followed her, and we should have seen all Europe involved in the extravagances of irreligion, immorality, anarchy and barbarism . . .. The devastation of the Species might be repaired, and at the end of a couple of centuries it is possible that Science, the fine Arts, and the politeness and gentleness of Society might again have been brought to the point at which they now are. Perhaps you may recollect that on the Decline and Fall of the Roman Empire a greater number of centuries was necessary for restoration. I really believe there is nothing exaggerated in this speculation.[28]

Sheffield is concerned with the collapse of civilisation—and if by civilisation one means the great patrician country-house society of 'Norman Abbey', then the Terror might serve as confirmation for Sheffield as it did for Burke. The force of this fear reads as real. One had to choose sides. Pitt warned Grey and the Whigs that 'anarchy and confusion' were 'worse, if possible, than despotism itself'.[29]

In that confrontation between 'anarchy' and 'despotism' ('the mob' and 'the Crown') the middle ground became almost untenable. A Whig sympathiser with the Revolution in France had to find a way between; a means of neutralising a very genuine fear. The Foxite method, it has been shown earlier, was to relate things back to the principles of 1688. A new phenomenon, therefore, was to be referred to the paradigm of the familiar and canonised, albeit improved with the further experience of America in mind. Here, in France, was another 'Resurrection of Freedom' (to adopt the subtitle of Barry's famous Whig print: *The Phoenix*). In this context it is worth completing Fox's praise of Washington already quoted in part. He was a man 'before whom all borrowed greatness sinks into insignificance, and all the potentates of Europe (excepting the members of our own royal family) become little and contemptible'. That monarchial parenthesis is not ironic. Fox was committed to a 'balanced' Constitution: 'I dislike absolute monarchy, I dislike absolute aristocracy, I dislike absolute democracy.'[30] Now, in France, a convention parliament, along the lines of 1688, would give the nation its just rights. It is needless to describe how rapidly such a reading was overtaken by Jacobinism. What is striking, however, is the eagerness to return to it whenever a change of events might seem to permit. It re-emerges at the other end of things. In 1815, Hobhouse, in his account of the Hundred Days, repeats the same analogy:[31] Napoleon was willing to become just such a monarch as William III. The liberal constitutionalists would restrain his inordinate appetite for power. *The Examiner* took the same line. So too, according to Hobhouse, did the French negotiators appealing to the allies: did not the French people have the same right as the English in 1688 to choose their monarch? Byron, in the Lords, was one of a tiny handful who voted for peace with France on a similar basis. One may be sceptical by this time whether anyone could still believe the old argument. (The modern Julius Caesar did not slacken his advance on Brussels). But it was expedient to appeal to Whig principle. What other for the party was there? But the Whigs were unable to contain the revolution within the limits of this inherited interpretation of history. The process, as part of the Byronic inheritance, is best illustrated through Fox himself, Mackintosh, Byron's 'classic' historian, and the admired Erskine. One sees a developing difficulty in maintaining the traditional discourse of the friends of freedom. Since Mackintosh and Erskine are heroic figures for the poet, they are summarised at length.

The language of Fox, in the beginning, is that of enthusiasm. He communicates the excitement of events. His remark on the fall of the Bastille has often been quoted. It is 'the greatest event . . . that ever happened in the world! and how much the best!'[32] But even the poet Cowper (whose Christian sentimentalism is scarcely Jacobinical) had written of those 'cages of despair/ That monarchs have supplied from age to age/ The sighs and groans of miserable men!/ There's not an English heart that would not leap/ To hear that ye were fall'n at last . . .'. More provocative was Fox's exclamation when the confederated monarchies of Europe were put to flight in October 1792:

No! no public event, not excepting Saratoga and York Town, ever happened that gave me so much delight . . .. The defeats of great armies of invaders always gave me the greatest satisfaction in reading history, from Xerxes' time downwards; and what has happened in America and in France will, I hope, make what Cicero says of *armed force*, be the opinion of all mankind, *Invidiosum, detestabile, imbecillum, caducum*..

If Louis favoured the 'Invasion of the Barbarians' it was 'necessary' for the French to get rid of him. His attempt to use royal prerogative against the Revolution provided constitutional provocation for the Jacobins. It 'goes a great way to justify the greater part of their conduct, and to palliate even the worst'. This is 'the great crisis for the real cause of liberty'.

Fox clung, in vain, to the Revolution to the very extremity of murderous anarchy. Many supporters had already become disenchanted. That process has been often chronicled. Brief and selected quotation is not intended either to reveal the range of Fox's reactions to the Revolution, nor to subsume those other elements of his party already fragmenting from his circle under the stress of daily events. The purpose is merely to show the kind of language which is the legacy of Byron. Classical history at once comes to Fox's mind (and separates his own discourse by its very education from that of popular radicalism). Salamis stands as a pre-eminent example of heroic resistance to tyrannical invasion. In the past: the barbarian autocracy of Persian imperialism; now: the new tyranny of the barbarous Brunswick manifesto. Byron's attitude to the Holy Alliance, and to Greece, clearly fits this model. Under stress the friends of freedom might be driven to 'excess' (what Erskine called the 'alloy' of what is 'wild and irregular'). Such an argument, which palliated Jacobinism might also, *mutatis mutandis,* serve as a defence of the Luddites of whom Byron would later speak with conciliatory sympathy.

These illustrative examples are drawn from unguarded letters rather than from Fox pursuing the intricate strategies of constitutional parliamentary debate. It is Fox in opposition, also, not as a Minister of All the Talents in the second decade of war with France. The selective filter remains Byronic. How much the poet knew of Fox's writings directly, how much came from the Foxite shrine of Holland House, is problematical. The party leader left no reflections upon revolution to challenge comparison with Burke. The task of more measured and philosophical exposition was undertaken by Mackintosh in the *Vindiciae Gallicae* (1791)—though Mackintosh soon afterwards went over to Burke.

Mackintosh echoed Fox. For the 'friends of freedom', the Revolution in France is the greatest effort made in history for the cause of all mankind. The Revolution is in the tradition of the 'noble resistance' of the American people, and then, turning to Ireland for illustration, he adapts Curran's phrase, the people 'will break their chains on the heads of their oppressors'. Such is the stream of human opinion now that the fate of the Gothic governments of Europe is sealed, and he cites the names of great Englishmen borne on the tide of freedom: Harrington, Locke, Molyneux, Sydney, to whom he adds Rousseau upon the social contract, and Voltaire, the advocate of toleration. No partial reform in France is possible of a system of government so afflicting and degrading as that of the Bourbons. To prune would be merely to strengthen oppressive power. The state must be returned to its first principles. What is incorrigible must be destroyed, and the enlightened principles of human rights be established by law.

Since he is writing at a time when optimism had not been shaken by bloody events, it is still possible to palliate alarm by likening the French convention to the English convention parliament of the Glorious Revolution. He sees in France not the 'despotism of a rabble'—and who could approve even of 'the tumult, venality, and intoxication of an election mob?'—but rather a government under the influence of the middle ranks of society, and he praises the part played by lawyers, favourably likening the role of the monied interest to that of the English Whigs opposed to Tory prerogative. He concludes with an appeal to the analogy of history, to the commonwealths of ancient Greece especially, as 'the only genuine example of governments truly legislative recorded'. What if the Revolution should produce 'excess'? Do not 'our sentiments, raised by such events so much above their ordinary level, become the source of guilt and heroism unknown before—of sublime virtues and splendid crimes?'. The academic tone of Mackintosh's prose is very different from Byron's typical style, but that last expression, with its sentimental and paradoxical conjunction of guilt and heroism, of virtue and crime, is a Byronic *leitmotiv* (and a ready target for the *Anti-Jacobin*). The detestation of the Bourbons and the Gothic governments of Europe will also explain Mackintosh's attraction for the poet.

The praise of France involves the writer, by corollary, in severe criticism of British society. The collusive government of the rich against the poor must not continue, and unless 'radical' improvement follows, radical even to 'subversion', the grievance of England will both produce and justify a change by violence. It is typical of this kind of discourse, that while seeming to offer a threat, it also withdraws it. Resistance to oppression abroad is no justification for revolution at home. The Constitution provides the means to reform itself, but genuine redress there must be. The people can no longer be fobbed off with 'impotent and illusive reforms'.

To Whig eyes the real threat of violence, and hence the provocation to that 'anarchy' which all rational friends of liberty deplored, came from the Tories. Erskine, in his *A View of the Causes and Consequences of the Present War with France,* took up the theme. The product of 'our invasion' of France will be 'to work by confusion against established authority; to stir up all the elements of misery and mischief'. That is to say, attacking France is anarchical, because it subverts an established government: 'What was this proceeding but the very system we had imputed to France, and proclaimed with horror to the universe?' Erskine's pamphlet was widely diffused. In the notorious caricature of the *Anti-Jacobin,* the '132nd' edition is borne aloft in the train of the Leviathan of Jacobinism. The year of publication was 1797. General Bonaparte concluded his devastating Italian campaign with the treaty of Campo Formio. Who was invading whom now? Opposition to the war with France was the work of the enemy within, so the Tories would claim.

In fact, *A View* is in full retreat from the Revolution, even while opposing the war. The essay is clear illustration of the way in which early support for revolution's principles on Whig grounds was destroying such vestigial unity, or even existence, as the party possessed. 'I am not defending France', Erskine protested, in the wake of the execution of the King, the expropriation of property, the Terror, and the internationalisation of Jacobinism at the point of the bayonet. The Revolution is 'the worst of all ills, except that confirmed establishment of tyranny and oppression for which there is no other cure'. It is the Scylla and Charybdis of anarchy and despotism. (Shelley's description, in the *Defence of Poetry*). What now, among the 'weather-beaten pieces of the wreck' of the friends of freedom—if anything?

It is the Tories who had produced these ills. Unable to reconcile Jacobinism to the principles of '88, the Whigs returned to the familiar polarities of domestic history. If only Britain has shown 'a just and generous compassion for the sufferings of the French people', had she become 'the cautious protector of the first revolution', well knowing from her own history the 'thousand difficulties' involved, then France might have been successfully launched upon the progressive removal of her gross and abominable corruptions. Sufficient men of property would have re-emerged in the passage of time to guide France through a process analogous to that of England in the seventeenth century. Instead 'a vast conspiracy against free states' (the Tories) had provoked the 'wild and visionary' elements of the revolution (the Jacobins), and the French people were confirmed in their excesses by foreign invasion. But the republic was more sinned against than sinning. If we put our own affairs in order, the call for international revolution might have met with derision. Again Erskine stresses his repudiation of 'French principles'. But now 'the holy communion of the robbers and destroyers of Poland' threatened the entire balance of power in Europe. He joined his voice to that of Fox, of Grey, of Sheridan, in asking for a 'Liberal peace' with the republic.

Like Mackintosh, Erskine links events abroad with the urgent need for reform at home, even 'radical' reform (although he offers the word only to overwhelm it with qualifications, to which, over the years, he continually added). The poor were cracking under the strains of war. 'Without peace, and peace on a permanent basis, this nation . . . cannot support her establishments, and must pass through bankruptcy into the jaws of revolution.' Between the horror of that revolution on the one hand, and the oppressive measures of Pitt, the war party and Toryism on the other, stood the Whigs who within the ancient Constitution of the realm must fulfil their historic destiny, to check the corruptions of power, and redress and reform abuses. Such was the course of history to which their principles accorded. But to whom was Erskine writing? The rump of the Foxite Whigs, in 1797, in despair had seceded from parliament altogether. The party no longer existed as a force.

The *Causes and Consequences* is indicative of the last attempt of sympathetic Whig discourse to reconcile itself to the new revolutionary principles. This is the pamphlet Byron had splendidly bound. If he identified himself with its arguments, then it may explain why the poet so rarely considers the French Revolution. It is for both writers an 'excess' of freedom, and they prefer to concentrate on the ills of a war fought by 'the Tories' for Tory ends: the power of the Crown. The Daedalian line of Whig constitutionalism is difficult to hold on to through the turmoil of Jacobinism, the change of the First Consul into Imperator, and the

Tory insistence on security for the legitimate monarchies of Europe.

These are large issues of principle. To relate everything in the break-up of the Whigs to the impact of the French Revolution risks obliterating the effect of specific issues in a rhetoric of generality. There is especially one major domestic issue which speeded the dissolution of the party, and with which Byron later was directly concerned. It is influenced by the Revolution in France, but the inability of the party to achieve their ends stretches so far both before and after the Revolution that the failure cannot be encompassed merely by assigning it to events across the Channel. The issue was that in the Duke of Richmond's mind on the day the Gordon riots broke out, and on which Byron spoke, in the most traditionally Whig of his parliamentary orations, in a debate during which his own party deserted him. That issue is parliamentary reform.

The idea of the balanced Constitution, and fear of the undue influence of the Crown, provided the justification for Whig support for parliamentary reform. There is no need to rehearse again the familiar material of the corruption of the eighteenth-century Constitution. In proposing the 1793 Reform Bill Grey estimated that 300 of 513 representatives for England and Wales were effectively in the gift of individual proprietors, and 11,075 voters returned a clear majority for England and Wales. The House of Commons, rather than being one part of three in a balanced Constitution, was an instrument of the peers and the Crown. A small circle of patrons, about 150, constituted a government as potentially powerful, and as separate from the real interests of the people, as the Stuarts at the height of their prerogative. A moderate reform of parliament would restore the Constitution by redressing the balance of property.

The Whig position was essentially different from that of the radicals, which was to be reiterated in the instant formula: universal suffrage, annual parliaments, secret ballot. That would be to establish 'absolute democracy' (in Fox's phrase), or 'the dictatorship of the proletariat' in the words of a later theoretician. It would be to destroy the influence of property, and to surrender the Constitution into the hands of demagogues. 'The Friends of the People'—the Whig reform society—had an initial subscription of two and a half guineas, and an annual subscription of the same.

26

Compare the penny a week of the radical Corresponding Societies. Country-house dinner parties with their toasts of 'Our Sovereign, the People' or 'Mr Fox and Parliamentary Reform' necessarily excluded, as Francis Place recognised, popular radicalism. When Byron later wrote that he favoured reform, but not 'the reformers' (meaning Orator Hunt, William Cobbett and their like) he was firmly in the tradition of 'the Friends of the People'.

But the radical influence was not easily shaken off. Whig principle meant that the rights of the people were dearer than the honour of the Crown (Coke's definition), and the demands of 'Our Sovereign, the People' were substantial. Philosophically considered it was difficult to deny a citizen a natural right to vote. The ancient Constitution of Anglo-Saxon England, as Major Cartwright expounded it, seemed to lend support to such a view, and Cartwright was no Jacobin. As Moore reports Sheridan, the *principles* of representation 'naturally and necessarily led' to annual parliaments and universal suffrage, but, he adds, Sheridan used to laugh the issue off as a 'wild scheme', 'wholly impractical': 'Whenever any one proposes to you a specific plan of Reform, always answer that you are for nothing short of Annual Parliaments and Universal Suffrage—then you are safe'.[33] Sheridan's defences of reform, wrote Moore, showed always 'the eyes of the snake glistening from under them'. Verbally some Whig politicians championed freedom, provided nothing was done practically. Fox refused even to join the Friends of the People. Grey was to complain that he wished Fox had kept him out of 'the mess'.

The 'mess' was the disintegration of the party and the flight from reform as a diminishing rump contrived into the 1790s to press an issue too dangerous to pursue. The great propertied magnates quitted at the threat of 'wild and visionary reform' at home precipitating Jacobinical revolution on the model of France. Portland, Devonshire, Fitzwilliam, Guildford, Egremont, Ashburnham, Stormont, Loughborough, Windham of Norfolk— the list of those going over to the other side reads like some passage in an Elizabethan history play. Perhaps an excuse to desert was convenient. However much the Whigs criticised the power of the Crown, they had never been backward in seeking its support.

The facts may be simply chronicled. Grey's reform motion of 1793 was lost by 282 votes to 41; that of 1797, for a household or rate-paying franchise, failed 256 to 91. The increased Whig vote was not seen as a positive sign. The rump of the Foxites, in despair, seceded from Parliament.

In 1792 Pitt, alarmed by the establishment of the Friends of the People, moved against the reformers with the Seditious Publications Act—the trials for constructive treason which followed provided Erskine, and the Whigs, with the last of their triumphs for freedom of speech. Habeas Corpus was temporarily suspended in 1794. In 1795 the 'Gagging Acts' against seditious meetings and treasonable practices prohibited meetings of more than fifty persons unless licensed by a magistrate, and made it treasonable to criticise the Constitution. These events may be directly paralleled during Byron's maturity by the temporary suspension again of Habeas Corpus (in 1817) and the Six Acts. By 1795 the nation was at war with revolutionary France.

Tierney wrote to Grey:

> In this extravagant ferment of men's opinions our task becomes every day more difficult. The Leveller and the Reformer, the King and the Tyrant, seem in the new vocabulary of Courtiers and Patriots to be confounded and considered as synonymous, and I much fear we shall neither gain proselytes from those who seem attached to the very defects of the Constitution, or those who seek to overturn it altogether.[34]

The middle ground has been eroded. Tierney complains that vocabulary is polarised at extremes: either 'Tyrant' or 'Leveller'—or, in the most familiar cant, either 'despotism' or 'anarchy'. Yet the most fervent of Whig discourse had always tended itself to run to such extremes in its defence of freedom, its claims for 'resistance', the appeal to 'the people', the opposition to the power of the Crown. It was, for many, an albatross hung about their necks.

The history of the limping return of the Foxite Whigs to Parliament after the secession, and even to brief coalition with 'the Tories' need not concern us. It may be said, in defence of principle, that Fox carried the abolition of the slave trade, and that the Whigs maintained their fatal allegiance to Catholic emancipation. But historians of the party agree that such reforming enthusiasm as it may once have possessed had in large measure evaporated. The commonplace charge against the older generation was 'apostasy' of having abandoned their principles, of having yielded to the allurements of the Crown. Such charges from the radical position are of no concern here. There was no need to wait on Marx to perceive that patrician parliamentarians preferred the interest of their own order to that of the proletariat. The allegation of apostasy would be familiar to Byron from his own side, however, and it is an issue raised in *Don Juan* even while the narrator proclaims allegiance to the 'buff and blue'. Lord John Russell admitted the case: 'the martyrs and patriots of the seventeenth century were succeeded . . . by a race of pettifoggers and peculators. Nothing can shew more clearly the necessity of perpetual jealousy than the corruption of the Whig party . . .'[35] Thomas Moore noted how, from the very beginning, 'apostate Whigs' had clustered round the Crown, even under William supporting the suspension of Habeas Corpus, corrupting elections, and while acknowledging the necessity of reform, 'they were able, by arts not unknown to modern ministers, to brand those as traitors and republicans who urged it'.[36] Hobhouse clashed strongly with Erskine on the issue of Whig apostasy in 1819, claiming himself to the the true heir of Fox, and Erskine as 'apostate'. Macaulay gave a substantial part of his *Edinburgh Review* article on Mackintosh (July 1835) to consideration of this party issue. Had Mackintosh betrayed Whig principles? Macaulay denied it. What is important for the understanding of Byron is the reactive quality of the debate—the way it moves backwards into the eighteenth century, and the world before the French Revolution. Moore draws heavily on Burke's *Thoughts on the Cause of the Present Discontents*. Hobhouse bases his analysis on that of Pulteney, Bolingbroke and *The Craftsman*, which saw Walpole as the pre-eminent example of Whig apostasy. Macaulay is the historian of 1688. Byron's admiration for Pope has its political relation in this context.

Criticism from without—from the 'Tories'—remained traditionally 'alarmist'. The revolutionary and libertarian language of the Whigs continued to encourage radicalism, Jacobinism, anarchy. Southey, in his history of Whiggery in the *Quarterly Review*, traced the origins of the party to the Cromwellian Levellers, and drew a direct connection with Jacobinism. Byron's language so frequently seems to provoke 'Tory alarmism' by the revivication of the inherited language, that to pursue this issue here would be to pre-empt much of the matter of the subsequent essays. One example from Byron's circle is of particular interest, however: Scott's *Old Mortality*. Scott accepted the 'alarmist' view of Whig discourse (as his pamphlets *The Visionary* clearly show), but his portrait of Henry Morton in the novel is extremely sympathetic. It may show not only how readily Scott and Byron could be friends, but also how chary one must be of using the term of Whig propaganda: 'Tory'. 'I will resist any authority on earth that invades tyrannically my chartered rights as a freeman', says Morton unjustly arrested, taking up arms and invoking the right of resistance. His demand from the Stuarts is for 'equal laws', 'freedom of conscience', and a constitutional monarchy.[37] The tragedy of this heroic Whig (and it is created by historical circumstance) is that to achieve this end he must league himself with religious fanatics, political extremists, murderers, wildly divided in their aims, anarchical, eventually insane (in short, in later terms, Jacobins and radicals). The fortunate conclusion of the story shows how, under William III, Morton's aims are secured. Scott's political skill is to make it appear that any Whig now who should invoke the right of resistance will fall straight into the jaws of Jacobinism, and after 1688, without good cause. It is an issue Byron was to take up also in historical fiction, in the Venetian plays.

It is a paradox that the Whigs should be accused, from the 'radical' side, of being apostate, yet from the Tory of being too revolutionary. The reasonable question anyone might ask, during the early years of the nineteenth century, was whether there was any living substance surviving between these contradictory charges. The party was not only fragmented, it was in danger of becoming a magnificent fossil. It had not enjoyed power during the entirety of Byron's lifetime. As Grey said in 1820, this 'system of conduct has during thirty-four years excluded me from office'.[38] There had been a momentarily magnificent defeat in the treason trials of the 1790s—to which the conversation of Byron's circle so readily turned—now the followers of Fox were the victim of a mythology which seemed to have permanently turned their vision backwards. The toasts were still loyally made to the good old causes and leader. So *The Morning Chronicle* records (27 January 1812) a Foxite dinner celebrating 'the recollection of his arduous and persevering efforts in the cause of liberty, civil and religious, and from the full conviction, that it is only by the intimate union of Aristocracy and Democracy, in the maintenance of the principles asserted at the Revolution, [of 1688] that we can hope to repair the injuries which the undue influence of the Crown has occasioned, and to save the Empire, by the quiet, safe and certain course provided by the constitution'. The loyal resolutions were made to 'The cause for which Hampden bled in the field, and Sydney on the Scaffold' (31 January): 'The rights of the People', 'The Cause of Liberty all over the World', 'Trial by Jury', and so forth. But the parliamentary fact of the matter was that Grey could scarcely bring himself up to London to attend the mummeries of Westminster, for the chance, as Mackintosh said 'of a few months of office in half a century'.[39] William Lamb would not even trouble to find a seat. The idea that here, *in potentia,* was Victoria's beloved Prime Minister would have seemed inconceivable fantasy. The toasts at country-house dinners were offered to the stone bust of a dead politician. It is an appropriate emblem.

Russell's summary of the principal Foxite causes in the Postscript of his *Memorials of Fox* indicates the extent of failure. With several Byron was to be concerned. On the power of the Crown, Fox's 'views may seem to have been defeated in 1784'; on the issue of 'religious liberty . . . he failed during his lifetime'. The motions for parliamentary reform 'which Mr Fox supported in 1782, 1783, 1785, and 1797', failed on each occasion. On the revolutions abroad, Russell asserts: 'Neither the pride which carried the nation forward in the assertion of dominion over America, nor the passion which sought to punish the crimes of the French people by the invasion and desolation of France, led him away from the great aim of honourable peace.' But this was the view of a 'small minority' in the American war, and of a 'smaller' in the French. Russell has little to say of the conciliation of working-class grievances by social legislation. Such minutiae lay outside the scope of the great general principles which Russell wishes to claim had survived the decades of failure.

> The loss of all prospect of power, the invectives of vulgar politicians, he was content to bear; the loss of friends, dearly loved, and of the national confidence, honourably acquired, were sacrifices . . . painful to his heart. But he never faltered, and never swerved from his purpose. The nation, inflamed by animosity, lifted up by arrogance, and deluded by the eloquence of men in power, assailed him as an enemy to his country, because he opposed measures injurious to her interests, and inconsistent with the great laws which regulate the relations between

man and man. In this deluge of folly and of fury, he sought in a return to literary pursuits an occupation and an amusement.

The doctrine of 'resistance' here has become a personal ability to stick it out and go it alone, although even friends have turned against one. (The rupture with Burke comes to mind, at which Fox wept.) In such circumstances the philosophical man finds occupation in literature. As Trevelyan wrote, the Whigs abandoned parliamentary hopes, 'not to make history, but to write it'. It is a paradigm to which Byron conforms.

One last example will close the chapter. It is Richard Fox's account of the life of Thomas Allen, librarian of Holland House, and the 'most liberal of men'.

His opinions were essentially Republican. He had early imbibed them, and was an ardent admirer of the early proceedings in France during the first Revolution. Although his kind disposition revolted at the horrors and cruelties that ensued, he still had hopes of a return to honest and philanthropic Republican Government, and was always indignant at the idea of reaction, and at the pretence made for arbitrary measures, that the Republicans must be such as Marat and Robespierre. It was not till Napoleon assumed the Imperial Crown that these hopes were blasted; and great was his despair and indignation when he heard of that event. The restoration of the Bourbons in 1814, the firm tenure of office in England of the Ultra Tories of that day, were to him as a close of all his political hopes and dreams; and from that time, he seldom devoted time to modern politics, and almost exclusively gave his attention to the early history of our Constitution and to the Anglo-Saxon language and history.[40]

Such is the ambience of the older generation into which the young Byron was taken up. Had the Whigs obtained power, of course, the story might have been different. Richard Fox, surveying history broadly, moves from Napoleon's assumption of the Imperial Crown, to the disappointment of liberal constitutionalists in 1814. He omits a year crucial to the development of Byron. In 1812, the Prince Regent assumed full powers subsequent on the final madness of George III. He had for long been the friend and associate of the Whigs. The reversionary interest had gathered round him. He wrote a letter to 'those persons with whom the early habits of my public life were formed' in which, in a notorious phrase, he

32

referred to a 'new era' in liberal politics. There was excited speculation that at last 'the wilderness years' had come to an end. This is the time Byron chose to enter politics. It was intended to be a fortunate conjunction.

In that same year, Napoleon launched the imperial armies against Russia. One aim was to throttle the British enemy by further extension of the Continental System. There was every reasonable expectation that he would win the economic war. Already more British troops were involved in the Midland counties than Wellington had at his disposal in the Peninsula. The main task of British arms was to control the Luddite disturbances.

It is a 'new era' very different from that dawn of nearly twenty-five years ago which Wordsworth celebrated.

2

Byron in the Lords:
The Languages of Resistance

Byron's ultimate disenchantment with parliamentary 'mummeries' was so extreme that it is easy to miss the hopefulness of the 'golden dream' with which Perceval mocked the Whigs. For more than a quarter of a century the party had been out of government. Now the cherry was *twice* knocked against the lips of men starved of responsibility, eager for office, first when the Regent assumed power in the early part of 1812, then when Perceval was assassinated in May. The editorial column of the Whig newspaper *The Morning Chronicle* charts the movement of excited expectation day by day as it flatters the Regent hopefully at one moment, warns of sinister influence behind the throne at another (as the Tories hang on), then flickers into anonymous hostility publishing lampoons which show how the great man would appear if he left his former associates. Byron, at one time preparing to attend a levée of 'our gracious Regent', at another writing anonymous scurrility, swings between the same extremes of hope and outraged disappointment.

It was not merely a matter determined by personalities. On great issues of principle ambition might anticipate a favourable change. Over a long period there was a progressive movement towards the cause of Catholic emancipation. On the issue of the Orders in Council the administration was in full retreat under pressure from Brougham and the manufacturing classes. Even the very violence of the Luddite riots might be seen as a symptom of a flood which might carry in the Friends of the People. The London Hampden Club, to which Byron belonged, appealed to the great men of the Whig party to support once more the issue of parliamentary reform. To no end. In a general political history of the period, 1812 is

34

merely another year of Tory administration. But Byron went through a day-by-day process which seemed otherwise. 'Ambition was my idol,' he wrote, wise after events. His political education was one in cynicism. 'I sate next to the present Duke of Grafton,' he wrote of the negotiations of 1812. 'What is to be done next?', Byron asked. '"Wake the Duke of Norfolk" (who was snoring away near us), replied he: "I don't think the negotiators have left anything else for us to do this turn".'[1] Such was the end of the 'golden dream'. It is a process analogous to what Byron later described (apropos of *Don Juan*) as 'scorching and drenching'. Yet, before the disillusionment, there came 'hot youth'.

Byron's three speeches in the Lords concern classic Whig issues: conciliation of the grievances of the people, reform of the Constitution, the right to petition without hindrance for such reform. The specific matters are the Luddite disturbances of 1811/12, Catholic emancipation, and redress for the veteran (and eccentric) parliamentary reformer, Major Cartwright, who had been harassed by the authorities.[2] The first two orations were delivered at the time of hope and are fervent, the last is a rebuke to the poet's party for their apostasy. All were ineffective. No member of the government troubled to reply to the speech on the Luddites, and it was only after Lord Holland backed Byron that the administration briefly rejoined. The Cartwright speech was merely out of order. The oration on Catholic grievances intrudes in a long and costive debate in which the Whigs evoked Magna Carta and the Bill of Rights (of course); arguing that Catholic exclusion was not a principle but an expedient of 1688 (back to the classic date), and that the time was now ripe to build on the concessions of 1793 and conciliate the wishes of four million petitioners and their natural leaders among the respectable classes. Byron had little time for such matters. His speech burns with indignation as he anecdotally lists specific examples of oppression: an eviction from two barns rented as a chapel; the acquittal of a Protestant German murderer; the abduction of two Catholic girls. At times he is violent, at others comic, always striving for effect. An illustration (Byron is borrowing from Sheridan)[3] may suffice as typical example. He is reminded of the story of

a certain drummer, who being called upon in the course of duty to administer punishment to a friend tied to the halberts, was requested to flog high, he did—to flog low,—he did—to flog in the middle, he did—high, low, down the middle, and up again, but all in vain, the patient continued his complaints with the most provoking pertinacity, until the drummer, exhausted and angry, flung down his scourge, exclaiming 'the devil burn you, there's no pleasing you, flog where one will!' . . . still you continue to lay on the lash, and will so continue, till perhaps the rod may be wrested from your hands and applied to the backs of yourselves and your posterity.

Underlying this colourful anecdote in principle is the idea of 'the right of resistance', but one may understand why Holland characterised Byron's oratory as 'full of fancy, wit and invective, but not exempt from affectation nor well reasoned nor at all suited to our common notions of Parliamentary eloquence'.[4] There is more emphasis on the dramatic incident than on the principle. The borrowing from Sheridan is 'literary' and is part of extensive reference in the speech to the Bible, the classics, Shakespeare and especially the eighteenth century: Johnson, Peterborough, Pope, Prior, Swift, Bayle, Montesquieu. Such allusion is typical of the patrician oratory of the time, but is emphatic in Byron. The language is not seeking to be merely a transparent medium for the communication of principles, but draws attention to the orator's education and verbal felicity in expressing indignation.

This may merely indicate that Byron, a poet, was out of his proper element in parliamentary debate. But writers choose their style, and if one turns from the Catholic oration to the Cartwright petition one becomes aware of a complete change. Instead of fervent attack the speech is a catena of routine formulae and respectful clichés:

The petitioner, my lords, is a man whose long life has been spent in one unceasing struggle for the liberty of the subject, against that undue influence [of the Crown] which has increased, is increasing and ought to be diminished . . .

This is familiar jargon. 'The whole body of the people' was insulted by the (temporary) arrest of 'this venerable freeman' Cartwright, and to whom should he turn, therefore, if not to the Whigs as Friends of the People and protectors of the Constitution? Remember trial by jury and the right to petition enshrined in the Bill of Rights. It was these very principles which Cartwright sought to protect, for his aim was 'the restoration of the true constitution of these realms, by petitioning for reform in parliament'. A key word here is 'restoration'. It distinguishes Cartwright, whom the Whigs may support, from those wild and visionary radicals (as they were called) who would bring in absolute democracy, and from the Tories who have arbitrarily subverted the balance of the state by 'an abused civil, and unlawful force' (remember the Stuarts). In making this claim Byron adopts a typical Whig strategy in carefully avoiding a commitment to any specific proposals for the reform of 'corruption'. Indeed, the entire presentation is hesitant, like the petition 'couched in respectful language towards their lordships' (unlike some radical petitions), presented only 'from motives of duty'. This is an utterly cautious and parliamentarian speech.

It is paradoxical that this series of Whig commonplaces marked Byron's break with the mainstream of his party. Since the petition was out of order—Cartwright should have appealed in the Courts—the speech was little more than an exercise in principled publicity. The Tories need say little. Their role was taken over by the Whigs. To receive the petition would be an injurious precedent claimed Fitzwilliam—the man recalled from Ireland for his support of the Catholics, and dismissed later from the Lord Lieutenancy of the West Riding for protest at Peterloo. The Duke of Norfolk, a founder member of the Hampden Club, and notorious for his Foxite toast, 'Our Sovereign, the People', praised the magistrate who arrested Cartwright. Only the 'Jacobinical' chairman of the Revolutionary Society of 1789, Stanhope, spoke on Byron's side. For the Tories, Sidmouth sought to rub salt in the wound by demanding after the petition was not received, that it should be rejected.

This incident, minor in the Lords, but major for Byron, may stand as a clear example of 'apostasy', by the Whig party, and of adherence to principle by the poet. He said to Moore, 'I told them that it was a most flagrant violation of the Constitution—that, if such things were permitted, there was an end of English freedom . . .'[5] Apply those commonplace generalities to a practical issue like parliamentary reform, however, and the party which had broken on the issue in the 1790s ran for cover again, leaving Byron in the lurch. In December 1813 he refused to present another petition (for W.J. Baldwin, a debtor in King's Bench) and he recalled how, on the Cartwright issue, 'Stanhope and I stood against the whole House, and mouthed it valiantly'. To be linked with Stanhope alone in defence of the eccentric Cartwright was to be politically outcast.

Two conclusions may be drawn from this affair. The first: how readily Byron, if he chose, could assemble the elements of conventional Whig discourse. The second: the importance of context in affecting what is said. Apply the standard language to Cartwright, and the Whigs did not want to be reminded of it. Further, what was claimed to be 'respectful language' in the Lords, advanced only for 'duty', is turned retrospectively into 'valiant' opposition and thus reworked into a myth of heroic and isolated resistance. That heroism itself was changed again for another audience. The anecdote from Moore already cited, with its high-sounding rhetoric, ends in a preposterous joke at cant political (covering over the humiliating repulse):

> 'But what was the dreadful grievance?' Moore asked interrupting him in his eloquence.'—'The grievance?' he repeated, pausing as if to consider—'oh, *that* I forget.'

Of course he had not forgotten. On the contrary, he had just been declaiming a speech he had troubled to commit to memory.

Hitherto the concern of this study has been with broad generalities of principle: the establishment of a benchmark. But as one approaches Byron specifically the issues of literary scholarship become critical. What is the form of the expression, when was it uttered, to whom, in what context? Is the poet consistent with himself in style, in strategy, in the roles in which he chooses to present his political principles? At one time he is content to rest in commonplaces. At another he fervently bypasses them. What is heroic opposition in one perspective, is a preposterous joke in another. The writer cannot be constructed merely by the scissors and paste method of assembling quotation. We must come to close analysis.

* * *

The Luddite issue is selected for detailed examination, for it best illustrates the crucial questions of the relation between form, content and context with which this study now will increasingly concern itself. The principle underlying Byron's argument for the frame-breakers is the familiar 'right of resistance'. This basic Whig idea undergoes substantial change depending on the audience to which Byron addresses himself and the form of that address. The speech (the poet's début in the Lords) was conceived within the context of party policy and, while in the planning stage, was summarised in a letter to Lord Holland. It was then followed by a poem published anonymously in *The Morning Chronicle* offering a partial account of the debate. Lastly, the Luddites' own position was imaginatively invoked in a song, sent in a letter to Moore, for his eyes only (and a few selected friends). The crucial issues concern Byron's grasp of the political matter before him, and the way principles evolve and change.

The initial letter summarises the content of the long speech, and is quoted in full. The bill to which Byron refers is one which would make frame-breaking a capital offence. The letter, self-evidently, is 'couched in respectful language' (like Cartwright's petition) towards the new member's mentor in the Lords. As such its decorum is therefore like that of the Cartwright speech.

[To Lord Holland]   8 St. James's Street
                                                    February 25th. 1812

My Lord—With my best thanks I have the honour to return the Notts letter to your Lordship.—I have read it with attention, but do not think I shall venture to avail myself of it's [sic] contents, as my view of the question differs in some measure from Mr. Coldham's—I hope I do not wrong him, but *his* objections to ye. bill appear to me to be founded on certain apprehensions that he & his coadjutors might be mistaken for the '*original advisers*' (to quote him) of the measure—For my part, I consider the manufacturers as a much injured body of men sacrificed to ye. views of certain individuals who have enriched themselves by those practices which have deprived the frame workers of employment.—For instance;—by the adoption of a certain kind of frame 1 man performs ye. work of 7—6 are thus thrown out of business.—But it is to be observed that ye. work thus done is far inferior in quality, hardly marketable at home, & hurried over with a view to exportation.—Surely, my Lord, however we may rejoice in any improvement in ye. arts which may be beneficial to mankind; we must not allow mankind to be sacrificed to improvements in Mechanism. The maintenance & well doing of ye. industrious poor is an object of greater consequence to ye. community than ye. enrichment of a few monopolists by any improvement in ye. implements of trade, which deprives ye workman of his bread, & renders ye. labourer 'unworthy of his hire'.—My own motive for opposing ye. bill is founded on it's palpable injustice, & it's [sic] certain inefficacy.—I have seen the state of these miserable men, & it is a disgrace to a civilized country.—Their excesses may be condemned, but cannot be subject of wonder.—The effect of ye. present bill would be to drive them into actual rebellion.—The few words I shall venture to offer on Thursday will be founded upon these opinions formed from my own observations on ye. spot.—By previous enquiry I am convinced these men would have been restored to employment & ye. county to tranquillity.—It is perhaps not yet too late & is surely worth the trial. It can never be too late to employ force in such circumstances.—I believe your Lordship does not coincide with me entirely on this subject, & most cheerfully & sincerely shall I submit to your superior judgment & experience, & take some other line of argument against ye. bill, or be silent altogether, should you deem it more adviseable.—Condemning, as every one must condemn the conduct of these wretches, I believe in ye. existence of grievances which call rather for pity than punishment.—I have ye honour to be with great respect, my Lord, yr. Lordship's

most obedt. & obliged Servt.

BYRON

P.S.—I am a little apprehensive that your Lordship will think me too lenient towards these men, & *half* a *framebreaker myself.*

The context of the letter, in general, may serve to remind how little those involved in events may know of them, and how little the individual can effect in history. On the ultimate cause of the 'grievances' Byron is silent. It is (of course) the war—the Pittite or 'Tory' struggle against revolutionary France. Hence the Continental System, the retaliatory Orders in Council, the imminent war with America. Exacerbating the recession thus induced is the loss of the American markets. In the Commons debate the Chancellor of the Exchequer asked, 'Could a committee open the continent and send the goods as formerly to the foreign European markets?' The answer was 'No'. He asked also, 'from whatever cause the [Luddite] riots arose, would anybody deny the necessity of putting them down?'[6] In a remarkable meeting between Sidmouth and Bamford the administration's view was summarised in three points: that 'the present distress of the country arises from unavoidable circumstances; . . . that his majesty's ministers will do all they can to alleviate such distress;—and, . . . no violence, of whatever description, will be tolerated but it will be put down with a very strong hand'.[7] The first and the last points are ineluctable facts. The war must be fought. It is not possible to sell goods for which there is no market. In what way may we suppose that Byron—or any other individual—can alter those facts? In the meantime, the administration has the power, and will use it, to maintain public order.

The letter also is imprecisely informed, but it is only the diligent enquiry of subsequent academic historians that places us now in a more enlightened position. Byron followed the Duke of Newcastle in adopting the mistaken view that new, 'improved' machinery had put men out of work. There were no new machines, and the issue was far more complex: it involved the production of cheap stockings by a 'cut up' method, the yarn woven on existing wide-framed looms; the use of cheap labour (women and children); payment by truck. There were too many workmen in relation to demand. Such markets as existed were saturated. Information is in the Home Office papers of the time.[8] In the summer of 1812 a petition specifically on issues of this kind was presented to Parliament (with what effect we shall see). But such precise information was not available to Lord Byron.

The opening of the letter reveals at once from how limited a viewpoint any one of us looks out upon the world. Consider only the address, and the first two sentences. The location, St. James's Street, is the very heart of fashionable London; the addressee, at Holland House, is Recorder of Nottingham, the writer, holder of the ancestral estates of the Byrons at Newstead Abbey. The language is that of 'polite' society; of one aristocrat to another: 'With my best thanks, I have the honour . . .'. It is a formula, but that word 'honour' is part of the system of discourse of gentlemen. It refers to a code of conduct by which they carry on their affairs (so a duel would be 'an affair of honour'). It is difficult to conceive of anything more remote from the experience (or the language) of a starving Luddite in Nottinghamshire.

From this distant, polite world, the writer is reaching out seeking to inform himself. He has stepped down a rank in the social order to *Mister* Coldham (the Town Clerk of Nottingham) whose letter he has. But Coldham was neither a Luddite nor a manufacturer. He found the riots a 'cause of serious alarm and permanent danger', but he feared that the government's Bill would cut off the information of spies and render the situation more dangerous yet. The voice is still outside Luddism. Finally comes the experiential claim (frequently important with Byron): 'I have seen the state of

41

these miserable men, & it is a disgrace to a civilized country.' As a Nottinghamshire landowner the poverty is obvious to him; but he does not claim as he might have done 'I have spoken with these men', or 'I have investigated the matter'. One may compare Cobbett on his rural rides on horseback, on the byways, talking with everyone. The experiential claim is raised again in the debate, and the language at once becomes more urgent: 'I have been in some of the most oppressed provinces of Turkey, but never under the most despotic of infidel governments did I behold such squalid wretchedness as I have seen since my return in the very heart of a Christian country.' The comparison sounds like a tourist view—I saw this on my travels—and the itinerant observer remains of the polite world of men of honour, members of what Byron calls a 'civilized country' compared with Turkey: *oi barbaroi*. By implication its despotic government is likened to the Tory administration, but for the insult to be effective the Tories must share the same general ideals of 'civilization' as the speaker—which they do. 'Civilization' represents the social and cultural values of the patrician order to which Byron and Holland, Liverpool and Eldon equally belong. Their Lordships would recognise that Byron was on the Grand Tour when he beheld Turkey, and the 'oppressed province' is Greece, whose dead language was the foundation of the humanistic education of a gentleman, and whose poetry, philosophy and history are thus part of the common stock of allusion of both parties (so Byron twice refers to the Tories as Draconian legislators). What Lord Byron has seen is a 'disgrace', something contrary to the 'honour' of a 'civilized' class in a Christian country.

It is not intended that this characterisation of Byron's approach should belittle his concern. We do not choose our window on the world; it is given by time, place, circumstance. He saw what he could see, and put it in the appropriate language. But what was the language which expresses the experience of Luddism? The problem is one of silence for we cannot go round Byron's speech, as it were, and compare it with the authentic language of the 'miserable men'. It does not exist. Illiterate work people, secret associations have not left written report. E.P. Thompson 'sees' them as Jacobinical; he leans to the more alarmist sections of the reports of the Committees of Secrecy of Parliament; Malcolm I. Thomis 'sees' a complex trade dispute without revolutionary aim.[9] But from the frame-breakers themselves there are mere fragments: an intimidatory letter, the claims of ignorance that Bonaparte would land to aid them, Major Cartwright would lead them, Sir Francis Burdett would rule England. There are also occasional poems which, by the very act of being literary, are abnormal:

> Chant no more your old rhymes about Robin Hood
> His feats I but little admire.
> I will sing the Achievements of General Ludd,
> Now the Hero of Nottinghamshire.

Then, much later, fictionalised folk memory emerging in Charlotte Brontë's *Shirley,* Frank Peel.[10] Beyond that, silence.

What is an appropriate language for this thing? How does one write of an issue so obscured by ignorance and complexity? Byron's line is to attempt to subsume ambiguous multiplicity into rounded generalisation: 'we must not allow mankind to be sacrificed to improvements in Mechanism'. It is the kind of statement which one might characterise as Romantic, for it is hostile to the mechanical, preferring the organic: 'mankind'. In context it suggests also the attempt to reduce difficult matters to a rhetorical formulation (with the coming debate in mind). The use of alliteration: *m*ust, *m*ankind, *im*provements, *M*echanism; the epigrammatic balance, like a couplet; the attempt to produce a general moral sentiment, all this suggests something of the kind of:

> Ill fares the land, to hast'ning ills a prey,
> Where wealth accumulates and men decay.

Alien matters are made comprehensible by reformulating them in the systems of language familiar to Byron's social system. Get them into appropriate language—an epigrammatic aphorism—and one creates the impression that civilized men can handle them.

In the debate the phrase is coupled with an attempt to formulate the language of Luddism:

The rejected workmen in the blindness of their ignorance, instead of rejoicing at these improvements in arts so beneficial to mankind, conceived themselves to be sacrificed to improvements in mechanism. In the foolishness of their hearts they imagined, that the maintenance and well doing of the industrious poor, were objects of greater consequence than the enrichment of a few individuals by any improvement, in the implements of trade, which threw the workmen out of employment, and rendered the labourer unworthy of his hire.

Both in the letter to Holland and here, Byron substitutes the phrase 'well doing' for the more usual 'well being', and in the speech attributes it to the poor themselves. It is backed up by the sentiments of civilised Christianity, by appeal to the Bible: the labourer is worthy of his hire. Such an attitude to 'the industrious poor' is that of a superior class, and the strategy is to show that the Whig lord, just as much as the Tory, appreciates the need for public order, i.e. the maintenance in peace of an industrious working class. It is part of a typically Whig balancing act between sympathy with those provoked to resistance by oppression, even to 'actual rebellion', and yet condemnation of such acts as 'excess'—in the speech 'excesses, however to be deplored and condemned, can hardly be subject of surprize'. The way forward is to substitute 'enquiry' for armed force and to conciliate. The objection to the death penalty is its inefficiency.

This line of argument, and language, was drawn by Byron directly from the House of Commons debate: 'Inefficacious', 'ineffectual' and (in Byron's speech) 'inefficiency' are other words employed. This vocabulary belongs to a different network of language than phrases like 'renders ye. labourer unworthy of his hire', 'mankind . . . *sacrificed* to improvements in Mechanism', with their religious overtones. 'Enquiry', 'inefficacy', are words which belong to scientific thinking. The implication is that enlightened investigation will show the facts of the case—of which the House is ill-informed—and when the facts are known efficacious measure will solve the problem. To call hanging a man an 'inefficacious' measure suggests even the language of Swift's modest proposer. It is certainly indicative of how much Byron in his letter is looking for a style appropriate to the decorum of the Lords. Witness the statement to Holland: 'I submit to your superior judgment and experience, & take some other line of argument against ye. bill, or be silent altogether, should you deem it advisable.' In the light of such a statement, the ambiguous postscript, which fears Holland may see Byron as half a frame-breaker, is leaning towards the 'firmness' which he states in the speech must accompany conciliation.

How reasonable it sounds! The opposition can thus avoid the issue which the administration must face. What is to be done *today* when men riot, steal and threaten murder? What too is Byron's (and the Whigs') view of the present law? It provided for fourteen years' transportation. Silence implies consent for this 'firmness'. One must press further. Does enquiry conciliate? The Committees of Secrecy enquired, and produced alarming reports of Jacobinical conspiracy, of para-military training, of intimidation and political murder.[11] Enquiry too about the specific conditions of the hosiery trade produced Gravener Henson's petition of the summer of 1812 to regulate wages, product and conditions of work. 'A Bill for Preventing Fraud and Abuses in the Frame-Work-Knitting Manufacture, and in the Payment of Persons Employed Therein' was presented to their Lordships. It had been emasculated in the Commons. The Lords were united in opposition to interference in the conditions of trade. The market must determine things, not themselves. Lord Sidmouth 'trusted in God' that no such similar Bill would again be sent up. Another voice added that the 'principle . . . of the Bill was a most mistaken and mischievous one'. The speaker carried especial weight, for he was Recorder for Nottingham—Lord Holland, Byron's mentor. The Bill was lost without a vote, Whigs and Tories equally opposed. The party, which had pressed for enquiry to conciliate in February, totally rejected conciliatory proposals in July.[12] Byron was silent. Meantime the facts of economic necessity led him to increase the rents on his Nottingham estates.

Enquiry was neither efficacious nor conciliatory. Nor is it a matter in which Byron was prepared to involve himself. There is a different strategy at work. It is determined by the context which may be simply expressed: nothing Byron said in the debate was going to affect the issue. The Whigs were in a minority. The death Bill had already passed in the Commons. Anyone looking at the benches of the Lords could count the heads, and would know that it would pass the Lords. The administration did not need to pack their supporters; it was a thinnish gathering; there was scarcely a debate. All the major speeches came from the Whigs. The administration presented the Bill as a routine extension of the law, clearly required given the violence of the disturbances. The opposition would put up the usual rhetoric.

The aim of the speech is therefore to put the administration in a bad light. Luddism was an opportunity, but the resolution of the dispute secondary to the attempt to hammer the Tories as barbarians, men without honour:

> When a proposal is made to emancipate or relieve, you hesitate, you deliberate for years, you temporise and tamper with the minds of men; but a death-bill must be passed offhand, without a thought of the consequences. Sure I am from what I have heard, and from what I have seen, that to pass the Bill under all the existing circumstances, without enquiry, without deliberation, would only be to add injustice to irritation, and barbarity to neglect. The framers of such a Bill must be content to inherit the honours of that Athenian lawgiver whose edicts were said to be written not in ink but in blood.

Grenville paid Byron the back-handed compliment that his 'periods' were 'very like Burke's'[13] (Burke was an ineffective speaker), and the comparison may also suggest that a man who speaks like this has an eye upon history. The speech, like Burke's, is to be published as 'literature' and is the record to the nation (and posterity) of that continuing evil, Toryism. The purpose is there again in an utterance like:

> You may call the people a mob, but do not forget, that a mob too often speaks the sentiments of the people . . . with what alacrity you are accustomed to fly to the succour of your distrest allies, leaving the distressed of your own country to the care of Providence—or the Parish.

The Whigs are the people's friends, the Tories render them an anarchical mob—*belua multorum capitum*—(and it was the Tories who have brought this distress at home, by the war against revolutionary France abroad). Later Byron evokes the popular myth of Robin Hood the Saxon yeoman who opposed the tyrannical John and the forest laws,[14] but was loyal to the good King Richard.

> Will you erect a gibbet in every field and hang up men like scarecrows? or will you proceed (as you must to bring this measure into effect) by decimation? place the country under martial law? depopulate and lay waste all around you? and restore Sherwood forest as an acceptable gift to the crown, [whose power is increasing] in its former condition of a royal chase and an asylum for outlaws?

Clearly one would not predict this kind of over-the-top invective from the cool summary and hesitant modesty of the letter to Lord Holland. It is a Philippic. The super-charged rhetoric is partly the product of the public chamber (compared with a private epistle), but partly also a symptom of irresponsibility. Since what is said will not affect what is done, form may dominate content and one may use rhetorical violence secure from violent consequence.

But how far were Whig attacks upon the Tories secure? At what point might violence of verbal attack prove support, or incitement to violence? The right of resistance does not surface in the letter to Lord Holland—there the word 'rebellion' is pejorative, although it is something to which the people may be driven. But the more violently one castigated Toryism as barbaric and tyrannical, the more one suggests the classic remedy: tyrannicide. It was a dangerous wave to ride. In the French Revolution the Whigs were overwhelmed by 'excess'. One might argue that later, in 1832, they more successfully rode the crest.

In the Lords debates the verbal threat of violence is more obvious in Byron's Catholic speech than here—because on the Luddite issue 'resistance' was a fact. It needed no emphasis. In earlier quotation one has seen Byron hinting 'perhaps the rod may be wrested from your hands and applied to the backs of yourselves and your posterity'—but that is a metaphor hedged around with a subjunctive. In the same Catholic speech, in a passage modelled on Junius's 23rd letter, he asked of the Ministers: 'To what part of the kingdom . . . can they flee to avoid the triumph which pursues them?' and wondered, 'if they can pass under Temple Bar without unpleasant sensations'. He hints at impeachment, and the fate of traitors. But again the threat is oblique. Do not Tory consciences make them fear for their lives? In the Luddite speech one might be forgiven for missing a similar application. It comes in the peroration—where decorum might suggest one could employ hyperbole. Byron imagines a Luddite arrested:

> suppose this man, and there are ten thousand such from whom you may select your victims, dragged into court, to be tried for this new offence, by this new law; still, there are two things wanting to convict and condemn him; and these are, in my opinion,—Twelve Butchers for a Jury, and a Jefferies for a Judge!

This is an argument about 'inefficacy', but that is not the thrust of the rhetoric. It is using classic Whig martyrology. One recollects Fox in his *History* of James II defending Monmouth as a man justified in resistance. 'Bloody' Judge Jefferies still is recollected today as part of that mythology of rebellion. He is a notorious instance of the corruption of the law by the Tories against the interests of the people. Tory law offends the laws of nature, and the spirit of the Constitution. Therefore: revolution. The argument is present only by implication. Byron, like Fox, in 1795, does not recommend violent resistance. But the violence of language, and the historical analogy, stimulate the idea. Byron told Holland he wanted enquiry, and efficacious policies. There is a very strong tension between that kind of enlightened discourse, and the emotional suggestivity of 'Twelve Butchers for a Jury, and a Jefferies for a Judge!'

Subsequent to the debate Byron wrote his verse account of what had happened in anonymous verses for *The Morning Chronicle*. The tensions and ambiguities of the debate on the issue arise more clearly. At first sight this is a mere popularist jingle, aimed at stirring indignation and laughter among the general public rather than swaying the *patres conscripti,* the men of honour, of the Senate. It was published as a rider to the *Chronicle*'s report of the Lords' debate, and it begins by subverting the arguments of Toryism by rewriting them, as it were, in a real language. The words of the poem indicate what the Tories truly meant.

> Those villains, the Weavers, are all grown refractory,
> Asking some succour for Charity's sake—
> So hang them in clusters round each Manufactory,
> That will at once put an end to *mistake*.
>
> The rascals, perhaps, may betake them to robbing,
> The dogs to be sure have got nothing to eat—
> So if we can hang them for breaking a bobbin,
> 'Twill save all the Government's money and meat:
>
> Men are more easily made than machinery—
> Stockings fetch better prices than lives—
> Gibbets on Sherwood will *heighten* the scenery,
> Showing how Commerce, *how* Liberty thrives!

This is written in the *persona* of a government supporter. Those whom Byron had called 'industrious poor', 'manufacturers', 'workmen', 'the people', and 'men'—our fellow men, members of mankind—are now 'villains', 'rascals', 'dogs', 'wretches'. This is what E.P. Thompson would call 'class hatred'. 'Tory' justice is equated in the next stanza with the deployment of 'Twenty-two Regiments'. Byron's own paternalistic emphasis on Christian civilisation is inverted in the attack on Charity, and his phrase 'we must not allow mankind to be sacrificed to improvements in Mechanism' becomes 'Men are more easily made than machinery'. One may note that this Tory gentleman has a more developed sense of the picturesque than he has of social welfare. The gibbets in Sherwood *'heighten* the scenery'.

The strategy is more complex than this, however. There remains the problem of the 'excess' of violence which in the Lords Byron had admitted must be met with firmness, while seemingly justifying it verbally. Throughout Byron's life a usual Whig response to Tory law and order policies had been the claim that they were alarmist—for instance, the threat of the French Revolution was exaggerated. Conciliate within the Constitution, as Erskine argued, and there was no threat at home. Thus, in this jingle, the foolish Tory is made to appear 'alarmist' by adopting a vocabulary to describe frame-breaking which minimises the disturbances:

> The rascals, perhaps, may betake them to robbing,
> The dogs to be sure have got nothing to eat—
> So if we can hang them for breaking a bobbin,
> 'Twill save all the Government's money and meat.

The Luddites only rob to stay alive. All this is no more than 'breaking a bobbin'. It was not what Byron wrote to Holland: 'Condemning, as every one must condemn the conduct of these wretches . . .'. Was it just 'breaking a bobbin'? Manufacturers were threatened with assassination (murder soon followed). Arms were regularly stolen. Reports of militarist training and of Jacobin delegations were regularly received—the matter of the Committees of Secrecy has already been noted. The gay little rhyme trips along with never a mention of such things. It is all Tory scaremongering.

But then the last stanza abruptly reverses the argument. There is a more overt development of what was latent in the reference to Jefferies: the threat of general insurrection.

Some folks for certain have thought it was shocking,
When Famine appeals, and when Poverty groans,
That life should be valued at less than a stocking,
And breaking of frames lead to breaking of bones.

If it should prove so, I trust, by this token,
(And who will refuse to partake in the hope?)
That the frames of the fools may be first to be **broken,**
Who, when asked for a *remedy,* sent down a *rope.*

This is no longer the Tory *persona.* It is clear why Byron did not put
his name to the poem. He will not identify the 'I' here who hopes
for violence (does he mean machines or bodies by the ambiguous
word 'frames'?) with the statesmanlike man of honour and
associate of Lord Holland who will work by enquiry to resolve a
complex problem. The lines are an invitation to riot—albeit a
jocular invitation, certainly not an appeal to Jacobin principles such
as the government feared—none the less an expression of hope that
the property (or persons) of pitiless Tories will get broken. There is
one language for Holland, another for a Senate Phillipic and a third
for a more popular readership (this will get down to Nottingham).
Lord Byron publicly associates his name with the Lords'
Phillipic—and dissociates it from this squib. The major problem
underlying all these utterances is the ambiguous sympathy for the
vaguely understood violence in Nottingham. In the light of the
poem, how Janus-faced the postscript of the earlier letter to Lord
Holland becomes: 'I am a little apprehensive your Lordship will
think me too lenient towards these men, & *half* a *framebreaker
myself'.* That ambiguous position is the dilemma of the 'right of
resistance' accepted in principle, feared in its 'excess'. At the same
time there is no practical 'remedy' which letter, speech or poem
offers specifically. (Byron never discussed the revocation of the
Orders in Council which was the one measure of practical relief
administration and opposition both agreed.) The thrust of the
argument is attack on the Tories, that being the classic Whig
strategy. But it is not a 'remedy'.

The last work in this sequence is the 'Song for the Luddites'. It is
in a letter to Moore, of 24 December 1816. The failure to find a
remedy had led to fresh disturbances. By this time the 'golden
dream' of the 'new era' was an unpleasant memory. The Whigs
remained 'Out' and the Tories 'In'. 'By the Lord! if there's a row,

but I'll be among ye!' Byron bursts out energetically (a thousand miles away). The lines that followed were 'written . . . principally to shock your neighbour—':

> As the Liberty lads o'er the sea
> Bought their freedom, and cheaply, with blood,
>   So we, boys, we
> Will *die* fighting, or *live* free,
> And down with all kings but King Ludd!
>
> When the web that we weave is complete,
> And the shuttle exchanged for the sword,
> We will fling the winding-sheet
> O'er the despot at our feet,
> And dye it deep in the gore he has pour'd . . .

He goes on to celebrate the renewal of the Liberty tree planted in the corrupted mud of tyranny.

This could not be published by *The Morning Chronicle,* and was not for publication at all. The lines, like the genuine Luddite song 'Chant no more your old rhymes about Robin Hood', have moved quite outside the language of Whig discourse. They are at an immense distance from the kind of utterance represented by the letter to Lord Holland. The poet is attempting to adopt the language and sentiments of the frame-breakers themselves. But since the poem is a fiction—the poet can only imagine himself as one of the 'boys' (compare 'industrious poor')—it has a function analogous to Byron's reading of Mr Coldham's letter: it is part of the quest of patrician Whig ignorance for information. It is an attempt to understand the frame-breakers by an imaginative act of (self-) dramatisation. It takes as its point of entry the only kind of contact which can now be established between the world of St. James's and the Luddites—a piece of literature. If the frame-breakers would write, then the polite classes might read and learn.

But this imaginative raid on what is unknown because inarticulate is exactly that kind of artifact the most alarmist of Tories would put into the mouth of a Luddite. (Conversely E.P. Thompson would use it to help substantiate his Jacobin hypothesis, were the lines genuine.) The 'Liberty lads o'er the sea' promiscuously combine American republicans, and the French. The Francophile Luddite threatens blood—which is cheap. (It was the Tory in the Frame-breakers Ode who also found life cheap: 'Stockings fetch better prices than lives'.) All monarchies (including the constitutional monarch in Britain) are identified with despotism. The verses proclaim *liberté* and *egalité* (without any reference, one notes, to *fraternité*). It is as extreme in its way as the Tory in *The Morning Chronicle* poem, and like that poem it is the fabrication of an alien voice: Byron in the *persona* of a Luddite. When the Whig imagines what the Radical is like he makes him in the way a Tory would conceive. Paradoxically this, one of the most extreme of Byron's utterances on the 'right of resistance', is also one which might most readily justify hanging Luddites as political assassins. On this evidence it can be seen why the Secret Committee of the House of Commons should report that:

> attempts have been made to create a persuasion amongst the persons engaged in these disturbances, that their proceedings ... are countenanced by individuals of a higher class and description, who are to declare themselves at a future time.

But not at that time. Byron was long since dead before the 'Song' was printed.

It would be meaningless to enquire which of these four pieces of writing—the epistle, the speech, Ode, or Song—most correctly expressed Byron's views on Luddism. Verses written in an alien *persona* to shock a friend, and an epistle written to conciliate a political mentor cannot be easily compared. What they show is a common preoccupation with a classic Whig issue: 'the right of resistance', but what they do not produce is a coherent, practical and effective strategy for resolving the problem with which they were faced. If there was a policy, it was given no chance to emerge. Byron made no progress in the party, and the party made no progress in Parliament, despite every hopeful expectation. This is not unconnected with the growing irresponsibility of these four passages. The later the date, the more violent they are. Perhaps that is 'Byronic', but Mackintosh saw it as an intrinsic danger in Whig frustration. He warned Thomas Moore, on 30 May 1819, of the danger of those in opposition becoming 'merely a sort of Tribunitian Band, who being unchecked by those hopes of succeeding to power, which at present moderate the temper of their opposition, & prevent them from committing themselves to rash opinions or impracticable measures, would run into all sorts of violence, & produce such shocks as would at last ruin the Constitution'.[15]

Byron, between his political failure in 1812/13 and the 'Song for the Luddites', may well have run through some sort of analogous process. The poetical squibs and expressions in letters and journals show a progressive sequence of anger and/or despair. Our concern is not political biography, but there can be little doubt as to the frustration of action which is such an important context for the written work post 1816. His own word for what Hume and Russell called the 'euthanasia' of the Constitution was 'Indifference'. He wrote to Lady Melbourne, 21 September 1813:

> 'Tis said—*Indifference* marks the present time,
> Then hear the reason—though 'tis told in rhyme—
> A King who *can't*—a Prince of Wales who *don't*—
> Patriots who *shan't*—Ministers who *won't*—
> What matters who are *in* or *out* of place
> The *Mad*—the *Bad*—the *Useless*—or the *Base?*

He suppressed an alternative categorisation of the Whigs: 'Patriots who *would not* . . .'. It was too harsh, and suggests patriotism as the last refuge of a scoundrel. 'Vain is each voice whose tones could once command' is a more sententious categorisation in the privately published *The Curse of Minerva.* His admiration for 'Fox, Horne Tooke, Windham, Fitzpatrick, and all the agitators of other times . . .' still held up, however (24 November 1814). 'I never was consistent in anything but my politics', he protests, and again: 'If you begin with a party, go on with them'. But it is clear that the present system of 'ins' and 'outs' had nothing constructive to offer him.[16]

Released from the need to formulate a language to persuade and carry through practical policies, there arise repeated expressions of hatred for the forces opposed to him, of which the 'Song for the Luddites', or his admiration for the classic Whig polemicist Junius, are typical examples ('I like him;—he was a good hater'). Since he does not know 'what liberty means—never having seen it', he typically works himself up with the argument, 'Whoever is not for you is against you—*mill* away right and left'. Especially, hatred for the Regent who let his side down (see *Windsor Poetics* and *The*

Waltz) combines with detestation for the restored Bourbons, who represent all that was worst in the *ancien régime,* provoking a stream of remarks which suggest republicanism—an 'excess' of Whig hostility to 'the Crown' of 'the Pym and Hampden times'.[17] But the attitudes change abruptly, and it would be a mistaken endeavour to reconcile them into a system. Consider two utterances, first 23 November 1813:

> But Men never advance beyond a certain point;—and here we are retrograding to the dull, stupid old system,—balance of Europe—poising straws upon king's noses instead of wringing them off! Give me a republic, or a despotism of one, rather than the mixed government of one, two, three. A republic!—look in the history of the Earth—Rome, Greece, Venice, France, Holland, America, our short *(eheu!)* Commonwealth, and compare it with what they did under masters.

Compare 16 January 1814:

> I have simplified my politics into an utter detestation of all existing governments; and, as it is the shortest and most agreeable and summary feeling imaginable, the first moment of an universal republic would convert me into an advocate for single and uncontradicted despotism. The fact is, riches are power, and poverty is slavery all over the earth, and one sort of establishment is no better, nor worse, for a *people* than another.

Ideas from both these passages re-emerge later, from the first in Hobhouse's commentary on *Childe Harold,* from the second reworked in *Don Juan* and *The Age of Bronze.* But it is impossible to reduce them to any sort of principle for they contradict each other internally by polarising politics into antithetical extremism: I believe in republicanism *or* despotism: and contradict each other in general, since the first looks for some political solution to problems, while the other not only regrets all existing governments, but rejects future government too. The aphorism 'riches are power, and poverty is slavery', rather than opening up a new line of thought, merely shuts out the 'people' from the political process altogether. Neither passage is going anywhere, because there is nowhere for them to go.

Scott claimed that there was no 'real conviction' in Byron's

'Liberalism'. 'Some disgusts, how adopted I know not, seemed to me to have given this peculiar and (as it appeared to me) contradictory cast of mind; but, at heart, I would have termed Byron a patrician on principle.'[18] Oddly enough, Scott too contradicts himself also, by denying Byron real conviction, and yet granting him patrician principle. It would be simple, on this line of interpretation, to compare Byron's hatred of the Prince Regent, when he ditched the Whigs, with his fulsome praise of George IV when he revoked the attainder of Lord Edward Fitzgerald.[19] The patrician conquers the Liberal. There are no consistent principles.

There is another interpretation for these violent twists and turns, however. 'Men never advance beyond a certain point . . .', Byron writes. What the patrician Whig is facing is a seemingly inevitable retrogression 'to the dull, stupid old system'. The Tories are putting back the clock all over Europe to 1780, even, at home, to 1680. Byron's explosion when he tore up his journal on 19 April 1814 is one of tragic rage:

> . . . the Bourbons are restored!!!—'Hang up philosophy'. To be sure, I have long despised myself and man, but I never spat in the face of my species before.—'O fool I shall go mad.'

The Whig tradition is one which celebrates the gradual progress of liberty, often checked by the wickedness of Tory tyranny, but which, like an incoming tide, if blocked in one place, flows on at another: from Magna Carta, to Habeas Corpus, the Bill of Rights, the American Republic, the fall of the Bastille. Leading the process for the people are the great patrician figures, men whom Byron named: Aristides and Washington, Brutus and Franklin, Fox and Windham, 'even Mirabeau'. What Byron was facing seemed, however, like a turn of that tide: retrogression. Abroad, the French Revolution issued in the restoration of the Bourbons; at home 'Vain is each voice whose tones could once command'. If 'philosophy' includes political thought, then the exclamation 'Hang up philosophy' is indicative of the failure of the inherited system of Whig libertarianism either to stop the reaction back to 1780, or to provide any practical hope of movement 'forward'. Hence the violent twists and turnings.

It is also highly histrionic. That cry 'O fool I shall go mad' casts Byron in the role of a tragic monarch, Lear, alone on the heath while the Bourbons hold power. The actual exiled monarch was Napoleon Bonaparte. The poet has identified one with the other. Political ambition in the British parliament was soon abandoned for that other ambition, to be the Napoleon of the realms of rhyme.

He did not 'hang up philosophy'. On the contrary, the move was towards it. *Childe Harold*—the subject of the next essay—politically considered, is an attempt to formulate, within a well-established poetic tradition, an overall historical philosophy of recent events in which frustrations of Whig idealism are placed as part of a larger pattern. There is a major tug of war, however, between the larger end and an alternative, insistent discourse which will relate philosophical history to contemporary events. The Whigs retired to write history rather than to make it, Trevelyan claimed. But the desire to make it was still there.

3

Harold in Italy:
The Politics of Classical History

In 1754 Richard Wilson completed his 'Landscape Capriccio with the Tomb of Horatii and Curiatii and the Villa of Maecenas at Tivoli'. His initials and the date are inscribed in the masonry of the ruined tomb as if the artist himself had passed into history as part of the landscape of Italy. The work was one of four purchased by Stephen Beckingham. Wilson's gentleman patron required a fitting memorial of his Grand Tour.

The capriccio is painted in the sombre yet glowing colours of Wilson's high classic style. In technique it alludes to the great masters of the seventeenth century, especially Claude Lorrain and Gaspard Dughet. It is, thus, a work about the past in the style of the past, a reminder to the knowledgeable connoisseur of a great tradition.

The tradition is elegaic. The evening light which falls upon the ruins, the deepening shadows, the memorials of a vanished civilisation inspire, in the receptive observer, a pleasing melancholy. The eye hears the stillness of time past. The few figures gathered in the foreground enhance the solitude of the great spaces of the canvas filled with emblems which remind mankind of mortality. Silence, solitude, the fading of the day, the ruins of Rome make Melancholy a moral exercise.

Although much is left to the individual imagination—for this high classicism is deeply romantic—the ruins provide philosophic guidance to the learned eye. The moralised image composes from the diversity of nature a history of Roman civilisation. The tomb commemorates the severe and simple virtues of the heroic republic; the villa recalls the elegant artistic achievement of imperial efflorescence, luxury and decadence. A modern patrician would ponder the causes and consequences of the grandeur and decline of Rome. History showed the precepts of moral philosophy working by example.

The fourth canto of *Childe Harold* provides an appropriate and traditional gloss:

– 108 –
There is the moral of all human tales;
'Tis but the same rehearsal of the past,
First Freedom, and then Glory —when that fails,
Wealth, vice, corruption, —barbarism at last.
And History, with all her volumes vast,
Hath but *one* page . . .

Byron supported his moralisation with scholarly authority, Hobhouse's note extracts a long passage from Conyers Middleton's *Life of Cicero*:

Rome, once the mistress of the world, the seat of arts, empire and glory, now lies sunk in sloth, ignorance and poverty, enslaved to the most cruel as well as to the most contemptible of tyrants, superstition and religious imposture: while . . . [Britain] anciently the jest and contempt of the polite Romans, is become the happy seat of liberty, plenty and letters; . . . yet running perhaps the same course which Rome itself had run before it, from virtuous industry to wealth; from wealth to luxury; from luxury to an impatience of discipline, and corruption of morals: till by a total degeneracy and loss of virtue, being grown ripe for destruction, it fall a prey at last to some hardy oppressor, and, with the loss of liberty, losing every thing that is valuable, sinks gradually again into its original barbarism.

Hobhouse gives no date for the passage. The *Life* was published in 1741. The message still seemed applicable in Regency Britain. Since it was 'the moral of all human tales' the date is irrelevant. The Roman lesson was universal. 'History . . . Hath but *one* page.' The painter, the poet, the scholarly commentator had chosen different media, but the underlying moral warning was simple, and commonplace.

The truths universally acknowledged by one generation, to another appear the determinations of culture. Middleton's language is that of 'Augustan' political controversy in the later years of Walpole. The argument between 'liberty' and 'corruption' has a local intention, whatever its claims to general applicability. The republication of the passage in 1818 by Hobhouse as a gloss upon Byron, redirects the commonplaces towards Regency 'Tory' Britain—its wealth, vice, corruption. The English, so Shelley wrote, were 'wilfully rushing to a Revolution, the natural death of all great commercial Empires, which must plunge them in the barbarism from which they are slowly rising'.[1] *The Political Register* or *The Examiner* more specifically pointed the accusatory finger at the unreformed luxury and corruption of 'The Thing' (Cobbett's term). Byron's pessimistic utterance is related to the frustration and despair of opposition political experience of Regency society.

The attempt of the verse, however, is to seek out the general rather than the particular; to philosophise current politics as part of a greater paradigm. It is the prose note which potentially tugs in the other direction suggesting the advance of British corruption from Walpole to the Regency. Byron's Spenserian stanza is the poetic equivalent of Wilson's classic style—a mode appropriate to embody a tradition. Harold's cosmopolitan outlook as citizen of the world may suggest comparison with Goethe in Italy searching for the *en kai pan,* or Madame de Staël's Corinne and Oswald discussing on classic ground the principles of cultural history. It is the relation between the poet's desire to assert permanent truths and the claims of the particular circumstances of post-Napoleonic Europe which is the theme of this chapter.

The point of view remains patrician. *Childe Harold* is a poem concerned with the lessons learnt by, and appropriate to, a gentleman and a member of the ruling order while on the Grand Tour. In the *Historical Illustrations* Hobhouse puts the matter clearly. On entering Rome, 'the city of the soul', he wrote of 'The education which has qualified the traveller of every nation for that citizenship which is again become, in one point of view, what it once was, the portion of the whole civilized world'.[2] That word 'civilized' has the same connotations as in the House of Lords debates discussed in the last chapter. It refers to the education in the classics common to all European gentlemen, and the application of the lessons learnt from that study to the present situation of the western world. To explore that matter fully would involve both a survey of the standard historiography of Rome in the classic and Renaissance eras, and the application of such historical example to British experience since 1688. Fortunately that task has already been accomplished by a number of fundamental studies.[3]

To confine enquiry merely to the Whig philosophy of history and to Italy would still remain a large undertaking. One need refer only to a few works to indicate the magnitude of the field: Robertson's *Charles V*—rich with the stories of the struggles of liberators and conspirators against tyrants—Roscoe's *Lorenzo de Medici* and *Leo X,* Eustace's popular *Tour Through Italy,* and pre-eminently, Sismondi's *Histoire des Républiques Italiennes du Moyen Age.* Such works tell how Italy had earlier given an example to Europe of the government of 'a free people by their common consent', lost through the invasion of foreign imperialism. The same cycle was run again in the late eighteenth and early nineteenth centuries, from the patriot resistance (described by Boswell) of Pasquale Paoli in Corsica, who established a republic: 'the best that hath ever existed in the democratical form', and through the great impetus given to participatory and legal constitutions by the French revolutionary armies, until the extinction of freedom again by the 'barbarians and invaders' of Congressional Europe. 'It has been the work of the coalition to destroy all; to place Italy again under the galling yoke of Austria; to take from her, with political liberty, civil and religious freedom, and even freedom of thought; to corrupt her morals; and to heap upon her the utmost degree of humiliation.' As with Roman history, several standard works explore these matters widely.[4]

The poetic moralisation of the classical landscape of Italy, and the political application of that moral to Britain, may provide a more specific focus on *Childe Harold.* The major Whig texts before the Romantic era are Addison's *A Letter from Italy* (1701), dedicated to Charles, Lord Halifax, Thomson's *Liberty* (1735–36), dedicatee, Frederick, Prince of Wales, and Dyer's *The Ruins of Rome* (1740). One may add Lyttleton's *Epistle from Rome* (1732), George Keate's *Ancient and Modern Rome,* and William Whitehead's *Ode to the Tiber* (both 1755).[5]

Thomson's title announces the main theme of the tradition, and the direct link with Byron: *Liberty.* Addison had pointed the way:

> O Liberty, thou goddess heavenly bright,
> Profuse of bliss, and pregnant with delight! . . .
> Thee, goddess, thee, Britannia's isle adores.

(119 f)

Rome had run the historical cycle from the heroes of the virtuous
republic to imperial tyranny. Though Italy remained the home of
the arts, to Britain had now fallen the role of custodian of ancient
freedom, and the proof of the acceptance of that historic destiny was
represented by the conquering arms of William III who had
destroyed Tory oppression on the Boyne and then brought peace to
Europe by humbling France (Gaul) and restoring the balance of power:

> 'Tis Britain's care to watch o'er Europe's fate,
> And hold in balance each contending state,
> To threaten bold, presumptuous kings with war,
> And answer her afflicted neighbours' prayer.

(145-8)

A subsequent generation, after Waterloo, was to reiterate the
message.

Dyer follows Addison and the Roman tradition closely. First
came the great republic, 'simple of life', creator of the empire.
Then the corruption of luxury prostituted the people to sell 'Their
ancient rights, their dignities, their laws,/ Their native glorious
freedom' (501-2). Britain, having inherited the Roman care for
liberty, now enjoys her own ancient Constitution, and with it the
prosperity of thriving agriculture and trade. Substantial quotation
may reveal the complacent self-gratulation of the plodding Whig
muse:

> O liberty,
> Parent of happiness, celestial born;
> When the first man became a living soul,
> His sacred genius thou; be Britain's care;
> With her secure, prolong thy loved retreat;
> Thence bless mankind; while yet among her sons,
> Even yet there are, to shield thine equal laws,
> Whose bosom kindle at the sacred names,
> Of Cecil, Raleigh, Walsingham, and Drake.
> May others more delight in tuneful airs;
> In masque and dance excel; to sculptured stone
> Give with superior skill the living look;
> More pompous piles erect, or pencil soft
> With warmer touch the visionary board:
> But thou, thy nobler Britons teach to rule;
> To check the ravage of tyrannic sway;

To quell the proud; to spread the joys of peace
And various blessings of ingenious trade.
Be these our arts; and ever may we guard,
Ever defend thee with undaunted heart,
Inestimable good; who giv'st us Truth,
Arrayed in every charm: whose hand benign
Teaches unwearied toil to clothe the fields,
And on his various fruits inscribes the name
Of Property . . .

(210-34)

The 'civilized' reader will recognise the same *locus classicus* behind Dyer and Addison: that cumulative passage in the sixth book of the *Aeneid* where Virgil (modestly) allows to the Greeks greater skill in the arts, but claims it as Rome's imperial mission to bring peace to the world: *pacisque imponere morem, parcere subiectis, debellare superbos.* With greater cause than Virgil, Dyer leaves art to others, but the heavy verse emphasises the usual Whig commonplaces: the defence of property (especially agricultural property), the rule of 'equal laws', and the opposition to tyrannic government. If one were to turn poetic apostrophe—O liberty!—into prosaic example, then for 'law' one might cite the usual triad, Magna Carta, Habeas Corpus and the Bill of Rights, and as 'tyranny', Stuart prerogative and the ambition of Louis XIV. For the defence of 'property', Locke is the obvious source. *The Ruins of Rome* is not primarily a political poem, but the contemplation of Rome had a moral message for the state.

Thomson's *Liberty,* on the other hand, *is* a political work, and to explore the sources of its ideas, their contemporary applicability in the poet's own age, and the details of Thomson's thought, would require a prolixity of detail inappropriate to the modest aim of this sketch. The theme of the progressive migration of liberty from state to state is linked with the functioning of Providence itself which directed freedom's course from Greece to Rome, and ultimately to what is described as its 'complete establishment' in England of 1688. The poet 'inflamed/ With classic zeal' on Roman ground celebrated as usual how that city in the republican era had once been free with 'equal' and 'essential' rights, but 'rash democracy', the 'unequal balance' of the classes of society, and the 'mixed rage/ Of boundless pleasure and of boundless wealth': 'Luxury rapacious, cruel, mean', had corrupted the state. Rome, under tyrants, lost her historic destiny 'To conquer tyrants, and set nations free'.[6]

Compare the happier, providential destiny of Britain. Liberty exclaims:

> Hence, Britain, learn—my best established, last,
> And, more than Greece or Rome, my steady reign;
> The land where, king and people equal bound
> By guardian laws, my fullest blessings flow,
> And where my jealous unsubmitting soul,
> The dread of tyrants! burns in every breast—
>
> (I. 316-21)

The development of progressive liberty has been the work of time: the Saxon constitution, Magna Carta, Hampden, Sydney, William III—here is the usual roll call of opposition resistance in defence of the 'long-contested rights' of the people in their struggle against corrupt and putrid courts and pestilential ministries. The poet's securities that the great cycle of historic change may have ended lie in the wise rule of the Hanoverians and their 'father senate', and, compared with antiquity, the better balanced Constitution of Britain, 'mutual checking' of King, Lords and Commons, and in the rule of law.[7] He celebrates the patriot hero who, independent through his possession of property, can quit retirement and, like a modern Cincinnatus, serve the state:

> Nought can his firmness shake, nothing seduce
> His zeal, still active for the commonwealth;
> Nor stormy tyrants, nor corruption's tools,
> Foul ministers, dark-working by the force
> Of secret-sapping gold. All their vile arts,
> Their shameful honours, their perfidious gifts,
> He greatly scorns; and, if he must betray
> His plundered country or his power resign,
> A moment's parley were eternal shame:
> Illustrious into private life again,
> From dirty levées he unstained ascends,
> And firm in senates stands the patriot's ground . . .
>
> (IV. 537-48)

If liberty were 'finally' established in 1688, or 'best' established, or most 'steadily' established, then these heroic lines contradict the congratulatory argument. 'Wealth, vice, corruption', to return to Byron's phrase, are here in the centre of political affairs where 'tyrants', 'foul ministers', 'dirty levées', and 'secret gold' are likely to drive the independent patriot out of office. To explore these tensions in *Liberty* would necessitate turning from the general to the particular: the circumstances of the poem's conception. All that is intended here is to show, laconically, certain commonplaces of the Italian theme in some of the better known of Byron's predecessors.

It is entirely appropriate, therefore, that Byron in Italy should address Britain as 'The inviolate island of the sage and free' (st.8). That is in the Whig patriot tradition deriving from 1688. In general terms, it is the Whig sense of the historical progress of liberty which underlies the famous prophecy:

– 98 –

> Yet, Freedom! yet thy banner, torn, but flying,
> Streams like the thunder-storm *against* the wind;
> Thy trumpet voice, though broken now and dying,
> The loudest still the tempest leaves behind;
> Thy tree hath lost its blossoms, and the rind,
> Chopp'd by the axe, looks rough and little worth,
> But the sap lasts—and still the seed we find
> Sown deep, even in the bosom of the North;
> So shall a better spring less bitter fruit bring forth.

How different this sounds in tone, however, from Addison, Thomson, or Dyer's:

> O Liberty,
> Parent of happiness, celestial born;
> When the first man became a living soul,
> His sacred genius thou; be Britain's care . . .
> . . . while yet among her sons,
> Even yet . . .

Byron's language is energised to communicate a sense of near desperation, of heroic resistance, the spirit of

> What though the field be lost?
> All is not lost; the unconquerable will . . .
> And courage never to submit or yield . . .

In Byron one finds that imagery of storm, that sense of striving against the forces of things, even a recognition of the destructive violence of freedom as thunderstorm, whose element is the tempest, which for convenient classification might be called Romantic in contradistinction to earlier Classicism. Freedom, as Thomson described it, was a Providential dispensation, but now has become a turmoil of natural forces. That appeal to a 'better spring' suggests (and perhaps is the very source of) Shelley's 'O wind, if winter comes, can Spring be far behind?'. Nature is politicised. The tree, which has lost its blossoms, is, of course, the Liberty tree—with all that might recall in the aftermath of the American and French Revolutions: so Jefferson, 'The tree of liberty must be refreshed from time to time with the blood of patriots and tyrants. It is its natural manure.'[8] That image in Byron of the renewal of the seasons may have its ultimate origin in the beautiful passage in Paine which ends the second part of *The Rights of Man:* 'It is now towards the middle of February . . .' in which he takes heart from the swelling of a single bud upon a tree—'It is . . . not difficult to perceive that the spring is begun' as the same appearance is promised everywhere, and from out of their vegetable sleep the trees will blossom. So too will it be with the political progress of mankind. Now Paine's optimism has yielded to something full of storm and stress. All that can be preserved is a 'seed' for the future. Such is the outlook post-Waterloo and the Congress of Vienna.

Such pessimism about the contemporary scene remains part of the Whig legacy, however, and is not the 'Jacobin' response of which Byron (with Hobhouse) was to be accused. It is easy to compare the pedestrian complacency of Augustan establishmentarianism with the *Sturm und Drang* of 1818, but the desperate tone in the rhetoric of resistance had always been typical of Whigs when in opposition. It is present, for instance, as early as Pope's late satires which give winged words to the essays of *The Craftsman*; or, to turn from verse to prose, in the vituperation of Wilkes and Junius, whose rhetoric has its part to play in *The Vision of Judgment*. It is as much part of the controversy over the American Revolution as the French, and is continually present in Ireland.

Consider, therefore, another image of art to contrast with Wilson's *paysage moralisé:* Barry's engraving *The Phoenix or, the Resurrection of Freedom* (1776). Time with his sickle is an active presence. He mows into the picture from the left scattering melancholy petals of remembrance. Beneath him are traces of the ruins of Athens, Rome, Florence—republican cities, and famous for their arts. On the right is Britannia's bier inscribed 'to the Memory of British Freedom' and attacking 'a Corrupt degenerate Nobility & Gentry, dissipated poor rapacious & dependent upon the Court'. Gathered round are the mourning figures of Algernon Sydney, Milton, Marvell, Locke and Barry himself. They gesture across a divide of waters (the Atlantic) towards a classical temple surmounted by the Phoenix of Liberty, and beside the temple dance the Three Graces, goddesses of the arts, associated by another inscription with 'human Rights'. In the lower margin is written:

O Liberty thou Parent of whatever is truly Amiable & Illustrious, associated with Virtue, thou hatest the Luxurious & Intemperate & hast successively abandon'd thy lov'd residence of Greece, Italy & thy more favor'd England when they grew Corrupt & Worthless, thou hast given them over to chains & despondency & taken thy flight to a new people of manners simple & untainted.

The tyrannical Court, in vain, seeks to forbid intercourse with this new people, and Habeas Corpus is shown in chains. Such is the situation of Britain under the Tory George III. The revolution of 1688 was not the 'complete settlement' which Thomson claimed. It had been betrayed. Liberty had taken flight yet again.

So, in *Childe Harold,* it is this old cycle, the *translatio libertatis,* which reasserts itself. One may observe the same preoccupations as Barry's underlying the comment on Waterloo and the world after that battle.

– 96 –

Can tyrants but by tyrants conquered be,
And Freedom find no champion and no child
Such as Columbia saw arise when she
Sprung forth a Pallas, armed and undefiled?
Or must such minds be nourished in the wild,
Deep in the unpruned forest, 'midst the roar
Of cataracts, where nursing Nature smiled
On infant Washington? Has Earth no more
Such seeds within her breast, or Europe no such shore?

This opposition between 'tyranny' and 'freedom' was intrinsic in

66

the treatment of the classic theme. Addison had made the comparison in 1701. So Wordsworth in the Ode of 1815 (notorious in its praise of 'Carnage' as God's daughter), Scott in *Waterloo*, Southey in *The Poet's Pilgrimage to Waterloo*, celebrates Britain's gift of freedom to Europe in the face of a new tyrant, Bonaparte. But for Byron (like Barry) the advance of historical corruption did not permit that optimistic dichotomy. Waterloo was merely a conflict between one tyrant (Bonaparte) and another tyranny (that of the 'base pageant' of the Holy Alliance). Wellington—the liberator—is never mentioned in *Childe Harold,* and, like Barry, Byron has to look outside Europe for the 'child and champion' of freedom. That phrase, a commonplace, is from Pitt, who had applied it to Bonaparte as the child and champion of Jacobinism. It is translated now to the patrician republican and revolutionary, Washington. For such national ingratitude Byron (Wordsworth thought) was properly in exile.[9]

The verse is attempting to establish major historical commonplaces by the generality of its reference. The rhetorical question: 'Can tyrants but by tyrants conquered be?' is not merely asked of Waterloo. But there is no way the poet can either disown the tradition in which he writes, not detach his verse from the date and context of its publication. Nor is such disingenuity expected. The prose commentary in which the poem is cocooned makes the particular application which the verse tangentially implies. The notorious dedication of the canto to the Bonapartist sympathiser, Hobhouse, writes of 'the bacchanal roar of the songs of exultation still yelled from the London taverns, over the carnage of Mont St Jean, and the betrayal of Genoa, of Italy, of France'. That word 'carnage' is directly critical of Wordsworth's Ode; the hostility to the restoration of legitimate monarchy in Europe is undisguised. Roberts, in *The British Review,* promptly responded to such a 'Jacobinical' challenge, attacking Byron as a 'character bred out of the French Revolution . . . estranged by ultra-marine habits and prejudices'. But we may see such reaction as part and parcel of the usual Tory strategy of labelling any opposition as 'Jacobin'.[10] Byron's moral and philosophical vocabulary, inspired by classical zeal on classical ground, is English and traditional. It is the historical context which has altered, so that the same words and poetic formulas shift their meaning by application elsewhere.

It may seem a paradox to state of a poem upon Italy that its central intellectual problem was to place the French Revolution and the Napoleonic wars for an English audience, but the Roman theme of the rise and fall of liberty demanded that 'the moral of all human tales' must apply at home and in France as it had applied on Italic soil. The French Revolution might be readily incorporated into the usual pattern. In twenty-five swift years France ran a cycle analogous to the tumults and contests of the pristine Roman republic, through wars of conquest to imperial luxury, decadence and eventual dissolution. Burke, who had inherited the paradigm, was in some respects only investing with the panoply of his language what as a schoolboy he had learnt from Aristotle, Polybius or Juvenal. France too had continually used the models of Roman history from the time of the adoption of the red caps of liberty in the 1790s, to the exploitation of Augustan ideology under the auspices of the eagles of the Imperator. To place France within such a pattern mummifies the Revolution as if its life-cycle were completed.

Yet it seems as if *Childe Harold,* a poem celebrating 'Freedom', adopts a variant upon this reductive formula to dismiss the extraordinary libertarian turmoil which had dominated Europe since Byron was born. The entire process is summarised with gloomy distaste:

– 97 –

> But France got drunk with blood to vomit crime,
> And fatal have her Saturnalia been
> To Freedom's cause, in every age and clime;
> Because the deadly days which we have seen,
> And vile Ambition, that built up between
> Man and his hopes an adamantine wall,
> And the base pageant last upon the scene,
> Are grown the pretext for the eternal thrall
> Which nips lifes tree, and dooms man's worst—his second fall.

This is the 'history hath but *one* page' argument again. The events of the 1790s (Jacobinism) are made commonplace. They are an excess such as belongs to 'every age and clime'. Bonaparte—the child and champion of Jacobinism—has his individuality suppressed (the name disappears) and he is reduced to a type of 'vile Ambition'. Even the Liberty tree loses its contemporary signification by the allusion to a 'second fall' and has become an amorphous version of the tree of life whose archetype stood in

Eden. There is little else about the Revolution, and although Byron repeatedly returns to the emperor, the pressure of typology continues to fit him into traditional role models. He is described as the modern Julius Caesar. Like the Romans of old he had the mission *debellare superbos:* he 'humbled once the proud' by destroying the monarchies of the *ancien régime*—'Too glorious, were this all his mighty arm had done'. But he became 'the fool of false dominion', and 'would be all or nothing'—a phrase which alludes to the Lucanic, and republican: *aut Caesar aut nullis.* Byron, philosophically, was contemplating that moment in traditional history in which turbulent republican liberty was involved with corrupting monarchical ambition. The continual pressure of the generalities is to step back from the local issues and fit them into an old order 'antithetically mixed'.[11]

But in 1818 it was difficult for the poet, and his audience, to achieve such broad detachment. Hazlitt preferred the bold commitment of the dedication to Hobhouse to this kind of writing which led the poet into contradictions. Byron, Hazlitt wrote:

> in his disdain of modern times, finds nothing to compare with the grandeur of antiquity but Bonaparte; and then 'as 'twere in spite of scorn', goes on to disdain this idol . . . Suppose what is here said of 'the child and champion of Jacobinism' to be true, are there not venal tongues and venal pens enough to echo it, without his Lordship's joining in the cry?[12]

It is noteworthy that Hazlitt, who would agree with Scott on little else, should claim that Byron is facing two ways. Scott categorised it as a dilemma of a patrician liberal, and as something temperamental. But a critical approach by way of language in Byronic discourse may also suggest that a process is occurring analogous to that of the Luddite debate. Alien events have to be contained within traditional language. But this pressure to compress and pass by is a late product of that difficulty of Whig attempts, already noted in Erskine, Fox and Mackintosh, to handle a very different revolutionary sequence from 1688. If there is a contradiction in the poet of freedom calling 'the child and champion of Jacobinism' a tyrant, the antithetical tension is not necessarily that of the Byronic temperament, but the problem of new wine in old bottles. The force and complexity of events cannot be contained in the old paradigm.

Similar illustration might readily be drawn from other contemporary poets. Wordsworth's sequence of poems dedicated to 'national Independence and Liberty' offers no consistent positive line. The ultimate celebration of the 'Dependence infinite, proportion just' of Congressional Europe: 'Lo, Justice triumphs! Earth is freed!' contrasts strongly with the earlier stern Whig view of seventeenth-century moral republicanism:

> Milton! thou shouldst be living at this hour:
> England hath need of thee . . .
> Oh! raise us up, return to us again;
> And give us manners, virtue, freedom, power . . .

It became commonplace to call Wordsworth apostate, and Byron's invocation of Milton in *Don Juan* was to be a rebuke to the man who had abandoned for Castlereagh his allegiance to 'The later Sidney, Marvel, Harrington,/ Young Vane, and others who called Milton friend'. But any sympathetic reading of the independence and liberty sequence will recognise the difficulty of choice which the exigencies of the war forced upon men (even Fox).

> If . . .
> Aught good were destined, thou wouldst step between.
> England! all nations in this charge agree:
> But worse, more ignorant in love and hate,
> Far—far more abject, is thine Enemy.[13]

But grant the myth of the pensionary corruption of Wordsworth by Judas's 'handful of silver', yet, what consistency is there in the voice of the most idealistic of the poetic friends of freedom? The first chorus of *Hellas,* and the general account of historical process in the *Ode to Naples,* may show how closely Shelley accepted the usual Whig commonplaces of the *translatio libertatis* from Athenian Greece to republican Rome to the England of *King* Alfred and *regicide* Milton (my emphasis). The pattern depends upon the familiar dialectical oppositions: freedom and tyranny, liberty and slavery. But then the French Revolution is hurried by on the way to millenarian prophecy. 'France, with all her sanguine streams', Shelley writes in verse, and in prose of a nation 'degraded by moral and political slavery to the practise [sic] of the basest vices it engenders'. The equivalent of *Childe Harold* (IV. 97) is the following passage from the *Ode to Liberty:*

> How like Bacchanals of blood
> Round France, the ghastly vintage, stood
> Destruction's sceptered slaves, and Folly's mitred brood!
> When one, like them, but mightier far than they,
> The Anarch of thine own bewildered powers,
> Rose: armies mingled in obscure array,
> Like clouds with clouds, darkening the sacred bowers
> Of serene Heaven . . .

The ambiguities here extend even to the syntax. The phrase 'the ghastly vintage' is unattached and could apply either to revolutionary France (whose 'Bacchanals' are Shelley's equivalent of Byron's 'Saturnalia') or to the allied powers. Bonaparte is both a mightier form of 'Destruction's sceptered slaves' (the legitimate monarchs of Congressional Europe) and yet the 'Anarch' of liberty (compare Byron's phrase 'Anakim of anarchy'). In such confusion the poet properly writes of 'bewildered powers' and of armies in 'obscure array'.[14]

The problem is that contemporary liberalism is unable to harness its idealism to any consistently successful force. The exclusion from office in Britain of a handful of Whig aristocrats would be neither here nor there if the Phoenix of Liberty were blazing in a new birth somewhere in Europe. 'I want a hero', wrote Byron in *Don Juan,* and ended by writing subversive burlesque. It is difficult to communicate the frustration of the 'Friends of Freedom' by brief quotation for that frustration is part of a continuing process. It would be appropriate, if there were world enough and time, to follow the political editorials of *The Examiner*[15] through 1813–15 as they expound the values of liberal constitutionalism and of emergent nationalities to the embattled powers of Europe who (of course) did not subscribe to the paper and whose dynastic aims were their own security and profit enforced by arms: *avec 600,000 [soldats] on ne négocie beaucoup.* Or consider Hobhouse's Foxite sequence of letters from Paris in 1815 explaining how France was now a pacific, constitutional monarchy in which the sovereign people through their representatives would control a chastened emperor. Waterloo was fought before Hobhouse got into print. Most revealing of all for *Childe Harold* would be Lady Morgan's 'fearless and excellent' *Italy*.[16] Lady Morgan three times had to chronicle the extinguishing of constitutional government in the peninsula, first by the very French armies who brought it, then by the liberating forces of Britain who reneged on her promise to Italian nationalism—'Oh! land of the Russells and the Hampdens, it is hard it should come from you!' But hardest of all was to be the failure of the Carbonari in Naples. The 'respectable' citizens, who would have diffused the principles of government through education and a free press, and who would have brought prosperity to the nation by the spread of 'trade . . . liberty and the arts' were deserted by their own people who refused to fight for the liberal cause and welcomed back the Bourbons. Having no 'property' to defend, the 'ignorance' of the people left them 'slaves' without 'national honour'. (One recollects the 'bacchanal roar of the songs of exultation' Byron detested in the London taverns. They were sung by the common people for a Bourbon restoration.) 'Opinion and illumination' had much to accomplish in the face of 'fast-striding evil, which . . . moves on, with the fearful lowering of a thunder cloud'.[17]

Such problems may further emphasise the stress behind Byron's '*Yet* Freedom! *yet* . . .'. In spite of everything one must once more assert the cause. In a prosaic study such as this, however, one must also ask what exactly that word 'freedom' is supposed to mean in such a context? The energetic resistance to the prevailing wind is excitingly heroic, but also vague. The problem of critical tact is how far to press the word for meaning? Thomson in *Liberty*, or Lady Morgan in *Italy*, explain their libertarian ideas in some detail. Byron, in general, relies on this Whig tradition. By tracking back to it he separates himself from the taint of Jacobinism. But how far can one read into the language of the poem specific ideas which the prophetic tone excludes? It would be false to the nature of the poetic—would it not?—to summon up the ghost of Byron for inquisition and demand does 'freedom' mean a constitutional reform of parliament (on what franchise?), equality before the law (whose laws?), a free press, a Bill of Rights, and a written liberal Constitution? Even more problematical: if the 'nations' of Europe are to be 'free', who is to draw their national boundaries?

Merely to ask such questions is to introduce the very insoluble complexities which, for instance, made Hobhouse's account of the Hundred Days out of date before it was published. It is to enter into the complexity and mire of events which continually frustrated the opposition. As a general political strategy, therefore, the function of the lines can be no more than to capture for one's own side an approved word, 'freedom', from the Tories celebrating Waterloo. Compare Wordsworth's 'Earth is freed!'. It is a familiar technique. The language of twentieth-century political journalism commonly employs it: 'freedom fighter' 'women's liberation', 'national liberation army'—such expressions establish a territory in language to which opposition is, by verbal definition, anti-libertarian, oppressive, chauvinistic, tyrannical. Who would be a 'slave' who could be 'free'? Byron's outburst has the same function, and by *not* defining achieves the widest possible support among opposition forces whether traditional revolutionary Whig, liberal Carbonari, or even radical: that is anyone who supports 'liberty' against 'tyranny'. The poetry works most successfully, therefore, by retaining an intense vagueness as to the present, and by the resonances of its historic tradition back to Washington, Milton, Alfred, Rome, Greece. In 1818 there was nothing much else which might embody the idea. Even in 1821 in *Hellas* Shelley was to prefer to substitute the idea of free Athens as a vision of the mind for what 'common fame' reported of the difficulties of the freedom fighters of Greece:

> Another Athens shall arise,
> And to remoter time
> Bequeath, like sunset to the skies,
> The splendour of its prime.

> (1084-87)

It is a retrospective kind of prophecy which sees an indefinite future in terms of an idealised past—'a Pallas, armed and undefiled'.

If it were not for Hobhouse the matter might be left there. But Byron's verse, which thrusts so strongly towards a philosophic historical generality, is enmeshed in a vast web of prose commentary which repeatedly introduces more directly provocative and local issues. There is the dedication to Hobhouse (which Hazlitt preferred in its commitment to the verse), the extensive notes (for which Hobhouse had authorial approval) and ultimately the *Historical Illustrations*. The reader of the context of the poem in its entirety is drawn into that very kind of propagandist exposition this chapter has just retreated from. The comment stands to the verse as Barry's politicised *The Phoenix* to the more general historical melancholia of Wilson's *Landscape Capriccio*. The same kind of distinctions also apply which were made when bringing together the different modes (and audiences) of Byron's writing on the Luddites. We are faced with variants upon the common theme conditioned by a local context, but one cannot telescope them together as if things written differently were one and the same.

When what hostile reviewers called the 'Jacobinical' intrudes, the nature of the discourse changes—most obviously from verse to prose. Consider the opening of the dedication to the notorious Bonapartist and would-be 'radical' candidate for Fox's old seat at Westminster:

To John Hobhouse, Esq. A.M., F.R.S., &c. &c. &c.

Those et ceteras devalue distinction. Compare, in the earlier tradition, the cautious way Addison had approached Lord Halifax in 1701:

the soft season and inviting clime
Conspire to trouble your repose with rhyme . . .

(7-8)

That is the Horation *nisi dextro tempore*. The humble poet approaches the great man with deference. The decorum of plebeian dedication to a lord applies. But now (1818) the lord dedicates to the commoner and 'to the public' to whose judgement Byron submits. It is far more democratic, familiar, informal. Though not too democratic. Hobhouse is a gentleman, as Byron tartly reminded the future Lord Broughton when he got too close to riff-raff like Hunt and Cobbett. There is another level: the mob, represented by the bacchanalian roar in the taverns of London.

How far is the 'Jacobinical' provocation intended to be carried? The dedication blows fierce.

What Italy has gained by the late transfer of nations, it were useless for Englishmen to enquire, till it becomes ascertained that England has acquired something more than a permanent army and a suspended

Habeas Corpus: it is enough for them to look at home. For what they have done abroad, and especially in the South, 'Verily they *will have* their reward', and at no very distant period.

Byron expects that this is the kind of writing which Hobhouse (or the 'fearless' Lady Morgan) will approve. The prose refers to local and specific events[18] and involves itself in the hurly-burly. The verse philosophises them into historical patterns. The function of the prose is both to encourage the dedicatee and to show that my lord is on the same side even though as a poet he writes in a different mode.

One representative example is sufficient to show the two kinds of writing functioning together, and also the extraordinary way in which Hobhouse, surging in with provocative contemporary explication, over-runs the text. Byron wrote:

> Alas for Earth, for never shall we see
> The brightness in her eye she bore when Rome was free!
>
> (737-8)

Hobhouse commented:

We have heard too much of the turbulence of the Roman democracy and of the Augustan virtues. No civil tranquillity can compensate for that perpetual submission, not to laws but persons, which must be required from the subjects of the most limited monarchy. The citizens of the worst regulated republic must feel a pride and may indulge a hope superior to all the blessings of domestic peace, and of what is called established order, another word for durable servitude. The struggles for supreme though temporary power amongst those of an equal condition, give birth to all the nobler energies of the mind, and find space for their unbounded exertion. Under a monarchy, however well attempered, the chief motive for action must be altogether wanting, or feebly felt, or cautiously encouraged. Duties purely ministerial, honours derived from an individual, may be meritoriously performed, may be gracefully worn: but, as an object of ambition, they are infinitely below the independent control of our fellow-citizens, and perhaps scarcely furnish a compensation for entire repose.[19]

Such inundation of the verse is a warning of the danger to any critic in over-explaining the text, and using it as an open door for the intrusion of self-opinion. How far can it be accepted as an explanation of the politics of the verse?

Both poet and dedicatee are challenging Whig tradition. Byron, in claiming that the republic of Rome was the apogee of freedom, is denying the more conventional doctrine that Britain, Rome's heir, surpassed, or perfected, her achievement (cf. Thomson). The emphasis of the verse is upon the melancholy nature of subsequent decline: 'Alas, for Earth . . .' and fits the general pessimistic *Weltschmerz* of the Harold *persona.* It cannot, in itself, be construed as a criticism of monarchy.

Hobhouse enlarges Byron's position as if it were critical even of constitutional monarchy, for under any kingly system submission to *persons* not *laws* (cf. 'equal laws' of the tradition)[20] induces servility. In his sneer at 'Duties purely ministerial, honours derived from an individual' Hobhouse is breaking a lance against all patrician values in Britain, and thus, by implication, attacking that tripartite balance of the Constitution—King, Lords and Commons—which is one of the central myths of the freedom of the realm.

This is typical of Hobhouse. The commentaries continue the matter of *Some Letters from Paris* in fiercely attacking monarchy, servility, flattery, superstition, and in praising republican freedom and national independence. If one turns to the reviewers it is apparent at once what happens. The copious gloss outrages the 'Tories'. Sometimes conservative reviewers hit the dedicatee with the same bolt, at other time—witness Scott—they distinguish between the merits of the poetry and the pernicious association with the commentator. But either way, the prose is being used to foster controversy in a way the verse is not.

The long gloss just cited was particularly offensive. *The Monthly Review* challenged Hobhouse in detail on this, recalling the career of the Whig, Lord Somers, 'who assisted in the establishment of a regular Constitution, and contributed his *ordinary* services under a limited monarchy, without feeling his "efforts palsied" or his "success mortified" by any of those considerations which seem to weigh down Mr Hobhouse's sensibility'. Roberts involved poet and commentator in a general attack on Jacobinical attitudes to the society, government, laws and usages of Britain. The country, he wrote, was now 'in the fullest enjoyment of liberty and law which has fallen to the lot of civilized man' (the 'Tory' is thus directly in the tradition of Thomson's *Liberty*). He continued by claiming that the 'covenanted contempt' of Hobhouse and Byron was part of a libertinism which pardoned 'every crime, except that of holding preferment, exercising office, maintaining order, practising devotion, advocating decorum, and suppressing tumult'. Scott categorised Hobhouse's commentary as a 'frenzy' improper to 'individuals of birth and education' (patricians), and Byron and his commentator showed that they were 'trained in the school of revolutionary France' (Jacobins). It ill became Byron to complain of British liberty when it was only as a result of the freedom which Britain had won that the poet might visit Europe (thus Scott is directly in the tradition of Addison's *Letter from Italy*).[21]

Further illustration might be rapidly multiplied. What is noticeable is that *both* sides claim to be speaking for liberty. Where they disagree is in their terms of abuse: slave/Jacobin. Conceptual similarities become most noticeable when the force of some of Byron's observations is acknowledged. Although Roberts sternly condemned the poet for abandoning his patrician duties and patrimony, yet the verses rightly proclaimed Britain was 'the inviolate island of the sage and free'. Why then did not the poet return home to 'reform abuses, or restore us to our Saxon estate?' The allusion is to the fabulous 'ancient Constitution' of seventeenth-century imagination, and Major Cartwright's. Might the Constitution, then, truly be in peril? Scott too reminded Byron of specific ills at home which required redress, of the 'vice and misery which luxury and poor's rates, a crouded population, and decayed morality can introduce into the community'. The door was open for Byron to work with others of 'birth and education' within the established order of society. *The Monthly Review* speculated that the poet's gloomy and contemptuous invectives against society 'rose from the "disappointment" and "ennui" which the "excesses of fashionable dissipation" induce'. High society, then, suffered the corrupting effects of luxury. It is a charge many accept, and fear the consequences.[22]

Remove the provocative association with Hobhouse, and the poem would lose much of its direct offensiveness. But the prose dedication and the commentary seem as if they were inviting the kind of adverse criticism which would keep Byron exiled from his patrimony. It is as if the Whig tradition, begun in opposition, based on resistance, is tending to become pathological, seeking to provoke situations in which action within the system is impossible and, therefore, not required. Addison, writing to Lord Halifax, Thomson to the Prince of Wales, even Barry publishing a political print, looked to influence events by the intervention of the great forces of the state to 'reform abuses, or restore us to our Saxon estate'. This is a task from which Byron, the Whig poet, has seceded just as the Foxites earlier abandoned Parliament. (Byron's notorious facsimile of Napoleon Bonaparte's coach shows the poet, like his former hero, defeated and retired into exile.) If there is a practical political job to be done it is handed over in the dedication as if by proxy to Hobhouse as commentator (and would-be MP). The poet, as champion of freedom, finds his burden almost intolerable:

– 93 –
What from this barren being do we reap?
Our senses narrow and our reason frail,
Life short, and truth a gem which loves the deep,
And all things weigh'd in custom's falsest scale,
Opinion an omnipotence—whose veil
Mantles the earth with darkness, until right
And wrong are accidents, and men grow pale
Lest their own judgments should become too bright,
And their free thoughts be crimes and earth have too much light.

Melancholy was always likely to be a part of reflection upon the Italian scene—witness Wilson's painting—but this is tending towards political *accidie*. It is not Hobhouse, but Southey, who pointed out the political implications. In *The Poet's Pilgrimage to Waterloo* false Wisdom takes the poet up into a high mountain and shows him the ills of all the kingdoms of Europe: the lost freedom of Italy and Spain, the extinction of the hopes for Liberty, Truth, the Rights of Equal Man, in blood at Waterloo, the restoration of the Bourbons by force, the threat that even Britain herself will fall 'By the wild hands of bestial Anarchy', the return of Europe to the old system of dynastic warfare:

Thus to the point where it began its course,
The melancholy cycle comes at last;
And what are all the intermediate years?
What, but a bootless waste of blood and tears! . . .
Rash hands unravel what the wise have spun;
Realms which in story fill so large a part,
Rear'd by the strong are by the weak undone;

Barbarians overthrow the works of art,
And what force spares is sapp'd by sure decay,
So earthly things are changed and pass away.[23]

So false Wisdom instructs the poet on the one page of history. All is
vanity, and the temptation is to yield to supine melancholia based
on materialistic epicureanism. Southey leaves no doubt to whom
such a wrong view belongs (and of the force of false Wisdom's
criticism). The preface points the finger directly at the 'Jacobins'
(or 'Liberals' as they now call themselves). That word 'Pilgrimage'
in the title indicates one gloomy 'Jacobin' above all others. But, for
the other party, Southey places his trust in divine Providence and in
the extension of recovered freedom once more from the British
people who 'do the will and spread the word of Heaven'.

No such trust in a Tory Christian God (or even a Liberal Supreme
Being!) is provided by Byron. If there be a way back to the light and
to freedom out of the paralysed solitude of despair, that burden rests
upon the isolated heroic individual, and especially upon the
promulgators of the written word, who have the almost intolerable
responsibility of carrying, often under persecution, the values of
liberty in societies no longer free.

Byron's frequent celebration of figures from the literature of
Italy in *Childe Harold* IV is not a mere act of connoisseurship. It has
often been observed how much the characters within the poem are
suffused with Byronic personality. It is less often noted how it is the
commentary's function to place these individuals in the history of
the rise and fall of European freedom. So we find Boccaccio
described as 'republican, philosopher and free man', Machiavelli
praised as a 'libertine', Alfieri as 'the bard of freedom', with Parini
the 'first noble exception' to centuries of submission. Men of
letters, Foscolo observed, are 'independent mediators between the
government which applies to force alone, and has a natural
tendency to despotism, and the people who have no less a natural
inclination towards licentiousness' (i.e. 'Saturnalia') 'and slavery'
(so Lady Morgan on Naples). 'Absolute monarchs hate the
historian, and the poet and the orator.'[24]

The most important example is Tasso. In *Childe Harold* he too
takes his place in the pantheon of poets as defenders of freedom. His
'offence was love of liberty'. His morbidity and sufferings were the
product of the social corruption in which he lived. 'It was one of the

extravagances of Tasso to discover that haughty spirit of a gentleman and a scholar, which made him averse to flattery.' Tyranny subjected him to humiliation, but 'the tried affection of an only sister, the unshaken though unserviceable regard of former associates, and more than all, his own unconquerable mind, supplied the motive and the means of resistance'.[25]

The analogy with Byron is self-evident. How changed, however, has that word 'resistance' become from Whig tradition: 'his own unconquerable mind, supplied the motive and the means of resistance'. The 'right of resistance' of the patrician revolutionaries of 1688 was the doctrine of a class and of a party. Now it has become an individual quality, dwelling in the mind of an isolated and imprisoned victim of tyranny, a poet and a madman. To that nadir the traditions of freedom might be reduced.

At one point even the fiery Hobhouse despaired: 'the gradual progress of reason is the dream of philosophy', he feared, quitting the optimistic tradition of the rebirth of freedom from generation to generation, from land to land, and he predicted for Italy:

> All the elements which, under the creative encouragement of a free, or even an independent government, might compose a great and enlightened nation, will mingle into their primitive confusion, and sedate ignorance establish upon the inert mass her leaden throne.

He quoted the apocalyptic ending of *The Dunciad* on the dying of the light.[26]

The paradox of the situation in 1818 is that the Tory writers are the forceful promulgators of the Whig celebration of Britain's mission to safeguard freedom by overthrowing European tyranny, while a Whig lord like Byron (and even his radical commentator) is on the verge of abandoning himself to despair, wanting, as Scott warned, 'worthier motives to action'. One might follow that darker strain of Byronic politics in poems such as *The Lament of Tasso* and *The Prophecy of Dante* which, in the dramatic *personae* of isolated men of letters, continue the pessimistic aspects of *Childe Harold* in developing images of imprisonment, exile and historical pessimism: 'All that a citizen could be I was;/ . . . And for this thou hast warr'd with me.' In *The Prisoner of Chillon* the spokesman of freedom offers an even darker view of the mind, which accustomed to slavery, comes even to regret its liberation. It is this aspect of

'Byronism' in 'the age of despair' which Shelley promulgated in *Julian and Maddalo*.

But to examine such poems in detail would be to reiterate, though vary, the bleaker aspects of *Childe Harold*. It is the alternative development which, instead, will be followed. Between 1818 and 1821 events in Britain and Europe suggested that reactionary Toryism might after all be violently forced back. Byron, in the '20s was to write of a 'second dawn'. It is a phrase which echoes the 'new era' of 1812. The cycle of hope for the Friends of Freedom rising from despair was to be repeated in a new wave of resistance: 'Yet Freedom! yet . . . '. But the outcome was tragic.

4

Venice Preserved

'In the first year of Freedom's second dawn/ Died George the Third.' The Liberal risings in Italy, Spain and Portugal of 1820 were followed by the insurrection in Greece in 1821. In 1822 Castlereagh committed suicide. That has been seen as the beginning of the 'age of reform'.[1] Henry Brougham welcomed the address from the throne of February 1823 as 'the signal for exultation to England'. It is the period of Byron's involvement with the Carbonari in Italy, and the Hellenes:

> The king-times are fast finishing. There will be blood shed like water, and tears like mist; but the peoples will conquer in the end. I shall not live to see it, but I foresee it.[2]

Byron's was not the prophecy of Cassandra. Revolution at home and abroad to many Britons seemed inevitable: Canning, Cobbett, Carlile, Queen Caroline, Hobhouse, Keats, Shelley, Southey, Wellington, Wooler, Wordsworth. The philosophical issue of 'resistance' was about to become practical. Against this background Byron composed his two Whig tragedies on Venetian history: *Marino Faliero* and *The Two Foscari*.

The first of these was written early in 1820 and completed a fortnight after the Carbonari rising at Nola (2 July). In Britain the immediate political events involve Peterloo (August 1819), the Cato Street conspiracy (February 1820) and the return of Queen Caroline (June 1820); the prosecution from Byron's circle of Burdett, Cartwright and Hobhouse. After the failure of the Carbonari Byron wrote *The Two Foscari* in June 1821. The plays convey an historical message for the times by analogy rather than by allegory. (Byron specifically rejected the kind of party political reading which had been made earlier of *Venice Preserved* or *Cato*. In vain. The audience of *Marino Faliero* interpreted even the censored text as local politics.)[3] The two Venetian tragedies show one of the great republican states famous to history, and traditionally likened to Britain, locked in a constitutional impasse. Good order is corrupted; decline seems inevitable leading to the euthanasia of the Constitution, corruption and extinction. In this situation revolution was provoked by misgovernment—as it was to be in France, or England. Byron's essay to Southey on *The Two Foscari* makes the explicit connection. The plays are home thoughts from abroad at a time of insurrection.

The Whig tradition was likely to inspire an aristocratic leader with revolutionary military ardour. It adulated Sydney, Russell, the men of '88, the 'buff and blue' of General Washington and Fox, and readily excused Lord Edward Fitzgerald. As Wilkes said 'a successful resistance is . . . not a rebellion'.[4] It was a defence of freedom that turned back the cycle of history to a less corrupt era. Such might be the aim of Byron as a *Capo* of the *Turba* of the Carbonari, or as an English Edward Fitzgerald. There are heady outbursts in some of the letters: 'Do let me know what there will be likely to be done—that one may lend a hand.—A revolutionary commission into Leicestershire would just suit me.' Croker and Scott did not take the tone of that seriously, however.[5] The note to Southey at the end of *The Two Foscari* is much bleaker:

> I look upon [convulsion] as inevitable, though no revolutionist: I wish to see the English constitution restored, and not destroyed. Born an aristocrat, and naturally one by temper, with the greater part of my present property in the funds, what have *I* to gain by a revolution? . . . But that a revolution is inevitable, I repeat. The government may exult over the repression of petty tumults; these are but the receding waves repulsed and broken for a moment on the shore, while the great tide is still rolling on and gaining ground with every breaker.

This is ambivalent. Seen as a great movement in European history 'Freedom'—in the *Childe Harold* sense—is a natural force, a 'great tide' which impels revolution, and which the writer supports. But seen in a local context—revolution in England—the writer fears for himself as an aristocrat. The split shows even more clearly in the

letter to Augusta, 2 January 1820, in which Byron claims he wants
to get out of Europe entirely to 'preserve my independence'. He
will fight only if the loss of his fortune no longer enables him to
remain 'aloof' from events in England: 'but . . . how I despise and
abhor all these men, and all these things . . . how reluctantly I
contemplate being called upon to act with or against any of the
parties.'

It is difficult to reconcile this distaste for revolution in England
with the familiar romantic image of Byron as armed Carbonaro and
Hellene. But Fox had been against the Wilkite mobs at home, and
yet palliated the excesses of Jacobinism abroad as provoked by the
Bourbons, and the Allies. What was local and what was distant
might be judged in different ways. It was much easier for Byron
(and his gentlemen friends) in Italy to act as liberal Carbonari than
to associate with radicals like Hunt and Cobbett at home. In Italy
(and Greece) politics could be 'simplified' to a 'detestation' of
government. 'Austrians Out' ('Turks Out') is a slogan which does
not demand much thought. Away with 'tyrants and usurpers!'. A
commitment to one issue activity—'national liberation'—
removes all complexities, for as a foreigner Byron had no
responsibility for what Italians might do when freedom was
obtained. The expectation of a Bentinck, Charles Kelsall, or Lord
Holland was that the peninsula would adopt a constitutional
government.[6] But at home the issues, because better known,
appeared far more complex and dangerous. Britain was threatened
with the destruction of the present social order in its entirety.

Compare Byron's letter to the Neapolitan insurgents with his
comment on Peterloo:

An Englishman, a friend to liberty . . . .. Having already, not long since,
been an ocular witness of the despotism of the Barbarians in the States
occupied by them in Italy . . . sees, with the enthusiasm natural to a
cultivated man [*ben nato*] the glorious determination of the
Neapolitans to assert their well-won independence. As a member of the
English House of Peers, he would be a traitor to the principles which
placed the reigning family of England on the throne, if he were not
grateful for the noble lesson so lately given to people and to kings,
I think . . . that if the Manchester Yeomanry had cut down *Hunt
only*—they would have done their duty . . . they committed *murder*
both in what they did—and what they did *not* do,—in butchering the
weak instead of *piercing* the wicked, in assailing the seduced instead of

the seducer—in punishing the poor starving populace, instead of that pampered and dinnered blackguard who is only less contemptible than his predecessor *Orator Henley* because he is more mischievous.—What I say thus—I say as publicly as you please—if to praise such fellows be the price of popularity—I spit upon it, as I would in their faces.[7]

As a Whig aristocrat in the tradition of 1688 he is the enemy of the unjust power of the Crown (at home or in Europe) and a 'friend of the people'. But as a gentleman, and a man of civilisation, he is also the enemy of barbarians, whether they are the troops of Austrian imperialism, or democratic demagogues like Hunt. The tone of the passage on Peterloo is violent: 'I spit . . . in their faces.' Elsewhere he says he would have run his sword-stick through Hunt's body. It is the language of a *Capo* of the Manchester Yeomanry. Fox said he was opposed to 'absolute democracy'. It was, claimed Burke, an illegitimate government. Byron went further. It was the worst of all governments, 'an Aristocracy of Blackguards', and 'a tyranny of blackguards'. Faced with 'a choice of evils with Castlereagh', he concludes 'a Gentleman Scoundrel is always preferable to a vulgar'.[8]

The same distinction separates Byron, stockpiling arms for the Carbonari in Italy, from the Cato Street conspirators at home who would have killed the Cabinet. Both events are immediate contexts for *Marino Faliero's* abortive conspiracy. In Italy Byron was following, in principle, Erskine's argument; to keep a firearm in the house to resist tyranny. The Liberty League in America, and Grattan's Irish Volunteers followed the same principle. The American republic and the Irish Parliament were established by revolutionary force. (The comparison of Grattan with Castlereagh must await *Don Juan.*) Cato Street sought to follow the same tradition. The very name 'Cato' recalled Addison's Whig tragedy and republican opposition to tyranny. Ings, on the scaffold, sang 'Give me Liberty or Give me Death' to the huzzas of the crowd, and Brunt's final words were an attack on the military government which ran the country. The crowd asked God to bless him, and shouted 'murder' at the execution of each victim. Those who expected 'inevitable' revolution would have had their fears confirmed.

But, as with Peterloo, Byron's reaction to Cato Street was to close ranks with his own order. Thistlewood was merely a criminal. 'Desperate fools' he called the conspirators:

> if they had killed poor Harrowby—in whose house I have been five hundred times—at dinners and parties—his wife is one of 'the Exquisites'—and t'other fellows—what end would it have answered? . . . but really if these sort of awkward butchers are to get the upper hand—*I* for one will declare *off*, I have always been . . . a well-wisher to and voter for reform in Parliament—but 'such fellows as these will never go to the Gallows with any credit'.[9]

So much, then, for the Ode on the frame-breakers Bill, and the 'Song for the Luddites'. His mind turns instead to the ill-effects of the Terror in France, and to 'Scoundrels' such as Hunt and Cobbett (ignorant of Tacitus, he remarks!). Revolutions are not made 'with rose-water', but if they are not made by gentlemen, Byron wants no part. 'Radical' was not a word in his vocabulary, he told Hobhouse, and he defined the new term pejoratively as 'uprooting', and a 'low imitation of the Jacobins'.[10]

Two references to the revolution in France at this time are particularly revealing:

> I am convinced—that Robespierre was a Child—and Marat a quaker in comparison of what they would be [Hunt and Cobbett] could they throttle their way to power.
> I can understand and enter into the feelings of Mirabeau and La Fayette—but I have no sympathy with Robespierre—and Marat—whom I look upon as in no respect worse than those two English ruffians.[11]

From Lord Liverpool this would seem Tory 'alarmism', from a 'Friend of Freedom' it is evidence of the way the mind is imprisoned by historical analogy. The Terror in France put back the case for constitutional reform in England half a century. 'In these times', wrote Lord John Russell, 'love of liberty is too generally supposed to be allied with rash innovation, impiety, and anarchy.'[12] What Byron had failed to see (from distant Italy) is the attempt of Hunt and the men and women of Manchester to break out of the vicious cycle in which mob murder and military murder continually provoked one another; to use the legal powers of the Bill of Rights to peacefully petition for the redress of wrongs.[13]

Instead, what Byron understands, more naturally, are the feelings of Le Comte Mirabeau and Le Marquis de La Fayette. One can only speculate what he imagined those feelings might be, but the dilemma of both men was that of the aristocrat in a popular revolution. Madame de Staël, who knew him, emphasised La Fayette's admiration for George Washington, his attempt to model the French Declaration of Rights of 1789 on 'the best part of those of England and America', his attempt to be 'faithful to his engagements to the King, and of establishing at the same time the liberty of his country'.[14] One thinks of the chivalrous captain of the revolutionary National Guard on his white charger putting down the very mob the revolution had raised, of Scipio Americanus against the Jacobins, of the eventual flight from France into an Austrian jail.

Le Comte Mirabeau is an even more Byronic figure: libertine, duellist, enemy of despotism who joined the *tiers état* proclaiming 'In all countries, in all times, the Aristocrats have implacably pursued every friend of the people'—witness the Gracchi ('history hath but *one* page'). Yet, with patrician imperturbability, he defended the absolute veto of the Crown because he feared more the tyranny of 600 irresponsible senators. Belonging neither to the Court nor to the Jacobins, he was none the less the supporter of the Queen. After his death his bust was removed from the hall of the Jacobins—an act of the same symbolic significance as the veiling of Faliero's portrait.[15]

This is merely imaginative speculation. But Byron's empathy is with aristocratic revolutionaries (and men who failed), and not with the radicals—the Clodius and Milo of the times, demagogues who seduce and mislead the people.[16] Hence the importance of the Queen Caroline affair for Byron and the Whigs, for here was an issue in which 'gentlemen', on a surge of popular protest, might emerge in their traditional role as leaders of 'the people'. It was the allusion of *Marino Faliero* to this affair which caused the play to be cheered in the theatre. This sordid, and intrinsically insignificant issue, of the Queen's honour has a contemporary and symbolic significance as important as that of Peterloo or the Carbonari in shaping the context in which the Venetian tragedies were conceived and in which they speak.

The affair seemed to confirm the further advance of the expected revolution. Such was the rhetoric of the press whether radical or establishment. *The Champion* claimed that not since the trial of the seven bishops produced the revolution of 1688 had the country been so roused by a legal issue. *The Times* claimed that 'the people's bosoms of this metropolis' were *more* agitated than at the landing of William III. If this sort of thing went on, Castlereagh commented, 'One cannot calculate on anything less than the subversion of all government and authority'.

In fact, what Caroline enabled the opposition to effect was a massive expression of support for the ideal of monarchy (embodied symbolically in the Queen), at the same time as attacking corruption (in the person of the King). Hundreds of loyal addresses from 'the people' (including the radicals) reached Caroline, often expressed in the traditional language of chivalry. Whig adherents of the Queen—Erskine, Fitzwilliam, Grey, Lansdowne—were celebrated, and the attachment of people to the party was enhanced, claimed Lord John Russell. A famous passage reappeared likening Caroline to Marie Antoinette:

> Little did I dream that I should have lived to see disasters fallen upon her in a nation of gallant men, in a nation of men of honour, and of cavaliers. I thought ten thousand swords must have leaped from their scabbards to avenge even a look that threatened her with insult . . .

But ' "The age of chivalry" was not gone; the "glory of Europe was [not] extinguished forever" ', the press commented. Caroline was saved from a corrupt king by a loyal people, and was herself the leader of revolution. Typical of the blend of monarchical and revolutionary imagery is Cruikshank's transparency design on the Queen's success, in which Britannia holds in her left hand the Liberty tree as her spear, but her shield bears the image of the Queen and rests upon a printing press. The motto would have delighted the heart of Wilkes or Erskine, for it celebrates 'the Victory obtained by the Press for the Liberties of the People'.[17]

It is extraordinary to realise that this affair drove Peterloo out of the forefront of debate; that it should have a revolutionary significance equivalent to that of the emergence of Liberalism. Caroline, the individual, was, of course, quite inadequate to carry the weight of symbolic suggestion with which the chivalry of a 'return to Camelot' invested her, and was soon forgotten (Victoria was to fulfil the role far better). Byron laughed at her as a 'tragedy quean'. Yet he recognised the significance of the agitation. Her acquittal 'will prevent a revolution—though it may *hasten* a *reform*'. If it were to lead to the Whigs assuming office 'as is probable' (hope springs eternal!) then help would come to the Italian patriots.[18] The matter speaks to him directly in a way the agitation of Hunt or Thistlewood did not because personal relations are involved. Caroline had entertained him as her guest (cf. Harrowby); since it is an affair of honour his hand searches for his duelling pistols (Brougham was in their sights).[19]

This matter is the contemporary analogy—and was recognised as such—for the strange motivation of the revolutionary plot of Doge Faliero: the insulted honour of Angiolina his wife. In Angiolina, and in Marina also (in *The Two Foscari*), Byron has created types of chaste, honourable, nobleblooded womankind for whom properly 'ten thousand swords' might be inspired. The idealisation of art supplies types which the particular matter of contemporary history did not offer—the symbolic significance of the name 'Marina' in a sea-borne empire is obvious—perhaps too obvious. Hostile criticism of what are admittedly imperfect dramas might liken the over-blown sentiments of a forced rhetoric to a process very analogous to the puffing of a new Marie Antoinette in Regency London.

But the Caroline affair is another instance of how, in a patrician society, principles of politics and matters of family honour are intimately involved, and how large issues thus may arise from small causes. This study cannot be concerned with the family quarrels, duels, intermarriages, debaucheries, debts, quirks, eccentricities and downright grotesqueries which are the day-to-day substratum of Regency politics (which the rhetoric of parliamentary oratory conceals rather than reveals). But the revolutionary issue of whether Caroline's name should go in the Prayer Book has a major place in the list of minor causes of political upheaval which Byron emphasises in the Preface to *Marino Faliero*:

a basin of water spilt on Mrs. Masham's gown deprived the Duke of Marlborough of his command, and led to the inglorious peace of Utrecht— . . . Louis XIV was plunged into the most desolating wars, because his minister was nettled at his finding fault with a window, and wished to give him another occupation— . . . Helen lost Troy— . . . Lucretia expelled the Tarquins from Rome— . . . Cava brought the Moors to Spain . . . an insulted husband led the Gauls to Clusium, and thence to Rome—a single verse of Frederick II of Prussia on the Abbé de Bernis, and a jest on Madame de Pompadour, led to the battle of Rosbach . . .

The list extends from Commodus and Caligula to Marie Antoinette, and Byron might, in art, have added Achilles and Shakespeare's Worcester. Their honour is moved to rebellion over a matter of the custody of prisoners of war. So, in England in 1820, the contents of a green bag might have led to the downfall of the monarchy, and if the monarchy went, what else might follow?

The emphasis of this contextual introduction has been rather on contemporary events in England which find their historical analogy in the Venetian tragedies, rather than on Byron's conspiratorial association with the Carbonari. The latter might suggest biographical empathy with Faliero in the context of Italian nationalism. An empathetic understanding is present, indeed fundamental in shaping both plays as Whig tragedies, but the Italian connection has only tangential signification. Let it be granted that when *Marino Faliero* was finished Byron wrote to Murray (22 July 1820) that 'We are here upon the eve of evolutions and revolutions' (in the same letter he discusses the Queen's trial). *The Prophecy of Dante* was published with *Marino Faliero* and both works contain visions of the future of Italy. But it is not possible to see the Venetian plays as advancing contemporary nationalism or liberalism. Marino's prophecy is not of the establishment of an Italian state; it concerns the further decline of the sea-borne empire (cf. Britain). His rebellion is not against an external power, but against the corruption of his class. The two Foscari refuse even to act against that corruption. Rienzi might have offered a hero indicative of 'the struggle of the people against tyrannous government',[20] if the poet did not object to a tavern-keeper's son. But Byron's heroes are not builders of nations. The issue they face is that of resistance against the corruption of their own class: whether the law of the state, made by their fellow patrician rulers of the state, should be broken if it is misused, or obeyed because without law there is no state. It is the dilemma of Tyranny against Anarchy once more, the problem of constitutional Whiggery in the 1680s, of the revolutionary Whig of the 1790s, and of Byron's own day when confronted with 'Tory' courts backed by yeomanry sabres.

The two plays form a mutually commenting pair. The first has attracted more attention for its revolutionary subject matter is more dramatically exciting, and it corresponds to certain popular stereotypes of Byronism because of the violent reaction of Faliero to corruption and his assumption of the role of the leader of the people in the cause of freedom. The 'ardent love of liberty and hatred of oppression' he shows derives from the tradition of resistance—the pervasiveness of that rhetoric may be shown by the fact that the 'revolutionary' phrase just employed was Henry Brougham's of his grandmother![21] But the tragic outcome of Faliero's resistance is indicative that there is something perverted, though noble, in the lengths to which he carries his action (beyond the 'prudential' boundary). The Aristotelian form of the drama suggests a fatal flaw. That flaw may not be merely Faliero's exaggerated and rash sense of family honour. Possibly it is in the very nature of violent resistance itself.

The Two Foscari takes the opposite case. It is a tragedy, as Jeffrey described it, of 'passive obedience and non-resistance'.[22] Resistance had only been justified in 1688 when the very Constitution was in danger, Burnet had argued. The normal, 'prudential' pathway was to use the law to uphold the state, and to reform the law to redress the Constitution. Wilkes escaped from the mob of his supporters and insisted on going to prison; Erskine told the mob to desist and he would free those charged with constructive treason by process of law. In the crisis of the Princess Charlotte in 1814 (proleptic of Queen Caroline) when she told Brougham she would throw herself on 'the people' for protection, the great Whig lawyer (defender of Hunt, champion of the slaves) admitted that if she did, 'the people' would pull down Carlton House and 'blood will flow', but he warned her, 'Through the rest of your life you will never escape the odium which, in this country, always attends those who by breaking the law occasion such calamities'.[23] She must obey the law, and the Regent. So, in Byron, the family of the Foscari honourably and legalistically follow the constitutional authories of Venice, and in so doing expressly draw a series of contrasts with Doge Faliero. But the outcome is equally tragic. Neither resistance, nor obedience, offer a way forward. Taken together the two plays are indicative of a total impasse producing, in Venice, decline and eventual extinction. What moral might that offer for Britain?

This impasse is a problem for the patrician. It is not the kind of issue which Hunt or Cobbett contemplate. For them the way forward was 'universal suffrage'—i.e. 'absolute democracy'. This study, several times, has argued that Byron's window on the world is that of his class, that 'Byronism' is not a phenomenon separable from time, place, social position. These plays, in the context of 1819–21, raise the class issue as a major theme. It is something of which they are aware, define and debate, because it is an issue pertinent to the writer and to his times. The political movement from which Byron was declaring 'off', even from his friend Hobhouse, was alien to him because he was a 'gentleman' rather than of the *Belua multorum capitum,* a man who possessed a classical education and who understood Le Comte Mirabeau and Le Marquis de La Fayette (or Lord Edward Fitzgerald, attainted like Faliero). The issue of what it was to be a gentleman is not the usual way in which the Venetian plays is approached, but in large measure it is what the plays seek to voice.

Stemmata quid faciunt? asked the bitter republican Juvenal: what does a noble pedigree do for a man? He gave the same answer as peasant Burns: 'a man's a man for aw' that'. The patrician would not always agree. 'The house' to which he belongs ('Our House', says Worcester beginning his complaint to Henry IV), helps create the sense of 'honour' which shapes his conduct. His education, his family connections, his inherited place in the state fit him for a particular role in government, and shape his mind with a sense of historical destiny. The Whig historian Lecky puts the matter thus:

> the essence of an aristocracy is to transfer the source of honour from the living to the dead, to make the merits of living men depend not so much upon their own character and actions as upon the actions and position of their ancestors; and as a great aristocracy is never insulated, as its ramifications penetrate into many spheres, and its social influence modifies all the relations of society, the minds of men become insensibly habituated to a standard of judgment from which they would otherwise have recoiled.[24]

Marina, in *The Two Foscari* speaks of her *stemmata,* and to personal 'qualities' joins the issue of breeding:

> We say the 'generous steed' to express the purity

> Of his high blood . . .
> And why not say as soon the *'generous man'*?
> If race be aught, it is in qualities
> More than in years; and mine, which is as old
> As yours, is better in its product . . .
> . . . get you back, and pore
> Upon your genealogic tree's most green
> Of leaves and most mature of fruits . . .
>
> (III.i. 290-301)

She is rebuking the villain Loredano, and the comment is authoritative, for her (invented) allegorical name indicates that she speaks as the voice of the bride of the Adriatic and Venice's traditions. Given the emphatic masculine composition of the patrician order, the rebuke is more cutting coming from a woman. Loredano is degenerate, and the Latinate use of *generosus* (of noble or eminent birth) distinguishes the language of one of classical education from plebian discourse and understanding.

As for the 'honour' of one's 'house': it is the very cause of the action of *Marino Faliero.* It would be an exercise of pedantry to list from both Venetian plays all the phrases linking house, name, family, birth, with honour, reputation, fame: typical are Faliero's references to the 'deep dishonour of our house', 'Their pure high blood, their blazon-roll of glories,/ Their mighty name dishonoured', and his invocation of the spirit of his sires, 'Your fame, your name, all mingled up in mine'; then, in *The Two Foscari,* the praise of the 'heroes' of 'the great house of Foscari', the Doge's rejection of pity as unworthy of 'my name', his lament that 'I have seen our house dishonoured'.[25]

This is the language of 'the age of chivalry'. The qualities which bestow honour on the men of generous houses are success in war and political service (and in their womenfolk, chastity, fecundity, obedience). Both plays particularly emphasise the military actions of the male protagonists in expanding the empire of Venice and repulsing her enemies. Byron, judging the historical record in his Preface, wrote of Faliero as 'a man of talents and of courage':

I find him commander-in-chief of the land forces at the siege of Zara, where he beat the King of Hungary and his army of eighty thousand men, killing eight thousand men, and keeping the besieged at the same time in check; an exploit to which I know none similar in history, except that of Caesar at Alesia, and of Prince Eugene at Belgrade.

As with Bonaparte in *Childe Harold,* classical typology places the great man in the list of captains: Caesar, Eugene, Faliero. The Roman analogy is invoked again concerning Doge Foscari's 'Thirty-four years of nearly ceaseless warfare' (II.i.14):

> The Romans (and we ape them) gave a crown
> To him who took a city . . .
>
> (IV.i. 312-13)

And Marina reminds the Doge too of the Spartans:

> these did not weep
> Their boys who died in battle . . .
>
> (II.i. 74-5)

Byron may be recalling also the famous scene in Addison's *Cato* in which the hero rejoices at the death of a son—these classic, imperial types are the role-models for a patrician hero.

Another classic duty of the great man was to be the patron of his clients, establishing mutual dependency within a hierarchical structure—a tradition of which Burke writes (of the Whigs) in telling of their 'long possession of government; vast property; obligations of favour given and received; connections of office; ties of blood, of alliance, of friendship . . .'.[26] Faliero, preparing the insurrection, says that around him

> will be drawn out in arms
> My nephew and the clients of our house . . .
>
> (III.ii. 255-6)

and noble Lioni, appealing to the responsibility of 'poor plebian Bertram' reminds him that he is his friend and

> the only son
> Of him who was a friend unto thy father,
> So that our good-will is a heritage
> We should bequeath to our posterity.
>
> (IV.i. 249-52)

Faliero carries the relation of patron to client to a feudal extreme. Like Worcester or Hotspur, when he rises against the authority of the state, he looks for support to 'my own fief', to 'our retainers', the 'vassals' of his district, the 'serfs of my country' who will 'do the bidding of their lord' (IV.ii. 1 f.).

This is not a window for looking into politics which one would usually expect in the times of Paine, Hunt, Cobbett. It recalls rather Burke's chivalric admiration for the 'antient opinions and rules of life'. But there is danger in quoting Burke too frequently lest he sound an isolated and eccentric voice. He is not. Consider the great Whig polemicist Junius attacking the corrupt Ministry of his day. The conceptual vocabulary, like Byron's, reminds the great lords of the 'house' from which they come, their 'ancestors', their 'illustrious name and great property' and the proper paternal attitude of a friend of the people. Consider the description of Lord Granby in *Letter* Two (from William Draper):

> Educated and instructed by his most noble father, and a most spirited as well as excellent scholar, the present Bishop of Bangor, he was trained to the nicest sense of honour, and to the truest and noblest sort of pride, that of never doing or suffering a mean action. A sincere love and attachment to his King and country, and to their glory, first impelled him to the field, where he never gained aught but honour.

The concepts are equally known by radical writers. Consider Godwin's Falkland, who is likewise motivated by name and fame: 'He believed that nothing was so well calculated to make men delicate, gallant and humane, as a temper perpetually alive to the sentiments of birth and honour.'[27] The examples of Burke, Junius and Godwin are particularly pertinent to *Marino Faliero* for they are describing an order, and its value, which they see in danger of extinction. One need only think, in addition, of Scott to perceive the kind of tensions between old and new a sympathetic writer might explore.

These parallels suggest that if we are to understand Regency politics it is just as important to turn to Plutarch or Polybius as it is to Paine: that is to say, to those writers who formed the thought of men of generous breed—'the antient opinions and rules of life'. The political typology of Byron's Venetian plays, indeed, might readily serve as a basis for instruction in the ideals of classical antiquity as moralised for an aristocracy by birth (or learning). To expand on the examples would be to overflow the chapter. It must suffice to list passim some of the historical names from *Marino Faliero* and comment laconically on the pertinence to the times of a few. Julius Caesar we have already seen here (and in the previous chapter); with Caesar, his assassin, Marcus Junius Brutus, who 'died in giving/ Rome liberty, but left a deathless lesson' (his ancestor, Lucius Junius, is the archetype for Doge Foscari's sacrifice of his son); with Brutus, Cassius; the Gracchi (violent friends of the Roman people); Manlius, called a traitor, but rather one who 'sought but to reform what he revived'; Gelon (conqueror of the Carthaginians, ruler of Syracuse, known as father of his people and patron of liberty); Timoleon (tyrannicide, who killed his own brother in the cause, law-giver, who lived as a private man, though chief influence in the state); Thrasybulus (the general who expelled from Athens the thirty tyrants, but would accept no recompense beyond a crown of olive twigs). Most important of all is Agis, sovereign of Sparta, who sought to restore the Constitution of Lycurgus, but who was killed by the magistrates (the Ephori). This is the type with whom Faliero climactically chooses to identify himself at his death:

> there's not a history
> But shows a thousand crowned conspirators
> *Against* the people; but to set them free,
> One Sovereign only died, and one is dying . . .
> The King of Sparta, and the Doge of Venice—
> Agis and Faliero!
>
> (V.iii. 16 f.)

In making the connection Byron may not only be drawing attention to history, but to another of those Italian patriot writers who had a major role to play in the politics of *Childe Harold:* Alfieri—one who showed 'a hatred approaching to madness against every species of tyranny'.[28] The allusion is both to Plutarch, and Alfieri's neoclassical tragedy *Agide* (1786). (The same writer's *Bruto Primo* was dedicated to George Washington.)

The use of these traditional paradigms is a formidable check to radical innovation by tending to reimpose old patterns upon historical events: to return to the archetype rather than to make things new. It is the theme of the return of liberty on classic models again, or the restoration of the principles of the state—revolution in the sense of turning back the cycle of history. The ideal which *Marino Faliero* especially evokes is *tyrannicidium:* kill Julius Caesar and the Roman republic will be restored. It is a simplistic solution to political problems, for in its basic form it necessitates identifying tyranny with an individual—Caesar or Castlereagh—so that the particular violent act can achieve the widest possible purgation. This chapter has suggested that simplistic solutions of this nature were attractive to Byron. History is a war between tyrants and liberators. Free Italy by expelling the 'legitimate' sovereigns. Since vocabulary is polarised into extremes, so, too, is action. Byron will be the liberator of enslaved people, a new Timoleon, the European Bolivar.

Such ideals got the man nowhere. The literary text, however, is more complex and one cannot read the tragedies directly in the simplistic way. The very number of the historical types suggests an uncertainty where to place the emphasis. The violence of the Gracchi was notorious (compare the Jacobins). The failure of Brutus and Cassius to restore a corrupt republic is even now a commonplace. Manlius was called a traitor (compare Lord Edward Fitzgerald). If I fail, Faliero fears, history will judge me as a Catiline (I.ii. 596) (the type of criminal revolutionary, not tyrannicide). The problem for Faliero is that he cannot identify his target as a corrupt individual to be cut off. It is an entire class of society which is to be exterminated, and it is his own: the corrupted *aristoi.* Nor has he an entirely 'new order' of things which he wishes to impose, and which the radical revolutionary might claim necessitates the 'uprooting' which a massive revolutionary movement seeks to enact. That phrase quoted of Manlius, that he 'sought but to reform what he revived' (IV.ii. 304), is straightforward Whig: the Constitution must be returned to its pure principles by reforming policies. The policy of the archetype Agis was to bring back the ancient code of laws of Lycurgus, not to make up a theoretical new system. As a man of great authority, like Faliero, his aim was to use 'true sovereignty' to establish 'freedom'. Thus, although the usual simplistic vocabulary of 'tyranny/freedom' is frequently employed, the dramatic situation is not conceived in the straightforward manner such terms imply.

The attempt by Faliero to explain his position to the conspirators reads very strangely, and one must consider not only what he says, but the dramatic inappropriateness of the utterance.

> Our private wrongs have sprung from public vices,
> In this—I cannot call it commonwealth,
> Nor kingdom, which hath neither prince nor people,
> But all the sins of the old Spartan state,
> Without its virtues—temperance and valour.
> The Lords of Lacedaemon were true soldiers,
> But ours are Sybarites, while we are Helots,
> Of whom I am the lowest, most enslaved; . . .
>   You are met
> To overthrow this monster of a State,
> This mockery of a Government, this spectre,
> Which must be exorcised with blood,—and then
> We will renew the times of Truth and Justice,
> Condensing in a fair free commonwealth
> Not rash equality but equal rights,
> Proportioned like the columns to the temple
> Giving and taking strength reciprocal,
> And making firm the whole with grace and beauty,
> So that no part could be removed without
> Infringement of the general symmetry.
> In operating this great change, I claim
> To be one of you—if you trust in me;
> If not, strike home,—my life is compromised,
> And I would rather fall by freemen's hands
> Than live another day to act the tyrant
> As delegate of tyrants: such I am not,
> And never have been—
>
>   (III.ii. 154-82)

In addressing 'the people' Faliero at once adopts the language of classicism. One need only imagine Orator Hunt using words like 'sybarite', 'helot' or Lacedaemon' on Peterloo field to perceive how little of the common touch the Doge possesses. The implication of the play is that the conspirators, though of lower order, share a common education, that they are members of what Hobhouse called in the Westminster election of 1819 the 'respectable classes'. The constitutional structure of the Spartan state (likened to Venice) is tripartite: 'prince' (Agis); 'lords' (whose magistrates, the Ephori, check the power of the prince);

'people'. Faliero (and Byron) sees Sparta, therefore, as analogous to the usual three-fold model embodied in Rome, Britain, America, that 'division of the whole legislative power into three estates' (Junius, 39). The fault of Sparta was that the austere military caste which embodied the virtues of the state—temperance and valour—reduced the people to slavery (helots). So, in Venice, the tripartite order has become unbalanced: its sovereign is a slave to a degenerate aristocracy just as much as the people are. The cause is the old, familiar, luxury which saps and destroys all Constitutions. Hence the use of the word 'sybarite'. Venice is monstrous; something out of the true nature of political order.

Hence Faliero's definition of a 'fair free commonwealth' as one in which rights are:

> Proportioned like the columns to the temple,
> Giving and taking strength reciprocal,
> And making firm the whole with grace and beauty
> So that no part could be removed without
> Infringement of the general symmetry . . .

The image of 'strength reciprocal' is in some ways preferable to the common notion of 'balance'—for the idea of checks and balances implies both the constant wavering into imbalance as one element becomes dominant, and threatens (in Fox's word) to become 'absolute', and also a constant state of 'class warfare' as the balance is restored. Faliero's ideal derives from writers like Polybius who explained the extraordinary success of the Roman people in their heroic ability to resolve their internal contests and dissentions in patriotic purpose. (Wordsworth's patriotic war sonnets have a similar class function.) It is appropriate therefore that the architectural image Faliero uses is of a classical building: a temple with columns. Any visitor to Washington may at once see on the Capitol that classic idea in architectural icon, and may read the words of Jefferson inscribed in stone declaring 'eternal hostility against every form of tyranny'.

This description reduces Faliero's speech to a rehearsal of commonplaces. It is not as easy as that. The commonplaces, to the ear of this critic, do not have the assurance and force manifested, for example, by the American founding fathers. Faliero leans heavily on the aesthetic of his description—words like 'grace', 'beauty', 'symmetry' show him like Burke aware of the poetry of politics—and he loads his discourse with words everyone would wish to associate with their cause: 'fair', 'free', 'right', 'truth', 'justice'. But the extensive use of these big, noble words is covering up the lack of any precision in the argument. It is like the use of 'Freedom' in *Childe Harold*, except that the context is different. Faliero is in a pragmatic situation. He is about to stage a *coup d'état*. Who is going to be killed? What happens tomorrow? Those questions demand immediate, practical answers.

Nowhere is the imprecision better embodied in the rhetoric than in the extraordinary wobble of the line:

> Not rash equality but equal rights.

Is there not a strong potential for contradiction in the claim that equality is not equality, or, if that is too abrupt a division, that right equality is not rash equality? It is a shuffle, and the kind of shuffle an aristocratic monarch is likely to make leading a proletarian rising. He offers equal status, and denies it.

To try to define what this means runs the risk of overrunning the text like Hobhouse in *Childe Harold*. Perhaps it is best left in its vagueness, and one should merely note that 'equal' and 'rights' are vogue words of cant political; that what Faliero does not recommend is hierarchical authority based on responsibilities and duties which might be more appropriate to his house and rank. The line is so tantalising in its implications, however, that, at the risk of overreading, a little more will be suggested.

In a Whig context that word 'rights' is linked with ideas such as the Bill of Rights, the Declaration of Rights—rights, that is, as codified by law, and expressed, in a phrase already familiar, by 'equal laws':

> by the English law and British constitution, the property and personal liberty of the lowest, the meanest subject, could not be injured or oppressed by the highest nobleman in the realm, by the most powerful minister, even by the king himself . . . the sovereign could not deprive the meanest of the people unheard, untried, uncondemned, of a single hour of his liberty.[29]

Compare Stuart prerogative, or the Bourbons and *lettres de cachet*.

Such a concept of right subsists with distinctions of rank and property. Junius put the matter simply in defending a balanced Constitution against one in which 'all ranks and conditions are confounded':

> However distinguished by rank or property, in the rights of freedom we are all equal . . . the least considerable man among us has an interest equal to the proudest nobleman, in the laws and constitution of his country . . .[30]

Clearly this separates a revolution like that of 1688, or even 1789, from Jacobinical 'levelling'. 'All men have equal rights, but not to equal things', wrote Burke in the classic rejection of egalitarianism in the *Reflections,* and he listed as rights: equal laws, the right to preserve the fruits of one's own industry, the right of inheritance, and the right to nourish one's own children.

Something of this kind, probably, Byron means by 'equal laws' in the *Ode from the French* (which laments the corruption of revolution), and also by Faliero's preference for 'equal rights' to 'rash equality'. Democracy would be a tyranny of blackguards, a dictatorship of the proletariat. Faliero, a libertarian Whig aristocrat, would lead a revolution, but not a Paineite, Jacobin, or radical *coup d'état.* Drawing the line, however, is not easy. This exposition of the context of his expressions should not smooth over the points of stress. On the contrary, the imprecise generalities of Faliero's speech, the inappropriateness of this kind of oratory as an appeal to the people, the potential contradictions in the notion of equality: these things are signs of unease.

What is the place of the people in this? Faliero is described as a 'liberal', one who recognises the rights of man, and a friend of the people. Israel Bertuccio describes him:

> his mind is liberal,
> He sees and feels the people are oppressed,
> And shares their sufferings.

> (II.ii. 174-6)

When he appears to the people they at once recognise him as their proper leader, so that his 'sovereignty' is not imposed from above but arises spontaneously as an expression of the general will to 'purify' the 'corrupted commonwealth'. It is an odd thing how easily this process of recognition of the natural leader occurs (the real life Carbonari in Naples, Byron noted, were far less successful!),[31] and then how much alarm is engendered in Faliero that this has happened at all. Is the adoption wish-fulfilment by the dramatist, or do people recognise an aristocratic class as providing natural leaders (witness the career of a recent scion of the house of Marlborough)? Perhaps that question is best left undebated.

The sufferings of the oppressed are carefully held at arms length. The specific complaint for which Israel Bertuccio seeks redress is that noble Barbaro has hit him on the face and drawn blood 'dishonourably'. Israel has the same code of values as the Doge himself (whose honour has been insulted), and is therefore a complainant within the aristocratic system. It is the same kind of conception which later leads 'honourable' Bertram as a client to turn to his patron when he betrays the revolution.

The pressure of Byron's model, Otway, operates here, for the motives in *Venice Preserved* are likewise personalised among members of the same class. Otway had to tread carefully in the political miasma of the 1680s. Byron too is writing in a highly charged political situation, but one must recognise that to a large extent form determines content. The decorum of the neoclassical tragic drama demands a 'high' style which of necessity excludes alternative discourses—including 'the voice of the people' who would use a different form of expression, and thus, different arguments. This is readily obvious by comparing a work already cited on the topic of 'honour': *Henry IV*. Byron, by preferring the neoclassical to the Shakespearian mode, has excluded that variety of style which is so typical of Shakespeare, and thus the variety of voices competing in dialectical debate. Falstaff's speech 'What's honour?' is an obvious example. Shakespeare creates the dramatic illusion that the people can speak for themselves. They do not, and they cannot, in *Marino Faliero*. In this respect, 'the people' in Byron's tragedy are in the same position as the Luddites in the House of Lords debates. The oratory of the leaders of state operates over an immense void of silence.

Thus 'the people' are seen from a height and from afar, and treated with brevity. Indeed, the text needs to be scanned for references to them![32] The issue of their disfranchisement is raised by the Doge: the people 'are nothing in the state, and in/ The city worse than nothing'. The matter is raised, and disappears. Israel offers the Doge a list of 'wrongs' under whose 'strong conception' the people groan: the foreign troups are in arrears of pay; the people are taxed for the war against Genoa, which is fought with 'plebian blood'; the class has suffered sexual 'oppression, or pollution' from the patricians. These matters also disappear. One need only consider what might have been made of the issue 'no taxation without representation'. It was the cause of Hampden, of the American Revolution, a crucial pragmatic issue for parliamentary reformers. To raise, then drop, such matters suggests that the playwright is listing just sufficient grievances to motivate discontent, but is not prepared to develop them to a point where the people must intrude as a radical force in the action. Compare, from Shakespeare again, the role of the plebs in *Coriolanus*. When, at long last, the citizens eventually appear at the end of *Marino Faliero* after the execution, their function is brief and choric:

> *Third Cit.* Then they have murdered him who would have freed
> us.
> *Fourth Cit.* He was a kind man to the commons ever.
>
> (V.iv. 21-2)

This is very similar to the function of *Il Popolo* (thus the speech prefix) in Alfieri's *Agide* who comment on the greatness of the protagonist, but do not save him. A chorus does not participate in the action.

The degree to which *Marino Faliero* suppresses any potential radical message may be further illustrated by comparison with Alfieri. *Agide*'s tragedy is provoked by his intention to abolish debts and re-establish community of property according to the laws of Lycurgus (the restoration of the Constitution). Thus luxury (*lusso*) will be purged and the hardy virtue of the citizen army preserved. (If this were popularised, what Agide is advocating is 'national socialism' more than 'capitalism'.) The austere chastity of Alfieri's high neo-classical form and language ensures that his provocative ideas are only for the intelligentsia (and Byron too, asking that his tragedy be only read, likewise shrinks from being clapper-clawed by the palms of the vulgar). Noble Agide commits suicide rather than lead *Il Popolo* in armed insurrection against the laws of Sparta. There must be no civil war. His name and fame will provide the necessary example. Isolated thus, it is easy for the corrupt *ephori* to destroy him.

The emphasis in Byron is different, despite Faliero's specific allusion to himself as a Patriot King like Agide. For the Doge readily uses violent 'resistance' as a means to his end, and the major emphasis of the tragic action is upon the disastrous consequences of forgetting the Foxite 'prudential' consideration in a bloodbath of the patrician order. The Doge talks of a balanced Constitution, but the obliteration of an entire order of state will leave only a father of the people sovereign by the popular will. There is nothing between the leader and his people.

Between Alfieri's eighteenth-century tragedy and Byron's, lies the French Revolution, and a clear indication of the dangers of democratic insurrection. What Faliero is about to unleash is the Terror. No sooner has he committed himself to revolution than he becomes a prey to doubt and riddled with guilt. This is the main theme of the action. To describe this merely as typical of the 'Byronic hero' is to subsume it into vague typology. There are specific political reasons (belonging to Byron's epoch also) why Faliero feels guilty. To be a 'Friend of the People' was commonly represented as a noble end for nobility. But who are 'the people'?:

> At midnight, by the church Saints John and Paul,
> Where sleep my noble fathers, I repair—
> To what? to hold a council in the dark
> With common ruffians leagued to ruin states!
>
> (I.ii. 579-82)

The comparison between 'noble fathers' and 'common ruffians' is pointed. The revolutionaries are 'malcontents' he thinks, and then, by implication, 'scoundrels':

> I cannot stoop—that is, I am not fit
> To lead a band of—patriots.
>
> (III.ii. 220-1)

The anachronistic allusion is obvious to anyone well-read in eightenth-century English literature. The pause places irony on the word 'patriot', and the emphasis will recall Johnson's definition of 'patriotism'. It is 'the last refuge of a scoundrel'. Others in the play are more direct. The armed Signor of the Night speaks of 'the bloodhound mob', and noble Lioni refers to those

> discontented ruffians
> And desperate libertines who brawl in taverns . . .
>
> (IV.i. 227-8)

One recollects the 'bacchanalian roar' from the London taverns in *Childe Harold.* A contemporary patrician reader might also readily call to mind the place of 'The Crown and Anchor' tavern in radical history.

Lockhart summed up the dilemma of the proud Doge:

> The conspiring Doge is not, we think, meant to be ambitious for himself, but he is sternly, proudly, a Venetian noble; and it is impossible for him to tear from his bosom the scorn for every thing plebian which has been implanted there by birth, education, and a long life of princely command.[33]

Thus the Doge is unable to exclude from his feelings a sense of mutual relationship between himself and his fellow patricians. The Terror will be directed at those who were his friends, or whose fathers were his friends:

> I loved them, they
> Requited honourably my regards;
> We served and fought; we smiled and wept in concert; . . .
> We made alliances of blood and marriage;
> We grew in years and honours fairly . . .
>
> (III.ii. 319 f.)

The key words here are 'blood', 'honour' and 'alliance', and the Doge distinguishes himself from Israel (the plebian Gracchus and popular tribune): 'You never broke their bread, nor shared their salt.' That heartfelt expression of the Doge's is not dissimilar from Byron's reaction to the Cato Street conspiracy. He was horrified at the attempt to assassinate his political opponent Harrowby. Had they not dined together hundreds of times? The point is introduced not to establish a crude biographical identification between Byron and Faliero, but merely to indicate that there is an empathy within the patrician order which the poet understands from experience, and which, therefore, he makes the Doge feel keenly. This is the tragic dilemma of Faliero. At the climactic moment of the play, when the bell rings too late for insurrection, and the tramp of martial feet Faliero hears is not that of the rebel forces but of the State's own soldiers, then the issue which he debates is the justification of terror, and the desperate tone of the soliloquy, its twists and suppressions, indicate how little he has truly convinced himself:

> And you, ye blue-sea waves! . . .
> Now thou must wear an unmixed crimson; no
> Barbaric blood can reconcile us now
> Unto that horrible incarnadine,
> But friend or foe will roll in civic slaughter.
> And have I lived to fourscore years for this?
> I, who was named Preserver of the City? . . .
> But this day, black within the calendar,
> Shall be succeeded by a bright millennium.
> Doge Dandolo survived to ninety summers
> To vanquish empires, and refuse their crown;
> I will resign a crown, and make the State
> Renew its freedom—but oh! by what means?
> The noble end must justify them—What
> Are a few drops of human blood? 'tis false,
> The blood of tyrants is not human; they
> Like to incarnate Molochs, feed on ours,
> Until 'tis time to give them to the tombs
> Which they have made so populous.—Oh World!
> Oh Men! What are ye, and our best designs,
> That we must work by crime to punish crime? . . .
> I must not ponder this.
>
> (IV.ii. 141 f.)

Byron's defects as a dramatic poet make criticism more than usually difficult. To claim that this argument is 'unconvincing' may be a comment more on the uncertainty of the writing than of Faliero's mind. It *sounds*, however, as if he is trying to convince himself about his policy, and failing. The echo of *Macbeth*—the sea 'incarnadine'—suggests the immense potential of evil to spread its stain everywhere. The counter-claim, that there will be but 'a few drops of human blood' may be the equivalent of Lady Macbeth's 'a little water clears us of this deed'—it is a statement necessary for the murderer to make, but untrue and not necessarily believed by the speaker. It necessitates a further distancing of the bloodshed—'the blood of tyrants is not human'—a statement in utter contradiction to everything Faliero has said earlier about the ties of blood which bind him to those whose bread and salt he has shared. It is, of course, a common strategy to dehumanise one's enemy; as non-human they cannot therefore claim 'equal rights' to life, liberty and the pursuit of happiness. But he does not sound as if he is convincing himself, and even less a potential audience. That question, must we work by crime to punish crime?, is *not* answered by the assumption that the end justified the means. It is much closer to the question in *Childe Harold,* 'Can tyrants but by tyrants conquered be?'. Of course Faliero is eager to demonstrate that, as a friend of equal rights, it is not he but his enemies who are wrong, but the new order he is offering is now no more than a form of words: 'a bright millennium'. There is not a single pragmatic proposal surviving in the speech—except the requirement to kill. The extinction of the patrician order in 'civic slaughter' *must* produce freedom. This view is utterly naive, and there is no reason to suppose from the text that it is anything more than the wish-fulfilment of an old man whose mind, he will soon admit, has become unhinged. Dagolino early in the play has indicated the likely extent of the terror. He was indifferent if 'thousands' should be exterminated. It is 'The spirit of this Aristocracy/ Which must be rooted out'. (III.ii. 40-1). The historical analogy is quite clear. Like Mirabeau or La Fayette, for the noblest of reasons, Faliero is committing himself to a disastrous course of action.

Faliero is enabled to preserve the nobility of his intention—to free the state from the corruption of its dominant aristocracy—only because the idea never issues in the execution of thousands. The betrayal of the conspiracy in many respects is more honourable than the (insulted) honour of the Doge and Israel Bertuccio. Bertram goes to Lioni for the best of motives. As a loyal 'client' to his 'patron' he wishes to save the life of this noble patrician. Nor is there anything to suggest that Lioni is unworthy of his regard. His concern for the state's safety as much as his own indicates his patriotism. In particular he shows the sensitivity and culture which belonged to a refined order of men. The over-long soliloquy in which he reflects upon Venice in the moonlight, her beauty and decadence, has often been noted as dramatically inappropriate. One of its functions, however, is to establish Lioni as a man of feeling, which is part of his true breeding, as much as his concern for his responsibilities to those beneath him who were his father's friends, and to his own class. Character analysis is not to the purpose, but after Faliero and Angiolina, Lioni is the most conspicuous example of a patrician and a senator in the play, and he is admirable. It is impossible to claim the whole order is corrupt when it contains such quality, and if that aristocracy were extirpated it would carry with it all that sense of patriarchal responsibility and all that fine feeling which Lioni embodies. In short, we are told aristocracy is corrupt, we are shown in Lioni (and Angiolina) types of its excellence.

The play is structured, therefore, upon paradoxes and contradictions. The resolution to which it moves is Faliero's prophetic curse. Since it was written after the extinction of the Venetian republic in this, at least, the Doge can speak the 'truth' about future times. Unlike Agide, he does not offer the consolation to posterity that the nobility of his death will ensure that the greatness of his ideals will be fulfilled some time in the future:

> Maturo è omai, credete a me maturo
> E il cangiamento: il ciel non vuol ch'io 'l vegga:
> Ma vuol ch'ei segua.
>
> (IV.iii. 292-4)

For the 1780s Agide's words have a prophetic upbeat. It is the equivalent of Byron's 'the king-times are fast finishing . . . I shall not live to see it, but I foresee it', and may have inspired Byron's expression. Both are greatly different from the curse on Venice and its degenerate aristocracy:

> Yes, the hours
> Are silently engendering of the day,
> When she, who built 'gainst Attila a bulwark,
> Shall yield, and bloodlessly and basely yield
> Unto a bastard Attila. [Bonaparte]
>
> (V.iii. 45-9)

Agide dies involved with his incorruptible virtue, rejecting even his family with the austerity of a Socrates or a Lucius Junius Brutus:

> i cittadini sono:
> Di un giusto re figli primieri.
>
> (V.ii. 44-5)

Faliero's sententious summary of his position is:

> I am not innocent—but are these guiltless?
>
> (V.iii. 40)

His crime has been against criminals. The line is obviously intended as a moral summary, and leaves the play locked in the basic contradiction which had produced its tragic outcome. In a corrupt state revolution itself corrupts: crime punishes crime. The name and fame of ideal virtue were the consolation of Sparta's king in his tragic failure. For Faliero there follows in history the obliteration of his image, and his ill-repute to posterity.

*   *   *

In his high moral idealism Sparta's king had rejected violent insurrection: 'Regenerar virtù non puote sangue.' The policy he had sought to adopt was to use the law to reform corruption, to restore the pristine virtue of the Constitution. It is, as we now know with the benefit of hindsight, the way adopted by progressive liberalism in the series of major reforms which gathered pace in England after 1820. Revolution, at least in Britain, was not 'inevitable'. A state which can reform itself from within cannot be entirely corrupt. The pessimistic question which history might put, none the less, is, can such restoration or reform be *necessarily* expected?

The tragedy of *The Two Foscari* arises from the rejection of 'resistance' as a principle of state, and the acceptance of the paramountcy of law. Jeffrey, in calling this 'passive obedience' would make the Foscari Tories and the Venetian regime in some sense an historical parallel to the Stuarts. But that avoids the dilemma Byron presents, for the Venetian state is not operating by arbitrary prerogative. Jacopo Foscari is condemned by due process of known law over which Doge Foscari properly presides. The 'ideal' form of that tragedy is the story of Lucius Junius Brutus, where the father has to condemn the sons because the state and its laws are superior to the ties of family. The Doge repeatedly in the last scene of the play draws attention to his rejection of the revolutionary cause adopted by 'attainted' Faliero and refuses to curse the State. Faliero was executed at the Giant's Staircase as a traitor: the Doge Foscari resolves to walk down the same staircase as a private citizen divested of sovereignty. 'Resistance' was criminal in Faliero. Legality is Foscari's prudential choice.

Like Faliero, Foscari expresses his conception of the ideal state. It is that in which he is chief 'citizen' of the 'whole republic' and of the 'general will'. In another context this might be the vocabulary of 'Jacobinism' (*citoyen, volunté generale*), but which is here effectively colonised by the patrician order. As chief of the legislature (the state's sovereign) it is Foscari's duty to obey the state's laws (Erskine or Brougham would agree). His view is put with the highest idealism:

> in all things
> I have observed the strictest reverence;
> Not for the laws alone, . . . but . . .
> I have observed with veneration, like
> A priest's for the High Altar, even unto
> The sacrifice of my own blood and quiet,
> Safety, and all save honour, the decrees,
> The health, the pride, and welfare of the State.
>
> (II.i. 248 f.)

That phrase 'all save honour', again recalls Faliero, and reminds that the chief citizen of the republic is an aristocrat, of generous blood, not a plebian.

The key scene for a political reading of the play is the debate between Marina (Jacopo's wife) and the Doge at the end of the second act. Marina's allegorical name and idealised role give her utterances authority. The Doge's patriotism is misguided, she exclaims. The state which he serves is now in the hands of an oligarchy whose code of laws is more than Draconian. Such a government is a traitor to the Constitution, not Jacopo. The oligarchs are tyrants. (Compare Hobhouse in *Examiner* 631 on 'the Oligarchical Conspiracy, which has ruined England, which can maintain its usurped power only by our perpetual enslavement: and which we must, therefore, determine to annihilate, if we determine to be free'.)

> The Country is the traitress, which thrusts forth
> Her best and bravest from her. Tyranny
> Is far the worst of treasons. Dost thou deem
> None rebels except subjects? The Prince who

Neglects or violates his trust is more
A brigand than the robber-chief.

(II.i. 386-91)

The awkwardness of Byron's theatrical writing as usual makes
critical assessment of the dramatic function of this difficult, but it
sounds as if part of a casuistical debate rather than an expression of
character, although as Jacopo's wife Marina has motivation 'in
character' for arguing like this. One might compare the tone and
function of Angelo and Isabella debating justice and mercy in
Measure for Measure. There is a morality play feel to the language.
The function of Marina's casuistry here is to identify the patrician
order as an oligarchical tyranny. Once establish the word 'tyranny'
as a correct description of the government, then the traditional
appeal to tyrannicide might be made: it is a 'right' of 'slaves' to
achieve 'freedom' by 'resistance'.

The Doge is given longer to reply, and that reply returns
repeatedly to the word 'law':'

I found the law: I did not make it. Were I
A subject, still I might find parts and portions
Fit for amendment; but as Prince, I never
Would change, for the sake of my house, the charter
Left by our fathers.

(II.i. 395-9)

This is liberal constitutionalism. The law may be used to amend the
law—that is the right of the subject. The Doge, as supreme
magistrate, is in the position of a judge. His function must be to
apply the rule of law such as is given to him. It would be utterly
corrupt to alter it unilaterally for family concern. That is what it
means to be a 'citizen'.

If we had not for many centuries
Had thousands of such citizens, and shall,
I trust, have still such, Venice were no city.

(II.i. 415-17)

Unlike Faliero, who cursed a degenerate state, Doge Foscari sees
himself as one citizen only in a great tradition stretching before and
after.

111

Like Agide, therefore, his example must stand as a type of ideal state service. He says that had he as many sons as he had years he would have given them all for the state (though not without feeling). The role models are, therefore, figures like Lucius Junius Brutus (another of Alfieri's heroes) or Cato Uticensis (Addison's Whig hero). Doge Faliero, in this tradition, is spoken of as a 'stoic of the state' and as showing 'more than Roman fortitude'. He claims that under her laws:

> Venice
> Has risen to what she is—a state to rival
> In deeds and days, and sway, and let me add,
> In glory (for we have had Roman spirits
> Amongst us), all that history has bequeathed
> Of Rome and Carthage in their best times, when
> The people swayed by Senates.
>
> (II.i. 400-6)

His ultimate message to Jacopo is brief:

> That he obey
> The laws.
>
> (II.i. 435-6)

The Doge's arguments in reply to Marina are—to the ear of this reader—as abstract as her own. The appeal is to an idealised concept of classical antiquity on which the great man of modern state should model his conduct. The Senate is the expression of the general will of an uncorrupted people. The supreme magistrate is the executor of that will legally embodied. The true patriot's function is service to the people, at whatever cost. An antique, and formalised conception—the true republic—is set in direct contrast to another: the tyrannical regime. Both are used to describe Venice. Action is dependent on which conception prevails.

Isolating a fragment of the play in this manner risks distorting the whole. *The Two Foscari* is far less of a political play than *Marino Faliero*. The major emphasis is upon the suffering of father, son and wife, and upon the extraordinary patriotism of Jacopo who prefers torture in a Venetian jail to exile elsewhere. His actions, like Faliero's, seem excessive, and the question of 'political justice'—are the laws those of 'the people' or 'a tyrant'?—only indirectly relates to the highly personalised motive of revenge which drives Loredano, like Shylock, to use the law to obliterate mercy.

With that caveat in mind one may, none the less, extend the political theme into the private story by observing that the law is not an abstract and ideal thing. It is made by people (and by ruling classes). What happens to the respect due to the rule of law and the Constitution when those who make the laws are corrupt? 'Political justice' may be justice politicised, and personalised. When the Doge proclaims his 'strictest reverence' for the laws he adds a proviso. Loredano has, 'strained' them, and he adds:

> I do not speak of *you* but as a single voice
> Of many . . .

At the beginning of the fourth act Loredano puts the matter bluntly:

> *Barbarigo.*   But will the laws uphold us?
> *Loredano.*   What laws?—'The Ten' are laws; and if they were not,
> I will be legislator in this business.
>
> (IV.i. 37-9)

A wilful patrician can use the acquiescent 'Ten', or the Senate, to push through what he desires as legislator. If the state is the slave of a tyrant, (or tyrants) who use its Constitution, its courts, and their power as 'legislators' to foster their own aims (as Loredano does) then 'justice' is merely the expression of the usurping self-interest of those able to manipulate power for their own ends. To use an analogy from the politics of Byron's time: 'the Ten', with Loredano pushing them on, are the historical equivalent to that power of the Crown which had increased, was increasing, and ought to be diminished. Barbarigo attacks Loredano for using 'your Giunta' for his aims.

> *Loredano.*   How!—*my* Giunta!
> *Barbarigo.*   *Yours!*
> They speak your language, watch your nod, approve
> Your plans, and do your work. Are they not *yours?*

Loredano.	You talk unwarily. 'Twere best they hear not
	This from you.
Barbarigo.	Oh! they'll hear as much one day
	From louder tongues than mine; they have gone beyond
	Even their exorbitance of power: and when
	This happens in the most contemned and abject
	States, stung humanity will rise to check it.
Loredano.	You talk but idly.
Barbarigo.	That remains for proof.

(V.i. 141-50)

Moore wrote in the *Life* of Sheridan that 'Law is but too often . . . the ready accomplice of Tyranny', and he sharpened the generalisation to a criticism of the Pittite system which used legislation to encroach 'upon the property and liberty of the subject'.[34] No Marxist criticism of the relation between class and power could put the matter more clearly. It is tempting to act as a latter-day Hobhouse, to point to the state trials of Hardy, the Hunts, Burdett, which must have been in Byron's mind, or even to look forward and observe how the submission of the martyrs of Tolpuddle to legal transportation mirrors the exile of Jacopo. But the text resists the local allegory. The debate is in terms of general principle only. Byron is concerned with the political philosophy which an historical record might teach, and, unlike *Childe Harold,* has no provocative commentator.

When the power of the State became 'exorbitant' then 'stung humanity will rise to check it' said Barbarigo. It is a Byronic 'prophecy'. It is the old theme of 'resistance' to 'tyranny' when the 'balance' of power is distorted. But one cannot isolate the passage this way to support a preconceived image of revolutionary Byron. Loredano is unimpressed: 'You talk but idly'. Loredano is quite correct. The historical fact about the Venetian State was that 'stung humanity' did nothing. Revolution was not inevitable. Faliero's curse was fulfilled. What followed was the 'euthanasia' of the Constitution. Barbarigo's fear of speaking out—his lack of a 'loud tongue'—is symptomatic of reluctant acquiescence sinking to servility. (Compare, if one will, a free press, or the poet's voice.) But, on the other hand, what use was Faliero's resistance?

As for an appeal to the people . . . Doge Foscari has the word 'citizen' often in his mouth, but *Il Popolo* do not have even a brief scene in this tragedy to express their admiration for a 'Friend of the People'. In any case, his name and fame rests on thirty-four years of war, not, for instance, on regulations concerning conditions of labour or the liberty of the press. Venice—all the citizens collectively—is embodied only in Marina whose attack on 'murder by law' is magnificent, but abstract. She accuses her country in the name of

> Men and Angels!
> The blood of myriads reeking up to Heaven,
> The groan of slaves in chains, and men in dungeons,
> Mothers, and wives, and sons, and sires, and subjects,
> Held in the bondage of ten bald-heads . . .
>
> (III.i. 240-4)

Marchand calls this 'the voice of rebellion that is never silenced by timidity or considerations of policy'.[35] But it is *not* rebellion. It is a protest delivered by an allegorical abstraction which has no result. Her demand for 'retribution' is as powerless as her earlier call for resistance. She represents no specific force within the orders of the State. It is only a voice, its helplessness emphasised by her sex.

But the man who acted, Faliero, likewise achieved nothing. Tormented by a guilty conscience he was executed as a criminal.

*　　*　　*

A recent lecture on 'Byron in Venice' spoke of Byron's 'iron revolutionary will'.[36] Wherever that may be found, it is not in the Venetian tragedies. They represent an impasse, and inevitable decline. It was a classic dilemma. Livy, beginning his account of the fall of the Roman republic, wrote that he would trace for his reader the process of the state's moral decay as the old teaching was abandoned and disintegrated, until the condition was reached when Rome could neither continue to survive because of her present vices, nor endure the remedies necessary to cure them: *ad haec tempora quibus nec vitia nostra nec remedia pati possumus perventum est.* No redress for grievances can be obtained, Faliero tells Israel, neither for himself nor for the people. In this the teaching of history, and the historical record, supported Byron as the sober language of Rose's *Letter from the North of Italy* indicates in an appendix to the text. 'A state without the means of some change is without the means of its conservation', wrote another classic historian. The words are those of Burke in the *Reflections on the Revolution in France.*

The traditional analogy between Venice and Britain suggests that the Italian experience is intended to carry a message for the poet's own country. The question for critical tact is to determine how far the role of moral historian and political poet overlap. The ancient subject matter and the rigid decorum of neoclassical tragedy distance the action and control the nature of what can be said. Perhaps the Brechtian concept of 'alienation' may help here. By distancing the action it is easier to understand the principles involved. Not that a fully detached objectivity is possible. If the lessons of history are pertinent to the contemporary situation, history is only understood through our own experience of the contemporary world.

In that respect, there are analogies, for instance, between Faliero's desire to lead his vassals in resistance, and Byron's vision of himself at the head of the men of Leicestershire; or the Doge's revulsion from the blackguardly conspirators and the poet's from Hunt and Cobbett. One might extend the analogies further and suggest that the relation between the overblown rhetoric of the plays and the exaggerated sentiments of the Queen Caroline affair is that both show aristocratic and chivalric ideals which are fast becoming anachronistic.

This is a matter of similarity, not identity. The plays are monitory: take warning from history. In so far as they relate, in general, to the situation of 'Tory' Britain they do not show any 'progressive' way forward. The choice is between class revolution or the continuation, *sine die,* of 'corruption' in the form of a reactionary oligarchy opposed by a party which has lost all guts for reform. Whig constitutionalism is a dead letter; joining the radicals will bring in Hunt and Cobbett, worse than Robespierre or Marat. Faliero is in a position analogous to La Fayette or Mirabeau (or Lord Byron if revolution came). Foscari is as helpless as Byron in the Lords. There is nothing to be done.

Advocates of Byron as the 'iron revolutionary' may indicate the substantial galvanic outbursts elsewhere in his writing, and life. But to what end? Compare the hard slog of step-by-step redress of a successful humanitarian liberal like Brougham (whom Byron hated). The poet conceives no such hero, and poets achieve no practical objective. The Venetian plays show how firmly the wheels of the juggernaut of state became stuck in the mire, and a happy Tennysonian vision of 'freedom broadening from precedent to precedent' does not correspond to the years of Peterloo, Cato Street, the Six Acts, nor to the lesson of Faliero's and Foscari's history. Byron's intermittent verbal explosions are the product of frustration.

As for Byron, the man of action, the *Capo* of the Carbonari . . .. He did not have the practical experience of a Cochrane to offer—a real liberator. The battlefields of Europe are littered with the bodies of those who believed that generous birth qualifies the rich to lead armies. But Byron never came under fire, and the Carbonari were snuffed out by professional soldiers in a twinkling. The call to the Italians to unite was merely the poetry of politics. Nothing came of it, and Byron's letters trace the swift ascent of hope to recrimination and bitterness. It was the usual cycle (compare 1812). Byron's disenchantment was part of general experience. 'I had no conception of the excess to which avarice, cowardice, superstition, ignorance, passionless lust, and all the inexpressible brutalities which degrade human nature, could be carried', wrote Shelley of the Venetians. How could a people degenerate for centuries acquire civic virtues under ' a foreign army and a barbarous code', asked Lord Russell to Lord Holland. The problem was, Lord Burghersh pointed out, that the Italians hated one another. Hence criticism of their 'cowardice, versatility, profligacy', their 'abject submission', their 'deformity of character'. 'Unworthy Naples', wrote Moore in his *Torch of Liberty*. It was not an issue worth a war, commented Canning, following in Castlereagh's footsteps; England should not, 'in the foolish spirit of romance, suppose that we alone could regenerate Europe'. To which one may add Byron himself on the Carbonari: ' . . . these villains.—But there is no room to be sufficiently bilious—nor bile enough to spit upon them.'[37]

Byron's political education, therefore, is not in revolution, but in disenchantment. It is a process of learning the hard way. But it is learning about things as they are. Compare the Venetian plays with Shelley's *Revolt of Islam,* whose delightful Laon and Cynthia belong to no age, no class, no race, but inspired by a pure disinterested love of mankind founded on reading the sages and poets of antiquity achieve social equality by the sheer force of their oratory. Byron's characters, on the contrary, have to deal with recognisable circumstances of time and place, social role, the corruption of human nature. Both revolutions fail, but Shelley's is pure fiction, Byron's part of real, historical record. One may ask practical questions of Faliero and Foscari, place them in relation to other historical types and situations, see in their dilemmas analogies to the contemporary state of Europe. A strong political tradition and a powerful historical imagination are at work.

How does one get out of the impasse? The conclusion of the major comic poems which conclude Byron's career is that there is no obvious way forward. The Whigs are where they had always been in Byron's life. *Plus ça change, plus c'est la même chose. The Vision of Judgment* shows God in his heaven—but God is a Tory. The Whigs are with Satan in hell.

5

The Reign of George III:
The Vision of Judgment

The matter of *The Vision of Judgment* was given to Byron by
Southey. The trial of George III, the choice of Wilkes and Junius as
chief witnesses for a Whiggish Satan, the king's admittance into a
Tory heaven—these are all in Southey's report which Byron
follows (comically) as if historical record. Even the fall of the
laureate into Derwentwater is suggested by the original: 'at the
chilling touch of the water,/ . . . my feet methought sunk, and I fell
precipitate'. Pope would have relished the Cibberian bathos. The
declared intention of Byron's parody was 'to put . . . George's
Apotheosis in a Whig point of view'.[1] The poem provides a direct
confrontation between Whig and Tory views on common matter of
history from the American Revolution to the King's death.

If the nature of the debate is to be understood, the Tory voice
must be heard. Southey's loyalism to the Court was particularly
valuable to established authority because it came from a writer who
had seen the error of his early Jacobinism. Although the poem has
usually been judged to be aesthetically ridiculous, it does not
necessarily follow that its ideology is ridiculous also. Little damage
will be done to the 'spavined dactyls' of Southey's panegyrical
hyperbole by separating Tory principle from poetic form!

If the poem had succeeded with later readers it might be seen as a
traditional panegyric of Augustan 'arms and arts' (the kind of
poem Dryden wrote). The peace and happiness of the 'free and
prosperous' people of Britain shows the operation of Divine
Providence of which the king is the agent: 'a trustee deriving his
interest in . . . [his territories] from God, and invested with them
by divine authority, for the benefit of his subjects'. Thus, Heaven
rejoices at the restoration of the 'ancient line' of the Bourbons, and

at the banishment of Bonaparte, the 'man of blood, the tyrant, faithless and godless'. The friends of the godless tyrant are, thus, the devil's disciples, the members of the 'Satanic school' of the notorious preface.

This yoking of God's purpose in history to a particular political viewpoint is 'reactionary' for it suggests something of the seventeenth century rather than the Enlightenment. A claim based on the 'right of birth and Divine assistance' has a Stuart ethos about it. *The Examiner* was to complain of the 'blasphemy' of recruiting the heavenly host as Tory agents 'in a piece of official servility'. But it is typical of the time (and of the kind of situation Byron had portrayed in *The Two Foscari*) that Lord Chief Justice Abbot and a Special Jury backed a Tory God and Tory laws. It was John Hunt who was prosecuted for publishing Byron's *Vision,* and James Scarlett (defending) appealed in vain to 'the truth of history'.[2] Religion and justice were functions of state power:

> Judge with my judgment, and by my decision
> Be guided who shall enter heaven or fall!

> (101)

Southey's strategy with the forces of hell is to deny them a voice in his poem. The devil and his witnesses, Wilkes and Junius, are tongue-tied and abashed. The reason is that factious Whig opposition had provoked rebellion of which the consequences were not foreseen: first America, then, by contagion, France (and Jacobinism). *The Examiner* (695) protested: 'JOHN WILKES, it seems, and not ages of oppression and misgovernment in France, and the blundering stupidity of British Councils, produced the French and American Revolutions.' But Southey is merely using Wilkes in the way the opposition used Castlereagh. The enemy, individualised, is not representative of 'the people', but embodies personal wickedness united with power.

Wilkes is an excellent target for Southey, for the hero of 'Liberty' was a notorious libertine as well as demagogue: 'the blasphemer of his God and the libeller of his King', said Pitt.[3] He is the type of the Satanic school's corruption of morals and politics, of 'everything in religion, in morals and probably in government and literature, which our Forefathers have been accustomed to reverence'.[4] As the 'Lord of Misrule' he is strongly contrasted with the modern

'Fabius, Aristides, and Solon, and Epaminondas', George Washington, who is recruited from the Whigs to the Tories. Wilkes provoked the American Revolution, but Washington and George III ('Rebel' and 'Tyrant' as they were called in life) in death are honourable admirers, acquiescent to providence in history, eager that nations learning from American and British experience should lay aside wrongful resentment and join in brotherhood. Southey is thus not the 'apostate' or 'renegade' he was called by the opposition, but is intent to show how legitimate government can reconcile liberal views with order. Abstractly considered, the union of Washington and George III makes sense if one recalls La Fayette's ideal of combining the best of the British and the American Constitutions against Jacobinism.

Conciliation is strongly emphasised throughout the poem. (It is the Whigs who divide the nation.) Charles the Martyr (a tyrant Stuart in the mythology of Whiggery) is at peace with the expeller of the Stuarts, William, of Glorious memory. Both are seen as part of the evolving tradition deriving from the Anglo-Saxon Constitution of Alfred, best of 'the Saxon Kings who founded our laws and our temples'. So too Milton, who has abandoned his regicide delusions, is at peace with Edmund Burke who broke loose from the trammels of party (the factious Whigs) and 'gave to mankind what party too long had diverted'. Southey is seeking to speak for an historically united people. Or, put another way, he retains the totem poles of the opposing tribe to which he had belonged in his hot youth.

But there can be no conciliation with the French Revolution. That issue is not fudged. The fear of imminent Jacobinism walks large in the poem. Between that hell and even a liberal heaven there can be no marriage. Consider Satan:

> Many-headed and monstrous the Fiend; with numberless faces,
> Numberless bestial ears erect to all rumours, and restless,
> And with numberless mouths which were fill'd with lies as with
> arrows.
> Clamour arose as he came, a confusion of turbulent voices,
> Maledictions, and blatant tongues, and viperous hisses;
> And in the hubbub of senseless sounds the watchwords of faction,
> Freedom, Invaded Rights, Corruption, and War, and Oppression,
> Loudly enounced were heard.
>
> (5)

This figure, derived from Virgil, Spenser, Shakespeare, and the many-headed beast of the Apocalypse, is intended as an allegorical representation of the *Belua multorum capitum:* the mob. Southey, in the *Quarterly,* argued that 'the Devil whose name is Legion' is the deity represented in the claim *Vox populi, vox Dei,* and recalled the Gordon riots and the Terror.[5] The mob, in the poem, has its mouth full of the discourse of the Whig/Jacobin opposition in a senseless babble of words like 'Freedom' ('Yet Freedom! yet . . .'), 'Right', 'Corruption', 'Oppression'. These are the forces of Anarchy, the foes of legitimate government, malicious and blasphemous in their rage and hate.

> Dimly descried within were wings and truculent faces;
> And in the thick obscure there struggled a mutinous uproar,
> Railing, and fury, and strife, that the whole deep body of darkness
> Roll'd like a troubled sea, with a wide and a manifold motion. (4)

What alarms the poet is that the devil's disciples are not confined to the hellish dead. As soon as George III is restored to his senses in heaven, one of the first questions he asks the assassinated Spencer Perceval is whether the spirit is quelled 'which hath troubled the land? and the multitude freed from delusion,/ Know they their blessings at last, and are they contented and thankful?'. It could be the opening for a Golden Age panegyric. But Perceval replies:

> Still is that fierce and restless spirit at work . . .
> Still it deceiveth the weak, and inflameth the rash and the
> desperate.
> Even now, I ween, some dreadful deed is preparing;
> For the Souls of the Wicked are loose, and the Powers of Evil
> Move on the wing alert. Some nascent horror they look for,
> Be sure! some accursed conception of filth and of darkness
> Ripe for its monstrous birth. Whether France or Britain be
> threaten'd,
> Soon will the issue show; or if both at once are endanger'd,
> For with the ghosts obscene of Robespierre, Danton, and Hebert,
> Faux and Despard I saw, and the band of rabid fanatics,
> They whom Venner led, who rising in frantic rebellion
> Made the Redeemer's name their cry of slaughter and treason. (3)

Southey's note refers to the assassination of the Duc de Berri in

France and the Cato Street conspiracy in England, but these are merely examples of something far larger rooted in a tradition extending from the Fifth Monarchy men of the seventeenth century to the Jacobins. The rhetoric is indefinite: a 'dreadful deed' threatens, a 'nascent horror', an 'accursed conception', but if that imprecision weakens the argument, it is nonetheless indicative of the alarm of the time. Some violent plot seemed to be hatching in obscurity. Why else the secret midnight drillings of massed workers, the systematic theft of arms, the circulation of delegates from district to district? Jeremiah Brandreth's rebels marched on Nottingham believing revolution's hour was come on rumours as vague as those to which Southey alludes. 'On whatever side I cast my eyes I see the restless and turbulent genius of evil inspiring every where ideas subversive and revolutionary.'[6] Such is the typical language of beleagured legitimacy.

The names of the provokers of anarchy which Southey selects are safe enough to unite potential readers. One notices the suppression of revolution's familiar Foxite martyrs: Sydney and Russell, for example (whom Southey claimed in the *Quarterly* would be well satisfied with the present Constitution). Likewise, the indefinite 'alarmist' rhetoric avoids specific issues on which the multitude were 'deluded': Peterloo, for instance. The emphasis is on the dangerous way a discourse of 'Freedom' and 'Rights' and tyrannical oppression in the mouth of the 'pale Catilines' of the Senate (the Whigs) lends support to the Jacobinical forces of 'the hircine host obscene' (the poet's goatish equivalent of the notorious 'swinish multitude').

Southey's contemporary heroes are men like Canning, a true *friend of his country* (compare 'friend of the people' in Whig cant political), and, provocatively, Lord Mansfield. He is

> just and intrepid;
> Wise Judge, by the craft of the Law ne'er seduced from his
> purpose.
> And when the misled multitude raged like the winds in their
> madness,
> Not to be moved from his rightful resolves.
>
> (10)

In Whig demonology Mansfield, who committed Wilkes to jail, was one of the major enemies of the freedom of the press because he invaded 'the province of the jury in matter of libel'.[7] The Whigs won from the judge the right of the jury to determine of libel, hence the motto 'Trial by Jury' on Erskine's coach. But what Southey prefers to recall is Mansfield's great speech on the theme *fiat justitia, ruat coelum* when the mob menaced his court. If justice were at the disposal of rioters then, in North's words, 'this constitution must be overthrown and anarchy ensue':

> If the security of our persons and our property, of all we hold dear and valuable, are to depend upon the caprice of a giddy multitude, or to be at the disposal of a giddy mob; if, in compliance with the humours, and to appease the clamours of those, all civil and political institutions are to be disregarded or overthrown, a life somewhat more than sixty is not worth preserving at such a price, and he can never die too soon, who lays down his life in support and vindication, of the policy, the government, and the constitution of his country.[8]

This book has already told how Mansfield was beaten up and his house looted and set on fire.

The justification for 'Tory' extreme measures was the continuance of disorder. The Wilkes/Mansfield issue is presented as clear warning to the present. One of Southey's notes describes the social problem. He quotes Benjamin Franklin (named also by Byron): an American revolutionary patriot, but who was appalled by the anarchy unleashed in London in the names of the rights and liberty of the people by Wilkes, 'an outlaw and exile, of bad personal character, not worth a farthing', and yet who can reduce London to mob rule. Franklin's views were pertinent still in the 1820s as Whig libertarian rhetoric fuelled discontent. Luddism, Peterloo, the Caroline riots were not new phenomena. God knows what might happen to a people misled by seditious men and publications intent on abusing the best of Constitutions.

> Even this capital, the residence of the king, is now a daily scene of lawless riot and confusion. Mobs patrolling the street at noonday, some knocking all down that will not roar for Wilkes and liberty; courts of justice afraid to give judgement against him; coal-heavers and porters pulling down the houses of coal-merchants that refuse to give them more wages; sawyers destroying saw-mills; sailors unrigging all the outward-bound ships, and suffering none to sail till merchants agree to raise their pay; watermen destroying private boats, and threatening

bridges; soldiers firing among the mobs, and killing men, women, and children, which seems only to have produced an universal sullenness, that looks like a great black cloud coming on, ready to burst in a general tempest. What the event will be God only knows. But some punishment seems preparing for a people who are ungratefully abusing the best constitution, and the best king, any nation was ever blessed with; intent on nothing but luxury, licentiousness, power, places, pensions, and plunder . . . . All respect to law and government seems to be lost among the common people, who are moreover continually inflamed by seditious scribblers to trample on authority, and everything that used to keep them in order.

In the light of such alarm one may perceive why the Constitutional Association prosecuted Byron's *Vision*. Because it 'defames the constituted authorities of the empire, and the reputation of public men' it is likely to 'inflame' disorder. The constructive argument against the 'Satanic school' is that Whig = Wilkite = radical = Jacobin = the devil. Personal immorality is the natural concomitant of disrespect for the institutions of church and state. In the vocabulary of a high Tory like Harriet Arbuthnot the terms Whig/liberal and blasphemer/rat at times are interchangeable.

It would fall into the trap which Southey sets, however, to accept either the polarity of his distinction between Tory virtue and Whig vice, or the constructive argument which, once it separates the Whig from his constitutional traditions, sweeps him at once into ultra-radicalism and revolution. The 'Whig point of view'—as Byron unfolds it—and the Tory have a great deal in common.

There are, for instance, common silences. By choosing the distant turbulence of the Wilkite riots as his major example Southey conveniently by-passed the other face of violence shown at Peterloo. Shelley exploited the issue in *The Masque of Anarchy*. But it is not available for Byron. As Wilkes is to Southey, Hunt is to Byron. Both demagogues 'seduce the populace' (Byron's phraseology), 'mislead the multitude' (Southey's). Democracy = anarchy = tyranny.

Yet one might expect a Whig poet to appeal to 'our sovereign the people' for whom kings are 'trustees' (to redefine Southey's terms). Byron's Satan claims that millions over whom George ruled were denied 'freedom'. Yet, when 'the people' appear in Byron, if they are not the anarchical many-headed beast Southey portrays, they do not inspire much confidence. Byron echoes

Franklin's reference to a 'great black cloud coming on, ready to burst in a general tempest' when he describes that 'little speck' on the horizon like a warning of a squall in the Aegean, which grows into 'a cloud of witnesses':

- 58 -

> But such a cloud! No land e'er saw a crowd
> Of locusts numerous as the heavens saw these;
> They shadow'd with their myriads space; their loud
> And varied cries were like those of wild geese
> (If nations may be liken'd to a goose),
> And realised the phrase of 'hell broke loose.'

There follows a babble of voices swearing, asking what is going on, clamouring to speak against George: 'Damn my eyes!'; 'By Jasus!; 'What's your wull?'; '*Our* president is going to war, I guess'. It is a dramatic way of representing the international hostility to Georgian policies. But there still remains something of the *Belua multorum capitum*. This babble of tongues is disordered, like the cries of 'wild geese'. That word 'geese' implies stupidity, and the word 'wild' may have a *double entendre*. The image extends from goose to locust, a destructive plague, and Byron eventually uses a phrase Southey would not disown: 'hell broke loose'. The people, broken out of their confines, are diabolical.

This mob is not as sinister as the Jacobinical force in Southey. The clamour sounds much like that of the lower class birds in *The Parliament of Fowls*. The comic tone in which Byron treats this 'squall' suggests that he is seeking to laugh the alarmism of the Tory 'tempest' out of court. The people are more given to boisterous and warm-hearted bad language than to Tom Paine. But the implication is that such folk, though they feel the right way about oppression, have not the intelligence to exercise political authority. Certainly no one in heaven or hell will grant it them. The words 'squall' and 'locust' hint at something dangerous. Maltreat the people and violence will follow.

Faced with a turbulent mob, Michael, a Tory, turns pale and asks Satan, as one gentleman to another, not to abuse his call for witnesses. The issue of George's trial is not to be decided by the clamour of the mob. Lord Mansfield would agree. But so too would Lord Erskine, and Satan (as a Whig). The aristocratic prince of hell confines himself entirely to 'gentlemen' like Wilkes and Junius when he tries to make his case.

It was convenient for Byron that Southey should have raised the Wilkes/Junius issue. What he ducks out of is any extended consideration of the ambiguous and shifting ground of the French Revolution. The 'Whig point of view' would be damaged either by admitting that the party had countenanced Jacobinism, or that Tory resistance was justified to the internationalisation of revolution and the tyrannical ambition (Byron's own words) of Napoleon. The preface makes the familiar opposition charge against the King (and his Ministers) of 'aggression against France', but then Byron writes that he will 'say nothing' of this, and keeps his word! It was a quagmire dangerous to enter. The war years are swiftly despatched in the stanzas so eloquently expressive of 'divine disgust'. Wellington and Pitt, Bonaparte and Fox (who joined the war administration) are all in hell's hot jurisdiction. The phrase 'crowning carnage' on Waterloo is double-edged. It attacks the crowned heads of the Holy Alliance (and their laureate Wordsworth), but the thrust of the attack conceals an awkward fact: had the French won, the same phrase would have applied. There is one important exception to the descent to hell. It is Louis XVI. His soul is saved, albeit under protest, because of his execution by the Jacobins.

The post-war years are even more swiftly passed by:

– 7 –

> Let's skip a few short years of hollow peace,
> Which peopled earth no better, hell as wont,
> And heaven none—they form the tyrant's lease,
> With nothing but new names subscribed upon't;
> 'Twill one day finish: meantime they increase,
> 'With seven heads and ten horns', and all in front,
> Like Saint John's foretold beast . . .

One is familiar with the Byronic prophecy that the king-times are ending, and it is skilful of the satirist to reverse Southey's image of the beast of the apocalypse, now likened to the despots of the Holy Alliance and not to the forces of Satanic democracy. But how little thrust there is to the expression of the friend of freedom about tyrants: ' 'Twill one day finish', especially when the line is completed 'meantime they increase'. Things, at this juncture in history, are going backwards. There is very little of revolutionary or ideal republicanism in a vague threat to the Holy Alliance from some indefinite process of history, and the word Byron applies to the rulers of Europe is 'tyrant', a term which any *British* politician, Whig or Tory, would distinguish from that 'constitutional monarchy' established in a free Constitution. The stanza does not apply at home.

In short, the poem says as little as possible about events in Byron's lifetime and prefers to concentrate on issues raised before what is described as 'the Gallic era eighty-eight'. It is an odd expression, because the Bastille fell in the Gallic era eighty-nine. *The Examiner* obituary for George III may provide a clue, for the condemnation of the political misgovernment of the King in large measure halts in 1788. It was the time of the first Regency crisis which set the Whigs by the ears—the King's first major attack of insanity. Intelligent opposition required a certain tact. Not everyone might, like Shelley, link the epithet 'despised' with 'old, mad, blind . . . and dying'. There is much in George's life demanding of pity.

There are good reasons, therefore, why Byron should move the debate on George's political faults back to before 1788. But if the issues of Wilkes and Junius, of American independence and Catholic emancipation are to provide the centre piece of an opposition attack upon the Crown, then the argument is likely to fall into the old pattern of Whig against Tory, and from an era before the opposition party broke up under the shock of the French Revolution. Since Byron's *Vision,* just as much as Southey's, indicates that the lessons of the times of Wilkes were pertinent to the present, then the view of historical process will be *plus ça change, plus c'est la même chose.* An eighteenth-century debate continues as if the French Revolution were a particularly offensive interruption in an old dialectic rather than a redefinition of the nature of the debate.

The dramatic setting of the action of the poem reinforces such a conservative view. It is the celestial equivalent of either the House of Lords, or Westminster Hall where George III is impeached before the aristocracy of heaven and hell. Satan, far from being the turbulent Jacobin thousand-headed beast of Southey's alarmed imagination, represents a permanent and traditional class in opposition, for he is a great patrician figure, an archetype of the

Whigs in general, or the sixth Baron Byron in particular (whose 'name' and 'fame' dates back to William the Conqueror). The poet plays with the fact that in comparison with the great families of the opposition, many of the Tories (like Eldon or Harrowby) were 'new men'. The tight circle of the great Whig families was not easy of access (as outsiders like Brougham discovered to their cost). There is an 'in' joke about party relations, therefore, in the meeting between Michael and Satan. The Tory

> turn'd as to an equal, not too low,
> But kindly; Satan met his ancient friend
> With more hauteur, as might an old Castilian
> Poor noble meet a mushroom rich civilian.

(36)

Throughout the debate Michael and Satan observe the 'great politeness' which is appropriate both to their former friendship and to their generous breeding. As the aristocratic leaders of different parties there is a familiarity between them which unites them as members of the same class, and separates them from lower orders. Michael seeks to exploit this relationship:

> – 62 –
> Why—
> My good old friend, for such I deem you, though
> Our different parties make us fight so shy,
> I ne'er mistake you for a *personal* foe;
> Our difference is *political,* and I
> Trust that, whatever may occur below,
> You know my great respect for you: and this
> Makes me regret whate'er you do amiss—

That word 'below' is not just a spatial description. Consider the view that Paul is a *parvenu,* or the apology necessary for Peter's 'condescension to the vulgar level' made by Michael. Satan, on his side, is widely separate even from Wilkes and Junius. His solitude, fierce pride and gloom are all typical of the Byronic hero, but the *Führerprinzip* of the hero is that he leads by the force of will from above. He speaks for the people whom he leads, but he is not of the people.

The main political difference between Michael and Satan is that whereas Satan's voice is that of freedom and opposition to tyrannical government, Michael is the devoted minister of his monarch (God). He

> ne'er nursed
> Pride in his heavenly bosom, in whose core
> No thought, save for his Maker's service, durst
> Intrude, however glorified and high;
> He knew him but the viceroy of the sky.

(31)

Satan, on the other hand, is filled with personal pride—so his haughty brow—and is the self-appointed leader of the republic of hell. If it is a defect of heaven that, as a Tory institution, it is sympathetic to kings, the defect of hell is that, if not sternly controlled, it will dissolve into storm. Satan is 'like the deep when tempest-tossed'.

What holds government and opposition together is, as it were, the Constitution of eternity. Heaven and hell in their spokesmen are locked in a never-ending debate, conducted with full regard to the proprieties of men of honour. In this Constitution it is the Tories who always form the government, supreme powers always sustaining their administration, and the Whigs are always in opposition and inevitably defeated in the long run. Part of the joke of the poem is that it suggests that the parliamentary order in Britain is a reflection of the Providential order of the universe. That is what Southey claimed, recruiting God for his party, and it is one of a number of Tory arguments that Byron does not deny. It lends a particularly dampening quality to claims such as ''Twill one day finish' on the *ancien régime* (when? at judgement day?), or an aside like 'whene'er/ Reform shall happen either here or there' (104). 'Reform', presumably, means parliamentary reform. But can one really imagine Satan or Michael, Whig any more than Tory, surrendering power to the lower orders? It is as if God should turn the universe topsy-turvy.

The poem, therefore, presents an order which is in constitutional stasis between opposed patrician forces. Just as in the Venetian plays there is no way in which this oligarchical system can evolve. This is one of a number of important distinctions between Byron and his fellow 'progressive' editors of *The Liberal* (Shelley and Hunt in particular), and may help to explain why the opposition journal so swiftly disintegrated. The interesting matter of Satan's speech is not the issue of principle on which he argues—freedom against tyranny—which is merely standard opposition fare, but the *context* in which the political argument takes place. The speech is that of a prosecuting counsel, and therefore weighted in one direction; the advocate is Satan in the *persona* of an aristocratic Byronic hero (with all the overtones of dark guilt and dangerous rebellion that implies); and nothing Satan says will affect the Providential outcome of things: 'God save the king!' Michael will retain his ministerial power. The 'Whig point of view' involves, therefore, polemic rhetoric, dangerous rebellious overtones, and exclusion from office and power.

Little need be said about the general principles of the attack. The vocabulary is familiar:

> He ever warr'd with freedom and the free:
> Nations as men, home subjects, foreign foes,
> So that they utter'd the word ''Liberty!''
> Found George the Third their first opponent.

(45)

So too are the major topics chosen: the American Revolution; the spread of that movement to France; Catholic emancipation; freedom of the press; freedom of election. 'He has all the private virtues, all the Christian virtues, but he wants to encroach on our liberties.' So Wilkes told Boswell.[9] *The Examiner* obituary covers the same ground, in principle and detail.[10] There is one significant issue which Byron omits: parliamentary reform. It was an embarrassment for the Whigs. If Horne Tooke had been called as a witness he might have raised it, but he is not allowed to take the stand. The arrival of Southey, twaddling, curtails the discussion conveniently early.

But does Satan inspire complete confidence? Consider the authorial voice introducing the prosecution case:

– 37 –

> He merely bent his diabolic brow
> An instant; and then raising it, he stood
> In act to assert his right or wrong, and show
> Cause why King George by no means could or should
> Make out a case to be exempt from woe
> Eternal, more than other kings, endued
> With better sense and hearts, whom history mentions,
> Who long have 'paved hell with their good intentions'.

131

Byron does not polarise the issue, as Southey did, into 'right' against 'wrong'. The word 'his' crucially alters the relation by making the interpretation of the moral values dependent on the character and point of view of the speaker. As the *diabolic* advocate sees the issue some acts are 'right' and some are 'wrong'. This is relatavistic, therefore, and emphatically so given that Satan is the speaker.

A similar relativity affects the word 'good' in the last line. If 'good intentions' pave hell, then one cannot abstract moral ideas of right and wrong from practical consideration of the consequences. The word 'hell' (sadly) is less ambiguous, and Satan is its prince. One might even argue that this advocate, the self-proclaimed champion of 'Freedom' (from the time of his resistance to a tyrannical God) has himself created hell in the pursuit of his good intention. (Like La Fayette or Mirabeau?). Be that as it may, there is no reason to accept that the prosecution is either disinterested or uncontaminated. The speaker is proud, tempest-riven, gloomy and autocratic. There is no objective 'point of view' out of the debate.

Satan tries to create one. His appeal is again a familiar one. It is to 'history'.

Whose
History was ever stain'd as his will be
With national and individual woes?

(45)

*   *   *

From out the past
Of ages, since mankind have known the rule
Of monarchs—from the bloody rolls amass'd
Of sin and slaughter—from the Caesars' school
Take the worst pupil; and produce a reign
More drench'd with gore, more cumber'd with the slain.

(44)

Such general appeals suggest the broad philosophical approach of *Childe Harold,* seeking to set contemporary events in the great patterns perceived by historical perspective. It was the duty of the historian to call the figures of the past before a moral tribunal and judge them in a way contemporaries could not. Thus, regard for posterity might serve to make men good, and the historian had a practical function. That is the tradition in which Satan places himself, and it may seem to have authorial approval. The poet had written *in propria persona* of George III: 'A worse king never left a realm undone' (although Byron then ruined the epigram by substituting in the Errata 'weaker' for 'worse').

But is the rhetoric convincing? Is there not something about it of an 'over-the-top' quality, forcing the issue to hyperbole, riding the emotions hard, more concerned with heat than light? Is it seriously being suggested by Satan (or Byron) that because a world war was fought during George III's reign that the monarch is personally responsible? That would be the counterpart of Southey blaming events in America and France on Wilkes. Has Satan forgotten—doubtless a temporary amnesia—another contemporary some called 'anti-Christ', one against whom 'the nations . . . finally rose up . . . for he had offended them more even than kings', whom in sending 'millions' to death claimed to represent 'the established order of God himself'? Bonaparte's soul is for hell.[11]

If the tone is debatable of the appeals to history, the ending of the oration more obviously gives the game away when, in Michael's words, Satan 'outruns discretion':

-48-

> Five millions of the primitive, who hold
> The faith which makes ye great on earth, implored
> A *part* of the vast *all* they held of old,
> Freedom to worship—not alone your Lord
> Michael, but you, and you, Saint Peter! Cold
> Must be your souls, if you have not abhorr'd
> The foe to catholic participation
> In all the license of a Christian nation.

By making this an *ad hominem* argument Satan is cheating. He knows that Saint Peter is hasty of temper (so the Bible tells, as well as this poem!), and he works on Peter's emotions here with great success, producing the Saint's explosion about 'this royal Bedlam bigot'. The pesonal element is as much in evidence, therefore, as the abstract principle of 'freedom to worship' (which, of course, was not denied,—Satan exaggerates).[12] The whole thing topples over into a joke both in the action (Saint Peter blows up again) and in the style (the rhyme of the familiar parliamentary word 'participation' with 'nation'). Catholic and Protestant are claimed to be equally licentious, and Satan, as an enemy of God, betrays that he does not take seriously the good effects of theology. (Authorially the joke also belittles Tory 'alarmism'. Catholic emancipation is not a dangerous issue.) The ending of the speech for the prosecution, therefore, like the beginning emphasises dramatically what sort of character is making the speech, to whom, and for what end.

Satan's role as advocate inevitably suggests an implied opposite voice (the speech by counsel for the Tories). Indeed, some of the ground is skilfully conceded: farmer George's undeniable domestic virtues, the influence of pernicious ministers on a *weak* rather than bad man—' 'Tis true he was a tool from first to last/ (I have the workmen safe)'. But Byron as satirist is not going to play fair and give the whole of the counter-argument. Let Southey stand before the public making a hash of it. But the question which 'history' may now put to the text is whether Satan's speech makes the case which the poet first seemed to set up for it, that George was the *worst* of kings?

The text creates the suspicion that the issue is not proven. There is about Satan's whole operation a feeling that he is merely going through the motions, that for all his oratorical skills in deploying Whig words and instances, his heart is not in it, and George is insignificant:

-64-
To me the matter is
Indifferent, in a personal point of view:
I can have fifty better souls than this
With far less trouble than we have gone through
Already; and I merely argued his
Late majesty of Britain's case with you
Upon a point of form: you may dispose
Of him; I've kings enough below, God knows!

This might be a strategy for establishing a disinterested concern for principle by an orator who had got overheated. But the tone is one of weariness. He had begun by calling kings merely a 'quit rent', and admitting that neither he, nor heaven, had any effect on what monarchs do. Now he ends by arguing only 'Upon a point of form'. The entire debate between him and Tory Michael is the equivalent of a parliamentary 'mummery'. Neither the opposition, nor the government, have any real power over events, and the evidence of contemporary history is dreadful. Paradoxically he is arguing from an analogous position to that attributed to Castlereagh in Hunt's introduction to *The Liberal*. Since certain things are 'unavoidable matters' they cannot be prevented by 'earthly means'—further evidence, if it were needed, of how 'unprogressive' was Byron's viewpoint. But again one must recognise that Satan is the kind of character who is likely to take this line. Since the celestial Tories will defeat him every time, it is a protection for his pride to denigrate the importance of the debate. Indeed, as leader of the opposition, he has a vested interest in letting a deplorable situation get worse, since all disorder reflects badly on the government. This mixture of large rhetorical outrage and cynical despair is recognisably 'Byronic'. But since the situation is fully dramatised, one must read the poetry as expressive of the dilemmas and tensions of a political situation, and not as an essay in verse autobiography.

How do Satan's witnesses affect the position?

The introduction of Wilkes and Junius raises, for the critic, the question of the limits of allusion. They stand for certain important matters in the tradition of opposition, yet the text remains silent on some of the *loci classici,* and the decorum of comic parody turns the witnesses into something of a joke. Michael asks for 'two honest, clean,/ True testimonies', but what hell offers is not a Washington and a Franklin, but a blasphemous libertine and an anonymous libeller.

The main link with the text of Byron's *Vision* is the issue of the freedom of the press: 'the *palladium* of all the civil, political, and religious rights of an Englishman'.[13] Wilkes's *North Briton* 45 and Junius's *Letter* 35 were both prosecuted as attacks on George III. Clearly Byron expects (and provokes) prosecution. (A fine of a mere £100 is anticlimactic in a continuing struggle!) The imprisonment of Burdett (1810), Leigh and John Hunt (1813 and 1820), and Hobhouse (1819) were major instances from the poet's own circle.

Freedom of election is the other classic issue. Junius backed Wilkes over the Middlesex election. The rioting the matter provoked was noted by Southey quoting Franklin. The use by the authorities of force to control the mob/people led to the notorious 'horrid massacre' in St George's Fields, the Whig equivalent of Peterloo.

Presumably, also, the two testimonies will recall Wilkes's support for the American colonists, but if pressed too far, might also raise the question of parliamentary reform. For Junius the palladium of property was the rotten borough. Its removal was no part of his palliatives for corruption. To go further, to the Gordon riots and the French Revolution, would be to show Wilkes, as a gentleman, and like Byron, declaring 'off'.

The language of Satan is a direct descent from that of Wilkes and Junius. There is a magniloquent generality about their kind of Whig rhetoric that pushes every issue to extreme and thus produces a highly destabilising effect upon the political order. The state rushes upon revolution as a last refuge against tyranny. Ultimately, this kind of discourse, by functioning only at white-heat, runs the risk of consuming itself in repetitive exaggeration. Let us set the discourse of Satanism, as dramatically created in Byron's poem, against that of historical exponents of 'the Whig point of view'.

Typical is the beginning of Wilkes's defence after his committal to the Tower:

> My Lord, . . . The liberty of all peers and gentlemen, and what touches me most sensibly, that of all the middling and inferior set of people, who stand most in need of protection, is in my case this day to be finally decided upon: a question of such importance as to determine at once, whether English liberty be a reality or a shadow. Your own free-born hearts will feel with indignation and compassion, all that load of oppression under which I have so long laboured.[14]

'At once' the rhetoric moves to the extreme case. 'Liberty' is threatened and the free Constitution at risk. There is a powerful sense of a present audience whose 'indignation' is to be aroused. It is a task of the superior orders to protect 'the middling and inferior set of people'.

What had provoked the government to move against this 'free-born heart' which begs compassion? *The North Briton* makes constant 'indignant' demands for 'justifiable resistance' in the spirit of Hampden against the 'slavish doctrines' of a Scottish, and thus Jacobite, administration. Number 19 is typical. Since the Jacobites aim at the destruction of the people, they have 'a right to resume the power they have delegated, and to punish their servants who have advised it'. The Tories are like the slaves of the evil Caesars of old. Recall the example of the freedom of Athens and

Rome. 'Ye worthy citizens of *London* . . . why do you not arise, and with honest indignation, tear them [ministerial libels] to pieces, and offer up the mangled fragments to *Vulcan?* . . . [You] have made tyrants tremble on their thrones, and dyed the scaffold with the blood of pernicious, wicked counsellors.' Under a 'fatal' 'Stuart' ministry is it surprising 'that the spirit of discord should go forth in the land, and the voice of opposition be strong in the streets'?

This is language not dissimilar to 'A Song for the Luddites'. Buy freedom with blood. It is an incentive to riot, and succeeded. 'If Mr Wilkes will turn patriot hero', wrote Horace Walpole, 'or patriot incendiary in earnest . . . he may obtain a rope of martyrdom before the summer.'[15] That hesitation—if he is in earnest—is significant. Anecdotes abound of Wilkes's insincerity. He called his supporters 'Middlesex fools', it was said, 'the greatest scoundrels upon earth'.[16] The truth or falsehood of such typical anecdotes is irrelevant. *The North Briton* is an incendiary publication (racist and libellous also!) written by a libertine whose sincerity was in doubt. One cannot separate the libertarian rhetoric of Wilkism—'The people of England . . . know they are FREE; and they will preserve that freedom which their ancestors purchased with their blood'[17]—from the reputation of the penniless pornographer who promulgated 'liberty' on a wave of riot.

That is one witness for Satan and the Whig point of view.

The *Letters* of Junius are less inflammatory, but run rapidly to an extreme: the Constitution is in danger. That is the standard complaint, whether the issue is the Middlesex election or the excise on cider. 'The noble simplicity and free spirit of our Saxon laws' which the Norman Conquest and the Stuarts sought to 'corrupt' is again under threat. The whole edifice of state is rotten: a degenerate aristocracy; a government in the hands of purveyors of place and sinecures; 'a settled plan to contract the legal power of juries'; government 'influence' on the judiciary, traitors to the public; the extension of the prerogative of the Crown 'more pernicious in its effects than either the levying of ship-money, by Charles the First, or the suspending power assumed by his son'. At times Junius sounds like a Marxist critic of 'structural violence', at others like a Whig equivalent of a Tory alarmist for whom the word 'Jacobite' has replaced 'Jacobin'.

Faced with 'the ruin of the laws and liberty of the

commonwealth', when the 'abandoned servility and prostitution' of the government has launched the Crown on the 'fatal course of Charles I', then the choice before the British people is whether they will be 'freemen or slaves'. Make no doubt, 'a convulsion of the whole kingdom' is threatened. To what that might lead no one can foretell, but the 'catastrophe will do no dishonour to the conduct of the piece'. Faced with the 'corruption of the legislative body on this side—a military force on the other' then he cries, 'Farewell England!' And so on (and on). Every issue is the thin end of the wedge. None of the 'King's friends' is less than a Jacobite, a Jefferies, a degenerate, dishonourable, slavish, venal, tool of tyranny. He attacks his opponents viciously by name, but will not reveal his own. He even accuses George III of 'personal resentment' as if that very quality did not flame in every indignant sortie against Bute or Grafton.

Eventually the administration was provoked. As with Wilkes's *North Briton* 45, the legal case arose from criticism of the king (which was unconstitutional). It may be, he writes in *Letter* 35, that the people will 'no longer appeal to the creature of the constitution [George III] but to that high Being, who gave them the rights of humanity'.

> The name of Stuart, of itself, is only contemptible;—armed with the Sovereign authority, their principles are formidable. The Prince, who imitates their conduct, should be warned by their example; and, while he plumes himself upon the security of his title to the crown, should remember that, as it was acquired by one revolution, it may be lost by another.

Add to this frequent claims of the kind, 'I would have the manners of the people purely and strictly republican', and it is obvious that if the letters were documents of the 1790s what 'constructive' interpretation a Pittite lawyer might put upon them. One cure for this monstrous corruption would be the removal of the King, the impeachment of the corrupt aristocracy, and the resumption of its rights by the republic.

That, however, would be the imposition of what Junius calls 'fatal democracy'. What then are the Whig cures for the monstrous ills of the state? They are a dissolution of parliament, triennial elections, an extension of county membership, and the return of a

Whig administration. Thence, the end of corruption, a king subservient to the law, and a people content under the government of their Friends. The gap between the weighted violence of the language and the light reformism of the aims is striking.

This is necessarily a partial account of the principles and language of Satan's two witnesses, but it indicates something of the problem of the polarisation of party polemic between tyranny, corruption and slavery on the one hand, and pure, patriot Hampdens on the other, with nothing but a sea of convulsion between. What brake does one put upon the militant tendency? Let us grant that a Pittite 'construction' is excessive. This kind of rhetoric, none the less, is always pushing in that direction. Hobhouse on monarchy in *Childe Harold* is an instance. In *The Liberal* itself, Hazlitt's essay 'On the Spirit of Monarchy' and Hunt's 'The Isle of Dogs' have the same radical implications. Hazlitt attacks all kings 'limited or unlimited' as creatures bent on 'doing all the mischief in their power', and his criticism of the principles of 'honour' and of 'hereditary' government would involve the aristocracy with the monarchy. Hunt merely calls the ruling class 'dogs'. It is not surprising that Lord Byron should have been warned about the company he was keeping, nor that he found he did not like it.

The question to be asked about the function of Wilkes and Junius in the *Vision* is in what way does their treatment by the poet qualify the commonplaces of their Whig point of view; at what point is the 'constructive' tendency towards radicalism, or Jacobinism, checked?

Junius is Satan's stronger witness. The first function of Byron's comic style is to pluck from him the mantle of outraged patriotic indignation which is an essential basis for his high-vaulting, high-principled Phillipics. The long description of his ambiguous appearance may be contrasted with the formidable gloom with which Satan is invested who, as a permanent force of 'resistance' in the constitution of eternity, *is* taken seriously. But it is difficult for the witness for hell to stand on his dignity after several stanzas of this kind of thing:

-79-
For sometimes he like Cerberus would seem—
'Three gentlemen at once' (as sagely says
Good Mrs. Malaprop); then you might deem

That he was not even *one*; now many rays
Were flashing round him; and now a thick steam
Hid him from sight—like fogs on London days:
Now Burke, now Tooke, he grew to people's fancies,
And certes often like Sir Philip Francis.

The suggestion that 'Junius' is Burke, *or* Tooke, *or* Francis may carry with it the implication that this kind of Whig discourse has little stamp of an individual author. The language of opposition is a basic rhetoric, even 'a thick steam', which anyone skilled in the manipulation of words can readily reproduce. We regularly view books 'written without heads', the poet laughs, and he teases the world for bothering 'if *there* be mouth or author'. A collective language has written the letters rather than a distinguishable 'hand'.

What of the content of that discourse? Junius declares:

– 83 –
'My charges upon record will outlast
The brass of both his epitaph and tomb.'
'Repent'st thou not', said Michael, 'of some past
Exaggeration? something which may doom
Thyself if false, as him if true? Thou wast
Too bitter—is it not so?—in thy gloom
Of passion?'—'Passion!' cried the phantom dim,
'I loved my country, and I hated him.

– 84 –
'What I have written, I have written: let
The rest be on his head or mine!' So spoke
Old 'Nominis Umbra;' and while speaking yet,
Away he melted in celestial smoke.

Michael's question, on behalf of the Tories, is reasonable. His exculpatory hint is that the Whig argument is too bitter, gloomy, exaggerated and passionate. The tone of the reply: ' "Passion!" cried the phantom . . .' dramatically grants at least part of the defence case. Junius is 'at once' in a blaze of 'indignation' (to use Wilkite words) and vanishes in smoke (an obscure element, not indicative of intellectual light). The angry polemicist spontaneously combusts.

The few words he utters are a catena of commonplaces, first from Horace, then from the Bible. His name and motto are likewise borrowed. The statement 'What I have written, I have written' makes George III a quasi-divine martyr (like Charles I) for the words were originally those of Pilate crucifying Christ. Junius, as a citizen of hell, appropriately speaks a Satanic language. The fine epigram 'I loved my country, and I hated him' may be original. However, it combines 'indignation' with one of opposition's cant words: 'country'. One does not need to read far in Whig polemic to find that it divides politics between 'the Court' party (which is evil) and 'the Country' (which is good).

'Junius' is thus an amalgam of other people's words, not always fortunate in his choice of allusion, and overpitched in tone. The *Letters* stand as a record to history of indignation against the Court. But as testimony in this 'neutral space' between heaven and hell, they leave the case non-proven.

Wilkes inspires less confidence. The 'merry, cock-eyed' unfashionable figure brings with him into the trial that shifty personal ethos which made contemporaries doubt his sincerity. He alludes to the classic issues of the Middlesex election (67), and the *North Briton* (69), but is denied the dignity of Junius's sententious commonplaces.

> 'If these are freeholders I see in shrouds,
> And 'tis for an election that they bawl,
> Behold a candidate with unturn'd coat!
> Saint Peter, may I count upon your vote?'

> (67)

This is the language of someone on the make at popular hustings. 'My friends', he launches forth, to people he has never met. The words 'freeholders' and 'bawl' indicate the not inconsiderable divide between the idealised liberty of the free Saxon Constitution, and the tumultuous canvassing of the bully-boys of a Middlesex election. His reference to an 'unturn'd coat' is crucial. He protests too much. He ended as a prop of the establishment, Lord Mayor of London, City Chamberlain (for which he was accused of venality), a torpid MP, an active repeller of the 'Wilkite' mob, and for his pains was received by the Court. In short, he is something of an 'apostate'. Accordingly, although he retracts nothing of his early criticism of Bute and Grafton (in hell, with him!), he *does* turn his coat on behalf of the King, and becomes a witness for the opposite side:

> 'for me, I have forgiven,
> And vote his 'habeas corpus' into heaven.'
>
> (71)

Good Whig doctrine is involved with this charitable conclusion, but the personal opportunism behind the constitutional facade is at once recognised by Wilkes's own party.

> 'Wilkes,' said the Devil, 'I understand all this;
> You turn'd to half a courtier ere you died,
> And seem to think it would not be amiss
> To grow a whole one on the other side . . .'
>
> (72)

As Southey might observe, Whigs become Tories in God.

There could be no better example than Wilkes and Junius of the militant tendency of Whig rhetoric, and the way in which those who blow hot, blow cold. Faced by a choice between the Crown and the people, Wilkes took his sword to the mob. Opponents spoke of apostasy, supporters of redressing the balance of the Constitution. Wilkes, as a Whig who ends up voting Tory, lends further support to the constitutional principle of eternity, as imagined by the poem, that the debate between heaven and hell is that of the 'ins' against the 'outs' in a system neither side will change. The paradox of the Satanic case is that however strongly the corruptions of George III's reign are urged, neither of the prime witnesses in life, or in the poem, was prepared to subvert the monarchical system. Their case against the Crown cannot be pushed to extremity for to do so would threaten the entire social order: witness Louis XVI.

One need only turn to Hazlitt in the second number of *The Liberal* to hear the usual charge against the Whigs. 'The distinction between Whig and Tory is merely nominal: neither have their country one bit at heart.' But that is a radical opinion. It would not be fair to apply it to Byron's *Vision*. 'I loved my country', cries Junius passionately. That is not a hypocritical expression—merely one which is, in context, exaggerated in its indignation at the Tories. Satan's commitment to the principle of freedom is sufficiently sincere for him to spend eternity excluded from heaven because of it, but it has regrettably divided him from Michael, the loyal minister of God. The specific instances of freedom which the case of Wilkes indicates (of the press, of election, *habeas corpus*) are vital to political liberty, but this is no guarantee of the disinterestedness of their champions. Hazlitt's charge against the Whigs is mere sentimentalism. He is still in pursuit of the idea of the sea-green patriot hero, a Prometheus unbound. What *The Vision of Judgment* is concerned with is the relationship between an ideal libertarian rhetoric and a dramatic realisation of its application and tendency in 'things as they are'. Space is 'neutral', but the people who fill it are necessarily partisan and imperfect.

Which includes the poet. The action of the poem follows that Whig strategy which Junius's *Letters* so clearly demonstrate. First the great commonplaces of freedom's rhetoric are launched against the corruption of the Crown, then, when hell seems about to be let loose, the balance is redressed by leaning the other way. Satan's witnesses let him down, and George gets into heaven (though damn his ministers!). Perhaps Southey was right. Even a revolutionary Whig (like Washington) has more in common with British constitutionalism than an emergent militant Jacobinism. But after the Gallic era eighty-nine the 'balancing' act was more difficult: 'God save the king! . . . God help us all! God help me too! I am,/ God knows, as helpless as the devil can wish . . .?'. This poet has no Utopian solution in his pocket for difficult times.

But, at least, his side is better than Southey. The enormous comic gusto with which the poet laureate is given a gentlemanly thrashing should not obscure the useful political role the 'renegade' has to perform. Relativity of arguments does not mean that all arguments are equal. Wilkes might be a far from ideal champion of liberty, the Whigs might slide towards their notorious apostasy on one side, and diabolic convulsion on the other, but Southey was beyond the pale, always at extremes, and always wrong. It is convenient to be able to level the charge of apostasy at the laureate Tory. It is even better that Southey had formerly been a radical: a revolutionary king-killer by construction from *Wat Tyler* (whose hero led what even Wilkes called the 'rabble'):[18] an ultra-democrat in his advocacy of Susquehannahian pantisocracy. If that was what radicalism meant, then it is clearly as ridiculous as Southey's Toryism with its ultra-monarchist drivel.

– 97 –

He had written praises of a regicide;
He had written praises of all kings whatever;
He had written for republics far and wide,

143

And then against them bitterer than ever:
For pantisocracy he once had cried
Aloud, a scheme less moral than 'twas clever;
Then grew a hearty anti-jacobin—
Had turn'd his coat—and would have turn'd his skin.

Michael rejects this as nonsense. So too does Satan. The first is a ministerial voice, the other spokesman for the principles of resistance. Neither will accept as part of their debate either Jacobinism, nor that prostitute slavery which praises 'all kings whatever'. Southey is, allegorically, thrown out of their parliamentary and legal system.[19] But his temporary appearance has helped to define the integrity of the middle ground.

He serves another function. The manner in which he is described further turns the clock back into the eighteenth century. Southey is Colley Cibber's heir. Byron, in administering chastisement, is in the tradition of Pope.

– 105 –

He first sank to the bottom—like his works,
But soon rose to the surface—like himself;
For all corrupted things are buoy'd like corks,
By their own rottenness, light as an elf,
Or wisp that flits o'er a morass: he lurks,
It may be, still, like dull books on a shelf,
In his own den, to scrawl some 'Life' or 'Vision',
As Welborn says—'the devil turn'd precisian.'

The first line alludes to *The Art of Sinking in Poetry*, and the literal application of the metaphor of sinking transfers to the Lake District the diving sports of *The Dunciad*. The word 'scrawl' derives from the desperate poet of *An Epistle to Dr. Arbuthnot*. The concept 'dullness' is a *leitmotiv* in Pope's war with the dunces, and it is linked politically with 'corruption' for the dunces are the hireling scribblers of Walpole's regime. This needs no development.

The passage may equally be glossed from the Preface to *The Liberal* which, in the first number, took the place of Byron's own introduction to his *Vision*. There 'corruption' is symptomatic of all slaves of 'legitimacy' whose 'pretended morality' equates the 'DIVINE BEING' with a bench of Crown appointed bishops. 'God defend us from the morality of slaves and turncoats', exclaims Hunt. If that is what 'religion . . . and legitimacy' mean, he prefers to be known as their enemy. That prepares the way for the appearance of Byron's Satan. At the same time Hunt turns to the example of Pope to refute the charge that the opposition threatens 'a dilapidation of all the outworks of civilised society'. On the contrary. The opposition has a fine literary pedigree. A clear and candid poet like Pope shows that 'There are other things in the world besides kings, or even sycophants'. A modern liberal incorporates the best of the culture of the old Whigs.

One sees, therefore, how Hunt and Byron at least began in step. A Popeian element is strong in the poem. The classic tradition of high art rejects the impoverished world of a Cibber or a Southey which has sold out to the Court. An independent gentleman shames the mercenary scribbler. The Augustan motifs are strong. If this is so, we are further back into history even than the reign of George III. Nothing has changed since Walpole's day. The same standards, attitudes, issues remain—and what Walpole was accused of was betraying the principles of 1688. The field of 'vision' of Byron's verse is the century 1688–1788.

Paradoxically, the Whig point of view, although 'revolutionary' in its origins, in its subsequent history emerges as potentially 'conservative'. Nothing in recent events is portrayed as fundamentally different from what it was before even the year in which Byron was born (1788). Things as they are, are things as they were, going from worse to worse. That is the implication of *The Vision of Judgment*. It is developed at length in *Don Juan*.

Perhaps that is why the comic voice develops. If nothing changes for the better, why the heat of Whig rhetoric? It is not going to effect anything.[20] The system provokes the justified voice of resistance. It rings forth, ideally. But the aim of resistance is to conserve the system. That is not (necessarily) cynicism. But it is a paradox.

6

There is no Alternative: *Don Juan*

The political subject of *Don Juan* is the *ancien régime*. The action of the poem first traverses the Europe of legitimate despotism, in which the siege of Ismail stands as the type of all wars fought by tyrant against tyrant for dynastic glory, then involves the corruption of liberty, even in Britain, once 'the inviolate island of the sage and free'. Had the work been completed it would have shown the outbreak of revolution in France provoked by the repressive power of the Bourbons, and the commitment by Juan to the Byronic role of gentleman revolutionary: citizen of the world, friend of mankind, symbol of disruption of the old order: an Anarchasis Cloots.[1] The historical Cloots was guillotined by his own side when Jacobinism overwhelmed constitutional monarchy. Byron's poem, in its uncompleted state, has reached a time just before the Terror in France, and the trials for constructive treason at home. The irony of Juan's fate fits the pessimism of much of Byron's writing. Revolution devours its children. 'Freedom' is kept alive for posterity only in the words of the poet. *Don Juan,* if finished, would be *The Dunciad* of political liberty.

This political structure is based upon the idea *'Idem semper'* (XVII. 11). In spite of all changes, all the multifarious miscellaneity of things, nothing has changed. Compare society before and after the Revolution. The old order remains just where it did. The constant anachronisms of Byron's narration, in which he intrudes the personalities and events of his own maturity into the events of the 1780s and early 1790s is a device which emphasises the similarities between then and now.

This sense of a frame—before and after—is clearly expressed in the Preface. The scene, we are told, is Spain after the restoration of

Ferdinand by the legitimate powers, and, thus, after the extinction of the liberal hopes raised in opposition to Bonaparte the tyrant. (A Bourbon army crossed the Pyrenees in 1823 to sustain legitimate power against the liberals.) From this historical viewpoint, post-Waterloo, the putative narrator, 'perhaps one of the liberals', tells his story which concerns the education of a modern Ulysses under the *ancien régime*. Juan will, like his archetype, see many countries and governments. Looking upon the scene of the narration are a few soldiers of the Napoleonic armies (first liberators, then oppressors). They are in prison. That political symbol requires no exposition. Although the elderly Spanish narrator soon vanishes to be replaced by the Byronic *persona*, the politics of the speaker—'perhaps one of the liberals'(!)—remains the same.

The events of the poem—before and after—span approximately Byron's lifetime. It is a period in which, Byron says, he retained his 'buff and blue': the colours of George Washington and his Foxite supporters. Yet, at once, the poet stumbles against a commonplace problem. Where are the old Whigs who sustain the true tradition—'Are none, none living?' Pope had asked that question more than half a century before of the patriot opposition, and ended the line: 'Let me praise the dead.'[2] If one looks at the parliamentary Whig party now, Byron's Preface claims, its members are merely apostate Tories, rancorous because they have received none of the rewards of state having backed the wrong faction. 'A modern Whig is but the fag-end of a Tory', Hazlitt wrote, lamenting that the old principles had been deserted, and Cobbett: 'Who thinks any thing more of the name of Erskine?'[3] The narrator of *Don Juan* likewise devalues a degenerate party (which had disowned him). He wishes, none the less, to record his adherence to the great historical principles which underlay it. Those principles blend with a wider humanistic tradition which leads the poet to look to the larger patterns in things. In the Dedication and Preface he turns especially to Milton and Pope as classic, heroic figures. By their standards the corrupt 'trash' of laureate Southey and legitimacy's tool, Castlereagh, may be judged. The dead condemn the living who 'want a Hero'.

Hence the indignant prosopopoeia which recalls literature's most famous tyrannicide:

Think'st thou, could he—the blind Old Man—arise

Like Samuel from the grave, to freeze once more
The blood of monarchs with his prophecies,
Or be alive again—again all hoar
With time and trials, and those helpless eyes,
And heartless daughters—worn—and pale—and poor;
Would *he* adore a sultan? *he* obey
The intellectual eunuch Castlereagh?

(Dedication, 11)

To *saeva indignatio* Byron joins political shrewdness, for the classical republican was a figure all admired. Milton is one of the heroes of Wordsworth's sonnets on national liberty, and of Southey's *Vision:* scholar, orator, statesman, poet, an incorruptible humanist and patriot. Yet, if he belongs to any contemporary force, he fits appropriately among those who claimed Hampden, Sydney, Russell, or even Junius as their predecessors. He wrote 'In Liberty's defence', that 'noble task',/ Of which all Europe talks from side to side'.[4] It is a typical strategy of Whig discourse that by choosing a figure like Milton as an example, republican principle should be implied, but not necessarily literally recommended. As a 'tyrant-hater' (st. 10), Milton resisted the Stuarts. Such a man, were he alive now, would see the Prince Regent as a sultan. He would not, therefore, 'adore' him, nor 'obey' Castlereagh. It is not stated, however, that he would return as a regicide. For Byron himself the preferred tradition of the 'buff and blue' in Britain was a constitutional monarch beloved by the people, such as the poet praises *in propria persona* in a more appropriate place (XII. 83-4).

The period of Milton's life which is imagined is not that of the Cromwellian regime. That would be a potentially unfortunate allusion on which one might expect Southey in the *Quarterly* to pounce. It is Milton as a helpless poet who is described *after* a restoration which has eclipsed his hopes of a major advance of liberty. The emphasis of the analogy is, thus, on the similarity between 1660 and 1815. It fits the usual Whig paradigm that the growth of the power of the Crown *now* was the return of the principles of Stuart prerogative *then* (an analogy heightened in *The Examiner* by the similarity of the morals of the Regent and Charles II). The heroic example of Milton ultimately is pessimistic. The old order has an immense capacity for restoration and the man of 'virtue and genius' is left in isolation.

The same sense of isolation affects Pope, upon whom Byron also freely draws. A link between Milton and the Augustan satirist is implied early in the Dedication, when Byron writes of Milton:

> *He* did not loathe the Sire to laud the Son,
> But closed the tyrant-hater he begun.
>
> (10)

This suggests *The Dunciad:*

> Still Dunce the second reigns like Dunce the first (1.6)

and a Southey/Cibber parallel. Byron alludes specifically to the succession of Charles II after Charles I (both 'tyrants') and to the future George IV's apostasy when, abandoning the Whig principles of his youth, in 1812 he followed his father's policy and adopted a Tory administration. So, in Pope, the death of George I in 1727 did not lead to the expected fall of Walpole, for George II did not recall the 'patriot' opposition. In all three instances the heroic poet was powerless to prevent the succession of corruption. Once perceive this kind of historical paradigm, then further sequences may be readily connected. There is a link between Rome's Eutropius (a eunuch), Pope's Sporus (Lord Hervey was a homosexual), and Byron's Castlereagh (an 'intellectual eunuch'). A similar historical relation exists between crazy fanatics like Brothers, the *demens poeta* of Juvenal and *Dr Arbuthnot,* and the Lakers. The Southey/Cibber parallel is pervasive (and already familiar):

> Europe has slaves—allies—kings—armies still,
> And Southey lives to sing them very ill.
>
> (Dedication, 16)

The general pattern is that, as history repeats itself, great qualities are constantly trodden down, and the old order of tyrannical dulness reappears.

The relation of Byron's own heroic alienation to Pope's is problematical, however. At the end of his life Pope emphasised his position as a solitary, but it is not his most typical political posture. The poems of the 1730s and 1740s cohere as an extended *apologia pro vita sua* grounded in the traditions of European humanism which he and his friends inherit. Twickenham is the symbol of the poet's independent status in which patriotic opposition to Court corruption is secure because Pope is 'unplac'd, unpension'd, no man's heir, or slave'. His home is a rallying ground for those 'To Virtue only, and her Friends, a Friend', and the recital of the good and great (driven to opposition) is familiar to any reader of Pope: Swift and Gay, Bolingbroke and Peterborough, Lyttelton and Cobham.[5] Although Byron's attacks on Southey, Castlereagh, and (soon to come) on pensionary Wellington, are such as Pope might have made—from what base do they originate? From a life grounded in the traditional standards of the Christian and philosopher, the *vir bonus*? From the independent property of Newstead Abbey? From the centre of a circle of good men who, though in opposition now, represent a great patriotic interest? Self-evidently not. Byron claims to be a poet in the tradition of Pope, and behind Pope, of Milton, but it is far less clear in his own age to whom, to what his voice—'perhaps one of the liberals'—is securely related.

Consider a number of those outbursts which seem so typically Byronic as he gestures broadly across the whole of Europe and the Congress system:

> Where shall I turn me not to *view* its bonds,
> For I will never *feel* them;—Italy!
> Thy late reviving Roman soul desponds
> Beneath the lie this State-thing breathed o'er thee—
> Thy clanking chain, and Erin's yet green wounds,
> Have voices—tongues to cry aloud for me . . .
>
> (Dedication, 16)

On this kind of rhetoric the image has been constructed of Byron the champion of the oppressed and freedom fighter, and a small anthology of such utterances may be readily collected from *Don Juan:*

> I will teach, if possible, the stones
> To rise against Earth's tyrants. Never let it
> Be said that we still truckle unto thrones . . .
>
> (VIII. 135)

> And I will war, at least in words (and—should
> My chance so happen—deeds) with all who war
> With Thought;—and of Thought's foes by far most rude,
> Tyrants and Sycophants have been and are . . .
>
> (IX. 24)

Here again is that great head of steam which is so noteworthy in *Childe Harold,* a commitment to ideological battle of a kind which, as Hazlitt wrote in his essay 'On the Late War', must be waged to 'extirpation'. But what is most striking is how solitary that 'I' has become, how insistent the reiterated 'I will', how vast and generalised the panorama. On one side 'I', on the other 'tyrants', and a cry 'I know not who may conquer' (IX. 24). The boiler sounds as if it is about to explode because the energy is not being translated into progressive motion. Or, if that is too metaphorical a description, one may compare these statements of political intent with the subject matter of the poem. The last thing Juan is doing in Europe is raising stones against tyrants. These libertarian outbursts have no correspondent action in the poem.

Rather than these passages representing the quintessence of Byronism, their anomality in the poem is evidence of the fragmentation of the language of opposition before the insistent, insidious and successful recurrence of the *ancien régime*—the element in which Juan lives and moves and has his being. 'I want a hero', the poet began, and the present age gave him as his *alter ego* Don Juan, *en route* to hell, in a pantomime. The choice of such a hero implies throughout the 'epic' poem a continuing exercise in self-parody. As in *The Vision of Judgment* one cannot separate political ideals from the context in which they must operate, nor disembody them as if they were immune from the limitations of humanity. 'Ambition was my idol, which was broken' the narrator says (I. 217), and the word 'idol' implies not only a false God, but—as far as Ambition's aims are concerned—one which may not even exist. What purpose might Ambition have? He encapsulates it at one time thus:

> Opposing singly the united strong,
> From foreign yoke to free the helpless native . . .
>
> (XIII. 10)

but that, he states, is the role of a modern Don Quixote—one whose ideals were sadly, and comically, not in the real nature of things. Tilt at windmills, and one is in for a rude fall. At another time, in an allusion to Pope, he speaks of his isolation:

> The consequence is, being of no party,
> I shall offend all parties . . .

(IX. 26)

Pope had boasted 'Tories call me Whig, and Whigs a Tory',[6] but that was to express the 'glory' of his 'moderation', his *independence* from *faction,* the disinterested patriotism which placed him in the 'Country' interest. Byron's role is that of a kind of political gadfly, one who attacks when the *estro* is upon him. Because he has no political base, he has no effective role.

Moreover, contemporary politics are a rotten thing. The great men among Byron's contemporaries are devalued—including another broken idol, the 'pagod' Napoleon. The poetic technique employed at the beginning of the poem is one familiar in Pope in which men become mere jangling sounds ('All [was] noise and Norton, brangling and Breval'):

> Each in their turn like Banquo's monarchs stalk,
> Followers of fame, 'nine farrow' of that sow:
> France, too, had Bonaparté and Demourier
> Recorded in the Moniteur and Courier.
>
> Barnave, Brissot, Condorcet, Mirabeau,
> Petion, Clootz, Danton, Marat, La Fayette,
> Were French, and famous people, as we know . . .

(I. 2-3)

So much for the revolution in France and the progress of freedom in Europe! If the poem had come to its political completion in the Terror, it would be apparent how the opening prepares for the end. Barnave, Brissot, Condorcet, Petion, Clootz, Danton, Marat were all spokesmen for *Liberté,* and were swiftly swept to dusty death. The paradoxical fate, and failure, of La Fayette and Mirabeau has already been discussed. As for the child and champion of Jacobinism—first, he is made just another general by coupling with Demourier, then the feminine rhyme disposes of both of them. Napoleon is bustled into triviality.

Strip humanist history of great men (in the contemporary world) and there is very little for positive faith to identify itself with, for the classic training of the patrician 'caste' (to use Byron's word) was the record of the lives of great men. What constituted true greatness, an honourable name and fame, was subject to debate, but history was made by the way that great men and women shaped the destiny of nations and empires. One recalls the famous procession recorded by Tacitus in which no image of Brutus appeared. Who is conspicuous in *Don Juan* by absence? Why the great silence since 1788? Are there none of the living with whom Byron can identify and draw into his circle as Pope named *his* early friends?

Early in his parliamentary career, Byron, one recalls, had written with enthusiasm of the heroic days of the 1790s. That was the time when he wished he had been a man, and he had hung on the words of the aged Erskine, Mackintosh and Sheridan. Now, in the poem, when young Juan visits England about 1790, one of his first acts, as an admirer of British freedom, is to visit Parliament (XII. 82-4) at a period when the poet states that the nation was '*really* free' (Byron's italics). He

> Had sate beneath the gallery at nights,
> To hear debates whose thunder *roused* (not *rouses*)
> The world to gaze upon those northern lights
> Which flashed as far as where the musk-bull browses . . .

It was the age of Fox and Pitt, Sheridan and Burke (and in Ireland, Grattan and Curran), those 'Who bound the bar or senate in their spell' (XI. 77). The great Whigs of this time, Moore claimed, were those 'patriot spirits' with both the 'courage' and 'eloquence' to come 'to the defence of liberty'—though how few were the defenders of the Constitution he lamented.[7] Byron might have compared such men *then* with Castlereagh and Wellington *now*, but the comparison is only hinted and passed by. Grattan (d. 1820) for a moment is set against the present ruling order, but the reader may be forgiven if the place in which he appears is not immediately recalled. The allusion is confined to the Preface to Cantos VI-VIII where Byron exclaims

> Let us hear no more of [Castlereagh], and let Ireland remove the Ashes of her Grattan from the Sanctuary of Westminster. Shall the Patriot of Humanity repose by the Werther of Politics!!!

That phrase: 'Patriot of Humanity' links Grattan with the prospective role of Juan as Cloots, 'the spokesman of the human race'. It is both magniloquent and vague. What is left of Grattan is only his ashes.

A short contextual gloss may indicate why Byron would find it difficult to describe the career of Grattan in detail. It is typical. The establishment of the Irish Parliament by the threat of armed resistance in 1782 was one of the great Whig achievements on behalf of freedom, but it was now an anachronistic event. Grattan was neither able to persuade the Parliament to reform itself (by the removal of corruption and a moderate extension of the franchise among the propertied classes), nor to carry a full measure of Catholic emancipation. *Idem semper.* The convulsion of 1798 removed the ground from beneath his feet. On the one hand, the Jacobinism of the United Irishmen and the Jacquery of a desperate Catholic peasantry. On the other, a privileged Protestant Parliament kept in office by British arms. In the middle, Grattan speaking for 'the nation', but voicing only the sentiments of a handful of patrician Whigs. 'I do not give up the country . . . I will not leave her . . . I will remain anchored here . . . faithful to her freedom, faithful to her fall.'[8] The famous prophetical treasonous orations against the Union are utterly Byronic in their solitary rhetoric of freedom, and their total inefficacy ('I will teach, if possible, the stones to rise against Earth's tyrants'). Castlereagh could not (and would not) speak like that, but, like Pitt, he had a policy. There was no way back after 1798 to 1782. Pitt and Castlereagh wanted Union *and* Catholic emancipation. Byron's 'Patriot of Humanity' was merely another unsuccessful and out-of-date Whig rhetorician. Perhaps it is unfair to Byron to enter into detail about a figure who is intended to represent a general type of patriotism, but the poet's silence about his heroes of the 1790s is striking, and explicable. There were problems best avoided by silence.

Perhaps the new world might redress the balance of the old? Earlier in this study we have seen how in Barry's print *The Phoenix* a small group of disappointed Whigs, led by Milton, look out from Britannia's bier from the England of George III to the America of George Washington. Byron likewise chooses a major example from across the Atlantic. The panegyrical portrait which he places against the great satiric attacks on Castlereagh, Southey and Wellington is that of Daniel Boone (d. 1820):

> An active hermit, even in age the child
> Of Nature, or the Man of Ross run wild.
>
> (VIII. 63)

Again Pope, as a poet of opposition, provides a basic allusion, for Boone in America is a type similar to John Kyrle. Yet that comparison further emphasises how little social and political function a good man now has. Kyrle, remote from the corruption of London in his sphere at Ross, exercised his proper roles as a paternalistic man of (modest) property. He built for the people of the town; he was charitable to the poor; he resolved controversies better than the courts of law; he was a good master; a pious supporter of the Church. While such men existed, though London corrupted, the heart of the country remained pure.

Compare Byron's description of Boone who

> shrank from men even of his nation,
> When they built up unto his darling trees,—
> He moved some hundred miles off, for a station
> Where there were fewer houses and more ease;
> The inconvenience of civilisation
> Is, that you neither can be pleased nor please . . .
>
> (VIII. 64)

It is paradoxical that Byron should mock Southey's Susquehannahian pantisocracy. Boone's small Rousseauesque family community preserves its health and vigorous virtue only by continual flight in search of an ever-diminishing Eden. It is a real life equivalent of Juan and Haidée's paradisical idyll, and equally fragile. In the opposition between solitary Nature and all the ills of luxurious society, there is no doubt which is the dominant force, and which is on the run. Kyrle, at Ross, was fixed as a landlord, and the land was related to the town. Boone 'fifty different times has shifted his abode westward . . ., nothing short of the salt, sandy desert can be expected to stop [him]'.[9] It is close to a parody of the old myth of the *translatio libertatis*. The axe is laid to the roots of the liberty trees of the fast diminishing forest. As a political hero for Europe after Waterloo, Boone has no function except to remind

155

that the vestiges of incorruptibility are now beyond the Atlantic, and retreating ever further westward.

Neither Boone nor Grattan supply the want of a hero. Both serve to remind, however, of nationalist resistance (in America and Ireland) to Georgian government. If there is an heroic cause in *Don Juan* to which wholehearted commitment might be expected, it is that of emergent nationalism. Since the poet was to die for Greece, might one not expect that at least Byron's own voice is that of a hero challenging the general corruption of the re-established *ancien régime:*

> The mountains look on Marathon—
> And Marathon looks on the sea;
> And musing there an hour alone,
> I dream'd that Greece might still be free;
> For standing on the Persian's grave,
> I could not deem myself a slave.
>
> (st. 3 between III. 86 and 87)

Here Byron wars in thought with tyrants, and was to do so in deeds.

Unfortunately the glorious idea crumbles on closer inspection. Even viewed in splendid isolation there is something odd about the stanza. The word 'dream' indicates the remoteness of the romantic ideal. Moreover, the interpolation of the lyric in *Don Juan* suggests atypicality. This is not the way things are in the poem. Restore the context and matters become still more problematic. Who is the 'I' who dreams? Not Byron. The context in which the lyric is set tells the reader that the poet is the Greek Southey, one who has settled for a 'laureate pension' because he prefers 'pudding to *no* praise'. What he has produced, in the special circumstances of Haidée's feast, is a 'national' air (after the manner and style of Moore's *Irish Melodies,* or the 'Tambourgi' lyric of *Childe Harold* II). Such poetic discourse can be produced by rote we are told: different nations, different songs, whether 'God save the king' or *'Ça ira'.* 'Pliable' is the word Byron uses of a poet who 'knew the self-loves of the different nations'. In *The Vision of Judgment* Byron preferred the term 'renegade'.

Behind the Southey figure stands a more noteworthy laureate. Byron tells that the writer of the lyric has returned here to the views of his 'warm youth' (when his verses carried with them the 'danger of a riot'). This is not merely an allusion to the Southey of *Wat Tyler* (or to the general criticism of the Whigs as 'inflammatory'). The great classical commonplace behind it comes from Horace:

> non ego hoc ferrem calidus iuventa
> consule Planco.
>
> (III *Odes*, XIV. 27-8)

That young idealist fought for the republic and liberty at Philippi, but in maturer years became the panegyrist of the very 'tyrant' he had fought against: Augustus Caesar. It is not only bad poets, therefore, whom history shows abandoning the ideals of their warm youth to reconcile themselves to an ineluctable political destiny. You cannot defend the republic when there is no republic to defend. To Horace and Southey one may add yet another poet—Byron himself:

> Some six or seven good years ago
> (Long ere I dreamt of dating from the Brenta)
> I was most ready to return a blow,
> And would nor brook at all this sort of thing
> In my hot youth—when George the Third was King.

He uses this Horatian allusion to introduce the long passage in Canto I (212 f.) in which he records his loss of political ambition and the worthlessness of fame.

To what extent should one extract the famous stanza on Marathon and freedom, therefore, from the qualification of this elaborate and subtle frame? Granted that Byron states that the Greek Southey has now made 'a short armistice with truth'—but what is truth? asked jesting Pilate. It is an insecure word in *Don Juan*. If we accept the lyric as 'true' we must accept it in its entirety, and even its positive recommendations are shot through with irony. A new Miltiades is demanded to liberate Greece. He is described as a 'tyrant'. The paradox is disturbing.

– 12 –

> The tyrant of the Chersonese
> Was freedom's best and bravest friend;
> *That* tyrant was Miltiades!
> Oh! that the present hour would lend

Another despot of the kind!
Such chains as his were sure to bind.

Ultimately that longing does not matter because the freedom of
Greece is only a dream to this audience. The refrain of the lyric is
'Fill high the bowl with Samian wine'. It is exactly what the
drunken revellers are doing in a feast recalling Samian Anacreon,
and it was the Samians who abandoned the Greek cause before the
Persian attack at Lade. Perhaps the poet rebukes his auditors, but
his epicurean message will be repeated by Byron later to Juan:
'*Carpe diem*, Juan, *carpe, carpe*'. The words are those of Horace,
who had no choice but to abandon the more strenuous course of
liberty. The alternative offered by the Greek Southey ends in mere
sentimentalism:

-16-
Place me on Sunium's marbled steep,
Where nothing, save the waves and I,
May hear our mutual murmurs sweep;
There swan-like, let me sing and die:
A land of slaves shall ne'er be mine—
Dash down yon cup of Samian wine.

Apart from the Werthers of political fiction, such as Foscolo's
Ortis, or, in a way, de Staël's Delphine, modern-day people do not
usually kill themselves from political despair—at least, not at this
feast where everyone is having too good a time.

This inebriated nationalism is abruptly interrupted by the arrival
of a Greek in arms. He is a recognisable equivalent to the real-life
Colocotrones and the self-styled Odysseus: the warlords and
profiteers of the Greek war. Lambro puts an end to the self-
indulgent orgy, and Byron describes *his* national sentiment in
different terms:

His country's wrongs and his despair to save her
Had stung him from a slave to an enslaver . . .
But something of the spirit of old Greece
Flash'd o'er his soul a few heroic rays . . .
'Tis true he had no ardent love for peace—
Alas! his country show'd no path to praise:
Hate to the world and war with every nation
He waged, in vengeance of her degradation.

(III. 53 and 55)

This is a disturbing kind of national 'hero', a kind of real life Corsair. Perhaps a trace of sentimentalism survives in Byron's liberal assumption that a figure such as Lambro possessed a concept of Greek nationalism, and that, therefore, he might be moved by national despair. That is questionable. Yet, granted the familiar Philhellene supposition, what is most noticeable about Lambro is that frustration has driven him to isolation, and that the corruption of things 'Had stung him from a slave to an enslaver'. Like Byron, he too has no political base. His situation is such that this friend of freedom is now indistinguishable from the Sultan he opposes. It was a familiar Whig apology in the nineties for the 'excesses' of the French Revolution that such were the acts that the degradation of slavery were likely to produce. The argument is still commonplace in Hazlitt's 'Advice to a Patriot'. But, if this is so, by what process can freedom advance if the slaves are as corrupt as the enslavers? It is the dilemma of Orwell's *Animal Farm.* One recalls the name of the new tyrant. It is Napoleon. 'War with every nation' is the result of the corruption of patriotism.

There follows the siege of Ismail—the political nadir of the poem. It shows the struggle between slaves and enslavers in the ultimate form of degradation. Lambro, the Greek 'patriot' has sold Juan to his country's enemy. Juan escapes to 'freedom' from the Turk, only to find refuge in the army of the 'tyrant' Catherine. The Turks and the Russians are at war in the interests of despotic rulers. Their 'slaves' perpetrate monstrous cruelties upon one another. Chivalry, love of family, love of home, total bravery in the face of death are good qualities utterly contaminated by an evil cause. Thousands die, and God is praised. Byron's castigation of the horrors of war rises bravely on the shoulders of Voltaire and Casti.[10] The verse suggests comparison with the images of Goya.

The immediate political concern, interwoven with the general theme, is established by the frame in which the cantos are set. The siege is prefaced by the second of the major attacks on Castlereagh, and Canto IX which follows is addressed, with great hostility, to Wellington. ('Could a Whig be proud of Wellington! Would this be consistent?')[11] These men, on the field of battle, or by diplomacy, had secured the restoration of the old order of things by 'the impious Alliance which insults the world with the name of Holy'. Superstition and tyranny are thus reunited, triumphant at Waterloo.

'Carnage' (so Wordsworth tells you) 'is God's daughter'.

(VIII. 9)

This contemporary context for the siege invites the usual comparison of the poem: then and now. The implication is that the late wars in general (or Waterloo in particular) are like the siege of Ismail. They are battles fought by dynastic corruption in pursuit of personal ambition, of pay, pension, title, 'corruption', and at the expense of free peoples. Byron rewrites the traditional epic panegyric of arms and arts to attack

> sovereigns who employ
> All arts to teach their subjects to destroy.

(VIII. 92)

The alternative is the just war, of which Marathon was a favoured type. The poet praises the struggles of a nation in 'defence of freedom, country, or of laws' (VII. 40). The names of the usual patriot heroes briefly emerge through the mists of carnage: Washington and Leonidas: 'Whose every battle-field is holy ground/ Which breathes of nations saved, not worlds undone' (VIII. 5). Such examples are 'A watchword till the future shall be free'. They are also safe enough. Leonidas is lost in the mists of time, and even Southey had permitted Washington to greet George III in Heaven. To approach more closely to the present might raise more difficult questions. Were the battlefields of the French republic 'holy ground' breathing 'a nation saved'? What then of the war of the Spanish against the French, or of the role of Wellington in the Peninsula? If Byron had fought in Greece, instead of drilling at Missolonghi, the poet might have seen also that the cause of nationalism can perpetrate horrors as dreadful as anything seen by Juan under the *ancien régime*.

The advantage of Ismail for Whig politics is that it is an unmitigated evil. One may simplify history into detestation of a manifest wrong. The Sultan and the Czarina are so obviously alien tyrants that no reader will hesitate to condemn *both* sides for no British interest is involved. The war is 'philosophised' as part of the recurrent pattern of history which involves Ajax and Achilles, Tamerlane and Ghengis Khan, Caesar and Suvarov, and thence

Wellington and Bonaparte. Typical is the invocation before the assault:

> Oh! ye great bulletins of Bonaparte!
> Oh! ye less grand long lists of killed and wounded! . . .
> Oh, Caesar's Commentaries! now impart ye,
> Shadows of glory! . . .
>
> (VII. 82)

In the attack on false glory, the contemporary political argument is presented thus as part of a general condemnation which no reader of feeling would wish to deny. Similar allusions flicker elsewhere in the text, sometimes in a phrase, when a term of British politics is applied to the Sultan—'passive obedience'—which likens the tyrant Turk to all Tories. At another time, more clearly pointing the historical connection, Byron reminds the reader that Catherine's son's son is the contemporary 'legitimate' Alexander. One sees the way Courts then and now remain 'leagued' against freedom (VI. 93 and VII. 79). Once recognise the continual presence of innuendo at work then a figure like Potemkin is both the historic individual and a type of avaricious commander whose like can still be found. He was

> a great thing in days
> When homicide and harlotry made great;
> If stars and titles could entail long praise,
> His glory might half equal his estate.
>
> (VII. 37)

As so often in this poem one detects the general influence of Pope and Scriblerian criticism of the Walpole system of false greatness and corruption, but the past tense of the verb 'made' is manifestly ironic. The emphasis that so it was *then* draws attention to *now*.

This kind of attack, arising out of revulsion at the siege, at times suggests a potential radicalisation of Byron, for the entire ruling caste seems to be involved. The progression of the following stanza is typical from its general satire on the false glory of war, to its condemnation of the sufferings of the poor (in Ireland) at the hands of the aristocracy:

Think how the joys of reading a Gazette
Are purchased by all agonies and crimes:
Or if these do not move you, don't forget
Such doom may be your own in after times.
Meantime the taxes, Castlereagh, and debt,
Are hints as good as sermons, or as rhymes.
Read your own hearts and Ireland's present story,
Then feed her famine fat with Wellesley's glory.

(VIII. 125)

The demotic tone reminds one of Byron's association with Hazlitt and Hunt (and of *The Age of Bronze*). The argument that aristocrats like the Wellesleys grow great by war, and the people starve, might be 'constructively' read with an internationalist and Marxist message.

This, however, is not the main thrust of the political satire in establishing the analogy of Ismail with Waterloo. Consider the more extended attack on Wellington—'Called "Saviour of the Nations"—not yet saved,/ And Europe's liberator—still enslaved' (IX. 5).

Though Britain owes (and pays you too) so much,
Yet Europe doubtless owes you greatly more:
You have repaired Legitimacy's crutch,—
A prop not quite so certain as before:
The Spanish, and the French, as well as Dutch,
Have seen, and felt, how strongly you *restore;*
And Waterloo has made the world your debtor—
(I wish your bards would sing it rather better).

You are 'the best of cut-throats': do not start;
The phrase is Shakespeare's, and not misapplied:—
War's a brain-spattering, windpipe-slitting art,
Unless her cause by Right be sanctified.
If you have acted *once* a generous part,
The World, not the World's masters, will decide,
And I shall be delighted to learn who,
Save you and yours, have gained by Waterloo?

(IX. 3-4)

The distinction Byron is drawing is between the old-style masters of the world who fight wars for dynastic power, and those who would fight on behalf of national liberation. It is not between masters as exploiters of the working class and an exploited proletariat. The allusion to France may be used to illustrate the point, and is one which the context of the age makes particularly provocative.

One must return briefly to familiar Whig territory. In the 1790s, the Foxites had condemned the Brunswick manifesto as an instance of the barbarous intrusion of monarchs upon the right of the French nation to choose its own form of government. Thence, in the Hundred Days, the line had been that the French had a right to elect Napoleon as a constitutional monarch as the British had chosen William III. Pacific non-interference was the correct policy. Waterloo was a disaster.[12]

The strategy of linking Waterloo with Ismail enables Byron to choose his ground of attack. As a supporter of the Holland House line on the Hundred Days he would be well aware, however, of how 'the World's masters' refuted the Napoleonists' criticism. Of course the analogy with William III was correct! The administration boasted of it. Had not William fought the tyrant Louis XIV and French ambition? The cause 'sanctified' by 'Right' (Byron's words) was that of the *vindex securitas Europae, assertor libertatis Britanniae*. The freedom of the nation and of the Constitution was guaranteed by Waterloo against Napoleon's lust for 'universal empire and military despotism'. The real 'friend of liberty' would rejoice at 'the destruction of detestable and slavish principles, and in the restoration of social order and representative government' in France. In short, Waterloo was like Marathon—a battle for freedom. The Whig opposition was hoist by their own petard. Their minority vote remained, as usual, small.[13]

Although the vigour of Byron's debunking attack on Wellington and Waterloo is compelling, one must recognise that the force with which he goes forward conceals the fact that there is little on which to fall back. One may preserve 'A watchword till the future shall be free', but at some point watchwords have to become things, to relate to practical policies and utilitarian purposes. Otherwise opposition is merely rhetoric. After Waterloo, Holland House policy had been to establish Napoleon in an English Stratfield Saye as if, after fighting against the British for twenty years, the emperor was now become a liberal country gentleman and an admirer of the Whig Constitution. It is difficult to imagine a more bankrupt policy, or one more fraught with dangers.

Byron now vigorously disowns his part in that. As Catherine to the Sultan, so, in *Don Juan,* Bonaparte to Wellington. That is the analogy of the siege of Ismail. But this is, as Casti wrote, *cangi il mal, nol togli:* to change the evil, not to remove it.[14] If history continues to repeat itself in this way, what sign of progress is there? It is no use looking now to a great man, the new Miltiades. We have seen how a Europe without heroes is left with the ashes of Grattan and an image of a transatlantic Noble Savage fleeing westward towards the Rockies. In this respect the fate of Juan in the siege may be read as a general political allegory. Because he has the 'generous' breeding of the old gentry of Spain, he shows the heroic characteristics expected of his class. He is brave in battle and chivalrous to women. He is also a man educated, as the poet points out, in languages and arts remote from common use. The patrician hero is no more than an elegantly decorated cork borne along helplessly in the tide of events (and into Catherine's bed). The man who destroys Ismail is the vulgar Suvarov, an effective professional soldier whose job is to marshal armies. His not to reason why. Theirs but to do and die. 'Wise men', writes Byron, sneered at Suvarov 'in phrases witty':

> He made no answer; but he took the city.
>
> (VII. 53)

Ismail is the nadir of the poem because of the depressing lesson it offers in *realpolitik.* In the contemporary world the poem's protagonist is not a maker of events, but the victim of them. There is little either that the powerless poet can do which will have any immediate effect. He *writes* that legitimacy is on crutches (newly repaired), but that cripple is quite vigorous enough to deal with the rhetoric of the opposition. The Whig fiasco of the Hundred Days would merely reinforce the lesson of 1812, repeated again in Italy and the failure of the Carbonari. It is this helplessness, the bankruptcy of any immediate, viable alternative, which at times provokes the language of numinous prophecy. One foretells the eventual and inevitable end of the system of Court tyranny without the necessity of asking what the next step might be, or what are the causes or consequences of the change. This is 'Romantic', but it is a romanticism created by the very effectiveness of Castlereagh, Wellington and the Congress of Vienna.

But ye—our children's children! think how we
Showed *what things were* before the world was free!

That hour is not for us, but 'tis for you:
And as, in the great joy of your millennium,
You hardly will believe such things were true
As now occur, I thought that I would pen you 'em . . .

And when you hear historians talk of thrones,
And those that sate upon them, let it be
As we now gaze upon the Mammoth's bones,
And wonder what old world such things could see,
Or hieroglyphics on Egyptian stones,
The pleasant riddles of Futurity—
Guessing at what shall happily be hid
As the real purpose of a Pyramid.

(VIII. 135-7)

This kind of writing is the closest Byron comes to millenarian Shelley. It is cast so indefinitely into the future, however, that one wonders whether the failure to set a date for the advent of ideal republicanism does not suggest self-criticism. Men only talk of a thousand years hence who prefer not to look at today. If that remark appears too cynical, it is supported by the poet's jaundiced attitude to the instrument of change. The force that is going to break 'legitimacy's crutch' is already familiar. It was embodied in the Foxite toast 'Our Sovereign the People'. Now the poet comments, 'The people by and bye will be the stronger'. The uncertainty with which a Whig viewed popular sovereignty is readily apparent, however, in the shifts of vocabulary in a typical prophecy:

The people by and bye will be the stronger:
The veriest jade will wince whose harness wrings
So much into the raw as quite to wrong her
Beyond the rules of posting,—and the Mob
At last fall sick of imitating Job.

At first it grumbles, then it swears, and then,
Like David, flings smooth pebbles 'gainst a giant;
At last it takes to weapons such as men
Snatch when despair makes human hearts less pliant.
Then comes 'the tug of war';—'twill come again,
I rather doubt; and I would fain say 'fie on't',

If I had not perceived that Revolution
Alone can save the Earth from Hell's pollution.

(VIII. 50-1)

This 'war' of which Byron writes does not seem to be now the patriot struggle of a Leonidas or a Washington. Indeed, there are no great leaders, who as 'Friends of the People' interpose between the Court and the mob. The middle ground has been eroded. Nor is the struggle described in terms of a great principle—for instance, government of the people, by the people, for the people—but is merely a trial of strength. So, in the analogous passage in his *Autobiography,* Hunt was to suggest how states change from monarchies to republics not because such a Constitution is chosen on rational grounds, but from 'despair created by the conduct of kings', and because monarchies 'exasperate the world'.[15] The Whig/Liberal alternative preferred in the nineteenth century was 'conciliation' (the word of the Luddite debate), or 'liberal reform' (a phrase of more progressive import) or 'the restoration of the purity of the Constitution'. Byron, on the other hand, sees historical developments occurring only by cataclysmic convulsion: 'revolution'. It is a violent purgative. This violence is the product of his continual experience of the day-to-day frustration of normal methods and hopes of reform.

The issue cannot be discussed merely in terms of ideology. Is there not something odd about the *tone* of the utterance? It is—is it not?—a little flippant. In *The Vision of Judgment* such a manner fitted a satire in which Whig and Tory go through the 'mummery' of parliamentary debate. Here, is there not something evasive about it, as if the writer were choosing not to think through a distasteful process? Thus even the syntax becomes uncertain. What is the meaning of ' 'twill come again,/ I rather doubt'? why adopt the archaism 'fie on't'? It suggests that the poet's very language is out of date, as if Lord Byron was an anachronism. If the lines are flippant, then the mob's revolution is devalued just as much as oppressive monarchs. What the historical process shows is that either kings are up, or mobs are up, and since this is a matter of power, not principle, not much good comes of it. One may readily guess how such an argument might have been extended to the revolution in France.

Byron returns to the issue a number of times. IX.25 begins with 'the people' and ends with 'the mob' and the poet's distaste is more clearly enunciated as he disowns too close an association with those called Jacobins, atheists, radicals, *et cetera de genere hoc:*

> It is not that I adulate the people:
> Without *me,* there are Demagogues enough,
> And Infidels, to pull down every steeple
> And set up in their stead such proper stuff.
> Whether they may sow Scepticism to reap Hell,
> As is the Christian dogma rather rough,
> I do not know;—I wish men to be free
> As much from mobs as kings—from you as me.

Steffan and Pratt in their edition gloss the verse by reference to Byron's letter to Hobhouse of 22 April 1820. It contains the kind of statement familiar from the chapter on the Venetian plays. Although Byron is a friend of liberty, he is the enemy of demagogues. 'I do not think the man who would overthrow all laws should have the benefit of any . . . I protest, not against *reform,* but my most thorough contempt and abhorrence . . . of the persons calling themselves *reformers, radicals,* and such other names. I should look upon being free with such men as much the same as being in bonds with felons.'

The letter, however, sounds firmer than the verse. Caught between 'the pestilence of despotism or . . . the tempests of democracy' the poet offers a line which totters with insecurity:

> I do not know;—I wish men to be free . . .

How different the tone from:

> Yet, Freedom! yet thy banner torn but flying,
> Streams like the thunderstorm *against* the wind.

What was before a positive force of resistance has now become an escapologist's wriggle from mobs or kings, from you or me, by a route the revolutionary logic of confrontational power struggles would seem to deny, and on what principle? 'I do not know', he writes. The heroic champion of freedom is reduced to this!

Nowhere is his dilemma more apparent than in the stanzas which contain what has been canonised, out of context, as one of the most famous of his calls as a freedom fighter, but which, restored to the poem shows the Whig, faced with the mob in power, like Wilkes turning to the other side. 'I was born for opposition', he wrote—an expression chosen by Marchand as the title for that volume of letters which relate to the rising of the Carbonari in Italy. There it enhances the image of political resistance to all forms of oppression. In the poem it voices the cumulative unease, even prevarication, which affects the aristocratic reformer caught between tyranny and the mob, and with nowhere to go:

I was born for opposition.

But then 'tis mostly on the weaker side:
So that I verily believe if they
Who now are basking in their full-blown pride,
Were shaken down, and 'dogs had had their day',[16]
Though at the first I might perchance deride
Their tumble, I should turn the other way,
And wax an Ultra-royalist in loyalty,
Because I hate even democratic royalty.

(XV. 22-3)

The 'weaker side' presumably is the Whig party into which the aristocrat is literally 'born for opposition' from generation to generation. Its role was, as Blackstone wrote, to stand as 'a screen and bank between the prince and the people'.[17] Thus, once kings were down, the party would have to defend the Crown from a new kind of tyranny, that of the mob. All the poet can do is to react against bad alternatives over which he has no control. It is a position of isolation, tending to disintegration under the upper and nether millstones. De Tocqueville foretold the end of Whiggery because its classic role between king and people was at an end. The danger to which it will finally succumb was the 'democratic spirit'.[18] These verses admirably illustrate the process.

Byron's heroic outbursts and his cynical self-subversion in *Don Juan* are interrelated, therefore. They both come from being of 'no party'—using 'party' in its widest sense—and of belonging to a patrician caste which, traditionally antagonistic to the Crown, has lost its historic function of speaking on behalf of the people. Don Juan, as anti-hero, represents something of this rootless isolation for he is separated from his own class among the gentry of Spain, and travelling from end to end of Europe is unable to integrate himself in any other social order, either the tyrannical courts of Sultan or Czarina, or among the people. In the shipwreck he has to restrain the sailors at pistol point; the soldiers of Ismail are brutalised. The shipwreck may serve as a form of political allegory expressive of the general experience of the first part of the poem, for the little society in which Juan has a gentlemanly role as passenger disintegrates, and eventually the hero is washed up alone, naked except for his impractical aristocratic ideals. The fragments of Whig discourse meantime bob about in the text like the fragments of the shipwreck!

*   *   *

The major exception to Juan's alienation is the subject of the second half of the poem. When Juan crosses the English Channel he moves from the despotism of the continent to 'the inviolate island of the sage and free'. He has arrived at the time when the young Fox and Pitt, Burke and Sheridan were at their zenith. He enters a society in which the Constitution of 1688, as yet not seriously challenged by Jacobinism, is guaranteed by the patrician class who made it. Juan is at once recognised by a great statesman (Lord Henry Amundeville) as a gentleman of his own kind; the doors of high society open to him; the wheels of the marriage machine begin to turn on his account. In bringing Juan to England Byron is following the advice given to another peripatetic hero: *antiquam exquirite matrem*. As every reader recognises, Lord Henry's Norman Abbey is Newstead Abbey. The 'exiled' Whig of 1820 is returning to his roots.

Juan, arrived from the corrupt court of the lascivious and arbitrary Czarina on the coast of Britain, at once falls into the usual Whig invocations:

> 'And here', he cried, 'is Freedom's chosen station;[19]
> Here peals the people's voice, nor can entomb it
> Racks, prisons, inquisitions; resurrection
> Awaits it, each new meeting or election . . .'

(XI. 9)

One recognises familiar issues: the freedom of the press and of election; equality before the law. These are matters of recent history: Junius defending the palladium of British liberty; Wilkes fighting the Middlesex election; the Tower disgorging this famous prisoner on a writ of Habeas Corpus. By the date Juan has landed, the most notorious of prisons established by tyranny abroad had fallen. The people had stormed the Bastille. The principles of freedom were spreading. In Byron's subtext lingers the old adage: *Vox populi, vox Dei*—'the rule of all good government . . . truly collected and freely expressed'.[20]

If one were to enquire what Byron meant by that 'freedom' he so often evokes, the definition would include Juan's principles. That cry to Britain as 'Freedom's chosen station' is in the tradition of *Childe Harold,* and must underlie Byron's own hopes as to what Britain could have achieved in Europe in 1815, his complaints of 'what might have been the noblest nation', of its 'decaying fame and former worth'. He writes of

> the once adored
> False friend, who held out freedom to mankind,
> And now would chain them, to the very mind . . .
>
> (X. 67)

He attacks Wellington:

> Never had mortal Man such opportunity,
> Except Napoleon, or abused it more:
> You might have freed fall'n Europe from the Unity
> Of Tyrants, and been blest from shore to shore:
> And *now*—What *is* your fame?
>
> (IX. 9)

Juan, therefore, gives voice to idealistic Whig sentiments of freedom which, in another context, are the basis of what Byron, *in propria persona,* advocated. It is 'buff and blue' principle.

Yet, no sooner has Juan exclaimed, 'Here peals the people's voice', then the demand of the highwayman proves a rude awakening. As in 'The Isles of Greece' lyric one cannot separate the ideal from its subversive context. The freeborn sounds Juan first hears are: 'Your money or your life!' He had been praising the rule of law: 'Here laws are all inviolate'—in practice a pistol is held to his head. The naive outsider's praise of the Constitution—'when *really* free the nation'—is confronted with mundane reality. A rhetoric of 'innocence' founders before the state of 'experience'.

This is typical of the satiric method of the poem. It fits the general argument advanced early in this chapter that the fragments of Whig rhetoric are unsupported by the context of the action. As a political allegory it may be reconciled with de Tocqueville's view of the subversion of the Whig patriarchy by democracy. The people hold a pistol to Juan's head (and in self-defence he shoots the people dead!). Granted this general schematic framework, one may press for further detail. What specific political significance may be found in the particular way the highwayman is presented?

Certain things he is *not*. Byron, with the Luddites in mind, might have represented him as an example of the 'excess' to which people might be driven by poverty. Was not Britain in worse case than the most oppressed provinces of Turkey? *Don Juan*, in general, points an accusing finger at an administration unconcerned at the burdens of high taxation and the national debt—'Though Ireland starve, great George weighs twenty stone'. Godwin, Byron's 'client', wrote of a people 'goaded to the commission of crimes' by nakedness, hunger and merciless laws, and Landor asked, 'is there no generous man who will proclaim aloud that misery leads to vice?'[21] The connection between poverty and crime was a criticism readily available to the opposition.

But the highwayman's cry, 'Damn your eyes! your money or your life!' is merely rapacious. He sees a rich man and he determines to take his money off him. The connection Juan makes in his own mind is with British innkeepers. They see a wealthy traveller and also rob him. In this the lower classes practise in their small way what the aristocracy practises in a great fashion. Everyone is on the make for money. 'Cash rules the Court', the poet exclaims. The social order is sustained by 'a wealth of tax and paper'. Even the narrator himself calls avarice 'a good old-gentlemanly vice' in a mock encomium. It would be redundant to multiply examples of such a common theme. Hence the allusion to the Gad's Hill robbery of *Henry IV* in the highwayman episode. Juan's assailant is 'the Moon's late minion', for which a fuller context is: 'gentlemen of the shade, minions of the moon . . . under whose countenance we steal'. One function of the robbery in Shakespeare directly parallels Byron. It shows how corruption in the state affects both high and low: Bolingbroke has stolen Richard's crown; the highwaymen plunder in their own way. By calling them 'gentlemen' Shakespeare reinforces the social interconnection. Theft is a 'polite' vice..

Byron unites with Shakespeare's theme another variant. It is from the opposition to Walpole and the Court, a common motif of *The Beggar's Opera* and *Jonathan Wilde*. The 'great man' of state is only a high class highwayman or pickpocket who robs by the force of the law (which he himself makes). The word 'great' is satirically weighted in this tradition. Thus, when Juan shoots Tom, Byron comments:

> He from the world had cut off a great man,
> Who in his time had made heroic bustle . . .
>
> Heroes must die; and by God's blessing 'tis
> Not long before the most of them go home.

Fielding is in Byron's mind here, and it is the hard magistrate of the *Inquiry into the Causes of the Late Increase of Robbers,* not the benign sentimentalist of *Tom Jones*.[22] In the novel Tom, like Juan, is attacked by an unsuccessful 'gentleman of the shade'. This unfortunate man, imprudently, but out of his goodness of heart, had stood bail and ruined himself for another. He is driven to robbery to preserve his family. Tom's charity saves him, reinforcing Fielding's message of prudent responsibility within the hierarchical structure of established society. In the *Inquiry,* however, Fielding expounded at length on a *general* cause of theft. It was the old, familiar demon of 'luxury'. The lower classes ape the manners of the aristocracy, and 'the very dregs of the people' aspire to 'a degree beyond that which belongs to them, and not being able by the fruits of honest labour to support the state which they affect, they disdain the wages to which their industry would entitle them; and abandoning themselves to idleness . . . those of more art and courage become thieves, sharpers, and robbers'. He quotes at length the passage on luxury from Middleton already familiar in *Childe Harold.*

This is the political context for Byron's

> Poor Tom was once a kiddy upon town,
> A thorough varmint, and a *real* swell,
> Full flash, all fancy . . .

(XI. 17)

'Poor Tom' is not 'unaccommodated man' naked on the heath, but would be like 'Captain Macheath'. He aspires to gentrification—' a real swell'. As Moore glosses the passage, he is ' A thief of the lower order, who, when he is breeched by a course of successful depredation, dresses in the extreme of vulgar gentility, and affects a knowingness in his air and conversation'. He is thus 'Full flash, all fancy'—a would-be gentleman. When Byron spoke in the Lords of 'the well-doing of the industrious poor' it was not the spread of luxury to the lower orders he had in mind. As Fielding wrote: 'The greater part of mankind must sweat hard to produce [the fruits of the earth], or society will no longer answer the purposes for which it was ordained.' Castlereagh agreed. Wealth would corrupt the morals, health and happiness of the working classes he said.[23] Gradgrind would not dissent.

'I do not adulate the people,' Byron wrote. This episode in which the highwayman represents 'the people's voice' indicates why. The common man is as corrupt as his rulers. If politics is a trial of 'strength' between the Court and the people, taking a pistol in your hand to rob the rich is an appropriate symbol of the process. Would you give a robber the vote? (It was a point Grattan made, arguing for a Whig, not radical, reform of Parliament.) This incident not only reinforces Byron's clear separation from radicalism, it also indicates how instinctively his criticism of the social order is grounded in a political outlook which goes back at least to the 1730s and 1740s—how *conservative* his attitudes are.

Hence the adulation of the balanced Constitution—the idea of an equipoise between the interests of classes rather than class war (for power and wealth); of a hierarchical structure of mutual duties and responsibilities in which 'the people's voice' is expressed not directly (in 'absolute democracy', which is mob rule) but mediated through 'the Friends of the People'. Juan's panegyric of British freedom is not unwarranted. If Britain had once 'held out freedom to mankind', if it had 'former worth'—then it existed in the proper application of the principles of 1688.

Juan visits Parliament. He hears the speakers who roused the nation. The passage is rarely quoted because it lacks the Byronic afflatus of the great libertarian outbursts, but it is remarkable because it is one of the few places in which he defines constitutional liberty. So important is it that it is given without an immediate ironic frame. One must recognise too that this is praise of the *unreformed* parliament, and that the prince so fulsomely praised is the future George IV.

> He saw . . . at the closing session,
> That noble sight, when *really* free the nation,
> A king in constitutional possession
> Of such a throne as is the proudest station,
> Though despots know it not—till the progression
> Of freedom shall complete their education.
> 'Tis not mere splendour makes the show august
> To eye or heart—it is the people's trust.
>
> There too he saw (whate'er he may be now)
> A Prince, the prince of princes, at the time
> With fascination in his very brow,
> And full of promise, as the spring of prime.
> Though royalty was written on his brow,
> He had *then* the grace too, rare in every clime,
> Of being, without alloy of fop or beau
> A finished gentleman from top to toe.
>
> (XII. 83-4)

Although this patrician panegyric does not soar to the heights of Burke on Marie Antoinette, none the less it celebrates the plumage of state: the august nature of ceremony, the proper pride of a monarch, the grace of royalty, the fascination of a 'prince of princes' whose highest commendation is that he is 'a finished gentleman'. The usual comparison is made: in Britain constitutional freedom, in Europe despotism. The usual tripartite structure is shown in place: King, Lords and Commons, with 'the people's voice' here expressed as 'the people's trust' in (presumably) their 'Friends'. From this basis one may expect 'the progression of freedom'.

It is not a complacent portrait for it compares 'former worth' *then* with the image of degeneracy *now:* witness especially the Prince Regent, 'whate'er he may be now' ('a hoary Hal', the poet writes elsewhere). The same implication divides the Parliament which *had* 'the people's trust' from Liverpool's administration now, constantly challenged by social unrest. The stanzas are, none the less, further indication of Byron as gentleman reformer. The poet's imagination is looking backwards to his ideal order, towards 'the restoration of the purity of the Constitution'. However violent his satire sounds elsewhere on a corrupt state, it is in the tradition of a writer like Junius and Fielding. The corrosive is applied to cleanse from within. The axe is not laid to the root from without.

It is a strong corrosive. Compare with the image of the 'finished gentleman' when '*really* free the nation' the portrait of the degenerate aristocracy of Byron's maturity:

> They are young, but know not youth,—it is anticipated;
> Handsome but wasted, rich without a sou;
> Their vigour in a thousand arms is dissipated;
> Their cash comes *from,* their wealth goes *to* a Jew;
> Both senates see their nightly votes participated
> Between the tyrant's and the tribune's crew;
> And having voted, dined, drank, gamed, and whored,
> The family vault receives another lord.
>
> (XI. 75)

That is to be the '*real* swell' whom poor Tom sought to imitate. Like the highwayman passage it derives from anti-Walpole satire. It is a variant upon the 'young Aeneas' passage in *The Dunciad* (IV. 275 f.): 'Stol'n from a Duel, follow'd by a Nun,/ And, if a Borough choose him not, undone.' As in 1740, so now in 1820, the aristocracy has degenerated to a caste of debauchees: 'So may the sons of sons of sons of whores,/ Prop thine, O Empress! like each neighbour Throne', wrote Pope (out of context he sounds Jacobin!). Byron's own formal invective is confirmed by the events which the dramatic action of the poem depicts (it is only the idealistic images he usually chooses to subvert). Compare the 'Paphian' mob outside Juan's hotel eager to sell their bodies to the rich and, in the salons of the great, the marketing of daughters by the Gynocracy to the highest bidder—after which the game of post-marital infidelity begins. A morally degenerate patrician caste devalues Parliament and a free Constitution. By a technique of verbal association Byron probably also learnt from the Scriblerians, the 'vote' is made worthless by its place in the sequence 'voted, dined, drank, gamed, and whored'.

Byron's view is bleaker even than Pope's because the ideal alternative is more constantly implied in the Augustan satirist rather than having to be rescued in fragments. The 'RIGHT DIVINE of Kings to govern wrong' of *The Dunciad* may be compared with the panegyric of *Windsor Forest* (Pope is more Jacobite than Jacobin). The subtle ironies of the Horatian imitations and the use of Virgilian ideals by comparison with George II establish a constant subtext of alternative possibilities from which the panegyrics of the good, and even the *great* and good, emerge as if recovering their natural element. Even in *The Dunciad* false epic constantly recalls the true. Pope is far less likely than Byron to write off both sides in a phrase such as 'the tyrant's and the tribune's crew'.

It is difficult to reconcile a passage in Byron which ends by showing 'a plague *in* both your Houses', with his earlier praise of the unreformed Parliament of 1790. Such abrupt contradictions are typical of the poem. The 'prince of princes' in 1790 is the 'Sultan' of 1820. 'The people's voice' is the foundation of a free Constitution, but it is represented by a highwayman. Greek freedom is a worthy cause, but Lambro is not a worthy Greek. Byron sets up, and he pulls down. One may call it 'paradox' or 'irony', but at times the satirist seems to be biting his own tail. All the 'right' attitudes of his inheritance make their appearance from time to time, but the medium in which they appear is unstable.

Is there a frame of any kind in which these fluctuations might be 'balanced', in which oppositions acquire some kind of reconciliation, where a 'free' Constitution may be perceived in extended operation rather than glimpsed for a moment, and then snatched away again? Is there a social base which justifies the claim that Britain is (or was) 'the inviolate island of the sage and free'?

If it is to be found at all, then Norman/Newstead Abbey is the best that is on offer. This examination of Byron began with idealistic description of the great country houses of the Whig revolution as icons spread across the English countryside. We return to where we began—just as Byron brought Juan back to where the poet belonged at Newstead/Norman Abbey. The country house, as the seat of power of the aristocracy, is the guarantee of the 'independence' of the ruling class from the 'influence' of the Court. It is a local source of reciprocal influence between the great landowner and the lesser gentry in his sphere. When Junius demanded parliamentary reform he asked for more county members (not for a democratic franchise for the industrial cities). He would have extended the power of the owners of landed property. That was the guarantee of the free Constitution.

One hesitates to propose Norman Abbey as an ideal. Clearly it does not have the same function for Byron, as Cobham's Stowe for Pope. The country-house set are the targets of laughter. Then so too, were the ideas of freedom in 'the Isles of Greece' or the libertarian rhetoric of Wilkes and Junius in *The Vision of Judgment*. The simple fact of Juan's experience is that on his Odyssean Grand Tour of Europe he has seen nothing abroad but the arbitrary power of Courts, the slavery they induce, and the crowning carnage of Ismail. In England the social element in which he moves is manifestly different and, with all its faults, better. One might use another satirist by comparison. There can be no doubt that the society of *Mansfield Park* is imperfect and infected, but the intention of the moral corrective of the satirist is, as it were, to 'restore the purity of the Constitution' by recalling the Bertram family to their Christian duties as patrician rulers. No criticism of the Bertrams' wealth is offered, for instance, on the grounds that the West Indies estates are worked by slaves. The ruling order is eventually reformed and absorbs Fanny Price from outside, but it is not democratised.

The idea that when Juan heralds England as 'freedom's chosen station' he is, in some measure, celebrating the political power of Lord Henry Amundeville is very far removed from some of the headier notions of revolutionary Byronism invented by the nineteenth century imagination. Yet it has been shown earlier that the word 'freedom' urgently uttered without context can be made to mean almost anything. To return that word to the dramatic substance of Byron's poetry and to Whig discourse inevitably locates it in a specific time, place, society, class. Byron had owned Newstead Abbey. From what other basis than that of an aristocratic nineteenth-century liberal would one expect him to contemplate politics at home or abroad? There were those who would have offered milord the throne of Greece. If he had accepted it, as an elected monarch he would have followed the precedent of William III and 1688. There was no other society to which he belonged. Nor is there any other society for Juan. In Russia he is Catherine's 'slave'. In France the Jacobins will guillotine him. If there is a chosen station for freedom, where else except at Norman Abbey can he find it, somewhere between 'tyranny' and 'anarchy'?

The recommendation to Juan to join that society is explicit. The passage on the corruption of the 'young noble' just discussed modulates into the famous *'Ubi Sunt'* stanzas (XI. 76 f.) and ends with that advice directly derived from Horace already cited in relation to Juan and Haidée's feast in 'The Isles of Greece':

> But 'Carpe diem', Juan 'Carpe, carpe!'
> To-morrow sees another race as gay
> And transient, and devoured by the same harpy.
> 'Life's a poor player',—then 'play out the play' . . .

The other literary allusion is to *Macbeth*. It may remind the reader that Shakespeare's Byronic hero/villain killed kings and was destroyed thereby. Best leave off that kind of activity and merge with the social world. This is ironic advice, of course, but that term 'irony' in itself tells one nothing. The poet at once goes on to call such a policy hypocritical and (in what tone?) villainous. Understand, *sotto voce,* in a different time, place, circumstance, there might be other things to do. (Brutus killed himself at Philippi.) For Juan, however, the choice is between Catherine's court, the Jacobins and England under the Constitution of 1688. 'Play out the play' the poetic voice recommends. There is no alternative.

The advice is offered at the end of a long passage of political cynicism. The *'Ubi sunt'* stanzas are one of the troughs of 'the age of despair'. The sequence is too long (and too well-known) to quote in full. One needs only to be reminded of the tone and characteristic argument:

> – 77 –
> Where is Napoleon the Grand? God knows:
> Where little Castlereagh? The devil can tell:
> Where Grattan, Curran, Sheridan, all those
> Who bound the bar or senate in their spell?
> Where the unhappy Queen, with all her woes?
> And where the Daughter, whom the Isles loved well?
> Where are those martyred Saints the Five per Cents?
> And where—oh where the devil are the Rents? . . .

> – 82 –
> Talk not of seventy years as age! in seven
> I have seen more changes, down from monarchs to
> The humblest individual under heaven,
> Than might suffice a moderate century through.

> I knew that nought was lasting, but now even
> Change grows too changeable, without being new:
> Nought's permanent among the human race,
> Except the Whigs *not* getting into place.

He goes on to review the political history of his maturity: the fall of Napoleon, the political role of Wellington and the establishment of the Congress system, taxes and the National Debt, the agricultural depression, Peterloo, class oppression, revolution . . . . It would be clumsy to gloss each allusion because the function of the rhetoric is to rush over the territory, to bring together matters major and minor—Napoleon and the Five per Cents, Castlereagh and Caroline—and by jumbling them in a catalogue to devalue them. It is not worth taking up a political stance to each event because, hey presto! it yields to another issue just as rapidly. In his 'hot youth' he cared. Where is all that now?

Yet, paradoxically, the recitation of the changes in the larger context of the poem indicates *Idem semper.* For, if the issues change with meaningless rapidity, the social structure of British society beneath them does not alter. Norman Abbey, as the name indicates, reaches back some 800 years. It is still in place, and Lord Henry is still in office. 'Change', Byron writes, 'grows too changeable, *without being new.*' The political implication of that is indicated by the joke:

> Nought's permanent among the human race,
> Except the Whigs *not* getting into place.

One reason why the Whigs were out of place was the fear of the governing order that the Whigs, as the party of reform, might precipitate revolution. That kind of change, among all the changes, was to be avoided. In that respect one must relate the *'Ubi sunt'* stanzas to the principal frame of *Don Juan* where the battle of Ismail before the French revolutionary wars stands as the equivalent of Waterloo which ended them, and where the imprisoned soldiers of Napoleon's armies look out from their jail on the aged narrator 'perhaps one of the liberals'. Europe is unchanged and just where it was. Like it or not, therefore, Lord Henry and Norman Abbey represent the best that is on offer, and what has survived twenty-five years of tumult unreformed.

To see Norman Abbey as a political emblem suggests relation to that long sequence of country-house literature in which the lord and his estate are used to represent fundamental social and cultural ideals: Penshurst, Appleton House, Twickenham, Stowe, Paradise Hall, Mansfield Park, Brideshead. Lord Henry's house has a fine library, rich with those classic authors which are the basis of a gentleman's education. He himself is a connoisseur of painting and architecture, a man of culture, therefore, as well as a politician. At his social table the lesser gentry sit in familiar converse, a rudimentary democracy founded on the reciprocity between the parliamentary and landed interest. Here, if anywhere in *Don Juan,* one perceives a social ideal implied beneath the comic surface of the satire.

That general ideal—one may trace it back at least as far as Pliny and Cicero—is specifically related by Byron to his own home. Biographical description has long recognised how Norman Abbey is modelled on Newstead, and thus, in so far as *Don Juan* contains elements of a *roman à clef,* Byron reminds his audience of his own (lost) patrimony, to which, one recalls, Scott wished him to return. Appropriately, therefore, the poet seems to include himself as a young political aspirant among the house guests:

> An Orator, the latest of the session,
> Who had deliver'd well a very set
> Smooth speech, his first and maidenly transgression
> Upon debate: the papers echoed yet
> With this début, which made a strong impression,
> And rank'd with what is every day display'd—
> 'The best first speech that ever yet was made.'
>
> (XIII. 90)

(Byron's Luddite oration, then, becomes another transitory thing—words without effect.) At the same table with the young orator sit Longbow and Strongbow: Curran and Erskine, the latter a role-model for Byron once. Although Lord Henry is probably a 'Tory' (for he has served as Privy Councillor) his political affiliations extend to the Whigs, and he values Juan because he stands 'well both with Ins and Outs' (XIII. 24). The differences between the parties are minimal, therefore. One may add one possible further biographical link. If the young Byron is present by implication as a guest at Norman/Newstead, the older Byron is potentially present in Lord Henry. If he had remained faithful to his patrimony, and succeeded in politics, it is thus milord might have developed!

The change of 'Newstead' for 'Norman' enlarges the political signification of the house. It indicates more, perhaps, than merely that the Byrons claimed proud descent from the aristocracy of William I. It raises the issue of aristocracy founded on the right of conquest. Had not Paine argued for the illegitimacy of the present Constitution because founded on that conquest? Yet Norman name and fame is intrinsic in Byron's 'House', and the Paineite criticism is one which Whig politicians easily turned aside. The historic destiny of the great families of the party was the restoration of the principles of the ancient 'Anglo-Saxon Constitution' as the aristocracy redressed the power of the Crown on behalf of the people. The Norman families, therefore, absorbed the Anglo-Saxon values of the race they had conquered. Scott's *Ivanhoe,* for instance, shows the beginning of such a process. Alfred's patriot name is stock-in-trade—so Alfred's Tower at Henry Hoare's Stourhead—and Gothic architecture (by process more symbolic than historical) becomes the sign of an adherence to the primitive values of the free Constitution—so the Temple of Liberty at Cobham's Stowe. Paine's argument that the Norman government of 1066 was still in place would seem historically naive to the patrician order. Lord Henry is not at the head of a plundering warrior band in a castle. His elegant house is the centre of a web of social relationships. The nature of the free Constitution was that it grew by organic process.

Thus Norman Abbey is described as of 'a rich and rare/Mixed Gothic' (XIII. 55):

> It stood embosom'd in a happy valley,
> Crown'd by high woodlands, where the Druid oak
> Stood like Caractacus in act to rally
> His host, with broad arms 'gainst the thunderstroke;
> And from beneath his boughs were seen to sally
> The dappled foresters . . .
>
> (XIII. 56)

The Gothic architecture of the house is in process of 'restoration' (a reformist, not a radical process of innovation!). It is a structure of

Huge halls, long galleries, spacious chambers, join'd
By no quite lawful marriage of the Arts,
Might shock a Connoisseur; but when combined,
Form'd a whole, which, irregular in parts,
Yet left a grand impression on the mind . . .

(XIII. 67)

These are pictorial equivalents of the development of the British Constitution—albeit implied rather than allegorically explicit. Caractacus rallying his host, none the less, points a moral of resistance to tyranny, and the oak's 'broad arms 'gainst the thunderstroke' is an equivalent of freedom's banner streaming against the wind in *Childe Harold.* Lord Henry, the owner of the 'happy valley' on which this oak stands like Caractacus, describes himself as 'a friend to freedom', and his addition 'and to freeholders' is not necessarily ironic. *The Freeholder* was the title chosen by Addison for his Whig periodical, and rightly so. The independence of the revolution depended on property. As for an image of the irregular growth of the free Constitution as resembling Gothic architecture, one need only quote to illustrate a commonplace Scott's *The Visionary:*

It was an excellent old mansion, which had been founded in the feudal times, but by additions and alterations, of which it was particularly susceptible, it had been adapted to modern ideas of convenience; so that, still retaining the exterior of the gothic castle, it was in the inside as warm and comfortable habitation as you could desire. In fact, the whole neighbourhood had long regarded it as a sort of public citadel.[24]

This *is* constitutional allegory, and Scott is defending the Gothic state against rash and radical innovation.

The ideal description of Norman Abbey is general and oblique. The main thrust of the comic satire is to ridicule the faults of high society, and they are legion. The dramatic context of the action, self-evidently, subverts the Gothic conception of a free society just as, for instance, using a Southey figure, or Wilkes, as freedom's spokesman elsewhere establishes ironic interplay between traditional Whig discourse and an imperfect world. One need only summarise the nature of the system as Byron describes it to perceive the tension between the verbal ideal and practical politics. Property, the keystone of the edifice, is secured by the operation of the 'Gynocracy'. Intermarriage between the ruling caste or the *nouveaux riches* is the means by which wealth is secured, and made available to purchase political power. The constant round of 'pleasure and ennui' which is the condition of life in the great house is part of this essential activity. While Lord Henry's role is to act as the head of the arch of lesser landholders—'All country gentlemen, esquired or knighted'—who sew up the borough system of an unreformed Parliament; the women's function is to be both the instrument and object of dynastic breeding, and thus preserve property.

To buy a parliamentary seat requires great wealth. Great wealth must, therefore, flow from parliamentary power to justify such expenditure. The 'cash' spent on the 'restoration' of the Gothic Abbey—and its pictures, library and lavish hospitality—is a manifestation of power, and the means necessary to sustain it. Such ostentation tends, traditionally, to the corruption of luxury, that lust for possession by which civilisations degenerate as the ruling orders sell their independence and patriotism becomes venal to feed the insatiable appetite for ostentation and enjoyment. Hence, according to Volney, the corruption of the laws, peculation in government, unjust taxation, and in the private individual a downhill path of borrowing, swindling, and even robbery.[25] There is a direct connection between the colossal banquets of Norman Abbey and the 'lower empire' described by Juvenal and Persius; between Longinus's classic description of the loss of freedom[26] to the thralldom of money, and the role of international Jewry in *Don Juan* and the clamour of the duns who gnaw at high society's roots.

As for 'the people'—apart from the poacher and the pregnant girl, they do not appear in the world of Norman Abbey. The numerous servants are treated as if invisible. Beyond the horizon of landed property the smoking chimneys of Leeds and Manchester are (literally) unrepresented.

Described thus, the society of Norman Abbey might justify Rousseau's allegations against the *ancien régime,* that law and morality were merely a cloak for power and 'self-interest' (Byron's phrase): or Madame de Staël's that hypocrisy was the predominant characteristic of the age—'cant' is Byron's term. Yet this is the system that is in place, the substructure beneath the political issues that changes from moment to moment, and which survives intact from before Byron's birth to the years of his maturity, shaking off the storm of Jacobinism and radicalism from its well-oiled surface. It is also, in Europe, the freest social order in existence; indeed, to return to Madame de Staël, the constitutional model she recommends. When Juan praised the rule of law, the date at which he does so immediately precedes the great Whig triumphs in the constructive treason trials (*Don Juan* alludes to Horne Tooke); real electoral pressures operate even upon Lord Henry; the very act of publication of a satire such as *Don Juan* testifies to the freedom of the press. The ancient British oak in the happy valley still stretches its arm against the storm. Politics is a more complex matter than stockpiling pistols for the Carbonari. What kind of positive principles are possible *within* the 'free' nation that Byron describes, not conceived in terms of an ideal rhetoric, but rather in terms of practical, empirical policy in an imperfect world, working with men as they are and things as they are?

The crucial political figure is Lord Henry Amundeville, possessor of the Gothic mansion in the happy valley, thus, as it were, symbolic of the principles of the ancient Constitution (in restoration), yet also, as a dramatic character, comically conceived, involved in the astringently funny social satire. His significance is greater than this, for, as owner of the surrogate Newstead Abbey, he is a type of what the Norman Lord Byron might have been, or would have had to be to succeed within the system. Lord Henry is the Whig revolution in practice.

To understand Lord Henry one needs a touchstone. Because his politics are not our politics (whatever ours are), it is easy to slide into facile criticism. To read Byron on Peterloo again may be a salutary check, or in praise of the unreformed Parliament. There is a great divide between us and the past. One must remember that many sincerely dreaded democracy and supported the influence of property on elections. Moreover, there were excellent reasons for holding such views. History is the record of people who do not share our opinions.

A contemporary 'benchmark' for comparison with Lord Henry, therefore, would be useful. Elizabeth Boyd has already noted his similarity to Lord Holland, William Lamb, and even Wedderburn Webster, but to pursue so many quarries so late might prove distracting. Lord Oldborough, in Maria Edgeworth's political novel *Patronage,* is offered instead as a character conceived as a representative type, and valuable as an example for that reason.[27]

For the last time in this study brief digression will seek to establish the language and attitudes of a Regency Whig writer. Since the novel is little known (undeservedly), it is summarised where appropriate.

Patronage is described as Whig for, in the novel, freedom is guaranteed by the landholding classes of England who stand as a buffer opposed both to despotism (as seen abroad) and to mob violence (at home). The tale centres on two propertied families. The ideal figures are the Percys who first lose their estates (to a bad landlord), but then are happily 'restored' to their property and 'dominions' to the delight of their contented tenantry and servants who celebrate their masters 'in due order'. The restorative process is achieved by force of law, and the lawyer son who saves the family inheritance is appropriately named Alfred. The Whig ideology is impeccable.

The active political figure in the novel is the great Minister, Lord Oldborough, and it is he who shares many of Lord Henry's characteristics. His own source of independent power is his great estate at Clermont Park (another Norman inheritance), and his name obviously alludes to the influence of property upon elections. The government to which he belongs inclines to those absolutist, aristocratic principles which the opposition called 'Tory'.

> The ministers agreed in an over-weening love of aristocracy, and in an inclination toward arbitrary power; they agreed in a hatred of innovation; they agreed in the principle that free discussion should be discouraged, and that the country should be governed with a high and strong hand. (I. 127)

This credo may serve to place Lord Henry on the political spectrum. He not only welcomes Whigs like Curran and Erskine to his table, but he is far more flexible than Lord Oldborough's ministerial colleagues in the face of 'innovation'. Addressing the landed interest Lord Henry states:

> He was 'free to confess' . . .
> That innovation's spirit now-a-days
> Had made more progress than for the last century.
> (XVI. 73)

He leaves the statement suspended thus with 'freedom', 'progress' and 'innovation' established as ingredients of his vocabulary, but not necessarily linked to any specific scheme of change, which he is equally free to disown. One may laugh at the shuffle, but it is not intrinsically different from the ambiguity of Byron's frame-breaker letter to Lord Holland. The point is that Lord Henry might go either way, whereas Lord Oldborough's Tory cabinet is firmly entrenched in reactionary attitudes.

Edgeworth's great Minister, however, is a man of integrity and principle. He is a faithful servant of his constitutional monarchy, dedicated to the patriot service of the state, not dependent, and not corrupt in the exercise of patronage (the evil alternative is shown in the fall of the family of the Falconers). The nature of the political system demands that he consider conflicting interests to survive; that he exercise power on behalf of clients through his control of the borough system and the gift of place, but his principle is to reward merit. That is what the system allows him. In real life he would have brought in Burke. Thus he best serves the good of the throne and the people, and secures both the gratitude of the king, and the praise of the ideal Whig, Mr Percy: 'notwithstanding the corruption of so many has weakened all faith in public virtue, I believe in the existence of . . . men who devote themselves to the service of their country', (II. 401). When Byron describes Lord Henry's service at Court, the description he employs is not intrinsically different. The great lord is 'Always a Patriot, and sometimes a Placeman' (XIII. 21). There is comic irony in Byron's description, absent in Edgeworth, but it is a fair description of how the system worked in practice. Without the use of place, there was no political power, and without power there is no effective patriotism.

It is appropriate that Lord Oldborough should offer the good Whig, Mr Percy a seat (as Lord Henry patronises the opposition):

it is his wish to see his Government supported and strengthened by men of Mr. Percy's talents and character; that he is persuaded that Mr. Percy would speak well in Parliament; that if Mr. Percy will join *us*, his lordship will bring him into Parliament, and give him thus an opportunity of at once distinguishing himself, advancing his family, repairing the injustice of fortune, and serving his country. (I. 165-6)

The acquisition of honour and the increase of the wealth of one's family are not bribes; they are the proper rewards for public service. It is easy to criticise such a system as 'self-interest', to see the exercise of political power by a Lord Henry Amundeville as the exploitation of the free Constitution for the profit of the ruling class; but Oldborough's offer is by integrity to integrity. Percy rejects it because he will not sacrifice independence to party. This too has its price, however. Percy cultivates his estate, but he is utterly removed from political power and influence. Somebody has to run the government, and Oldborough's use of patronage is the best available.

It is a sign of Oldborough's rectitude that at different times he is attacked both by the Ultras as wishing to become 'the *independent* minister of the people' (rather than of the Crown), and is also stoned by the mob for his aristocratic hauteur. He defies the mob with personal courage, threatens their ringleaders with the law (remember even Wilkes!), and complains that they are seduced by evil men. His judgement recalls that of Byron on the misled people at Peterloo:

> Poor people, they are not ungrateful, only mistaken. Those who mislead them are to blame. The English are a fine people. Even an English mob . . . is generous, and just, as far as it knows. (II. 293)

At the end of *Patronage* Whig and Tory motifs are intertwined when Oldborough retires to cultivate Clermont and classic authors, and discovers a son who will inherit land, position and power, while Caroline Percy (the heroine) marries Count Altenberg, a continental nobleman expatriate because of his antagonism to revolutionary Jacobinism and reactionary absolutism in his own land. He comes to England:

> to live in a free country . . . where he had property sufficient to secure him independence . . . a country where he could enjoy better than on any other spot in the whole compass of the civilized world, the blessings of real liberty and of domestic tranquillity and happiness. (II. 389)

That definition of British liberty might have been inspired by Sismondi.[28] Its guarantee is that men like Oldborough may still be found to labour in the labyrinthine paths of political corruption to serve Crown, country, and—to put the matter directly in Byron's phrase—'the landed interest'. Like Mr Percy and Count Altenberg, Lord Byron had opted out. One risks contamination otherwise. Yet Oldborough is not a hostilely-drawn caricature. His principles are sincere and rational. The king should choose his Ministers; Ministers should control their boroughs; patronage should reward ability with place; great estates should be preserved as the basis of independence; the aristocracy best know the interests of the people who, when well led, are duly grateful; the mob and demagogues must be defied. This is what it is 'to live in a free country'. That is the system described by a Whig writer. There is no alternative.

Using this touchstone—contemporary, sympathetic—how closely does Lord Henry relate to Lord Oldborough as an honourable politician? Byron introducing the owner of Norman Abbey describes him thus:

> He was a cold, good, honourable man,
> Proud of his birth, and proud of every thing;
> A goodly spirit for a state divan,
> A figure fit to walk before a king;
> Tall, stately form'd to lead the courtly van
> On birthdays, glorious with a star and string;
> The very model of a Chamberlain—
> And such I mean to make him when I reign.
>
> (XIV. 70)

It is not an attractive portrait. Nor is Oldborough an attractive man. Politics are not about personal charm. Yet it is not entirely hostile. There are ambiguities which depend upon viewpoint. Pride, for instance, is not necessarily a fault. It is a quality which goes with being a man of honour, of holding high office, of participating in the ceremony of state, of ancient ancestry. Mr Darcy is proud. So too is Juan. He is recommended for it, and Lord Henry likes him for it:

> Proud with the proud, yet courteously proud,
> So as to make them feel he knew his station
> And theirs:—without a struggle for priority,
> He neither brook'd nor claim'd superiority.
>
> (XV. 15)

Byron hated 'rash equality' one recollects.

The description of Lord Henry hints at criticism of the court. The word 'divan' suggests Oriental despotism; 'star and string' could be an allusion to worthless bribes; even the reference to 'birthdays' may recall the Cibberian laureate odes. Yet these are only potential innuendoes suggested rather by the comic tone than by direct allegation. Lord Oldborough would see 'a star and string' as a proper reward for office. Byron does not call it a bribe, for Lord Henry is a 'good, honourable man'. That is not ironic. If Chamberlains are necessary, then this is 'the very model' of an officer of state.

Earlier the poet tells something of the furniture of the politician's mind. He congratulates himself on the advantages of the British Constitution compared with what Juan knew on the continent:

> bold Britons have a tongue and free quill,
> At which all modern nations vainly aim;
> And the Lord Henry was a great debater,
> So that few members kept the House up later.
> . . . and then he thought—
> It was his foible, but by no means sinister—
> That few or none more than himself had caught
> Court mysteries, having been himself a minister:
> He liked to teach that which he had been taught,
> And greatly shone whenever there had been a stir;
> And reconciled all qualities which grace man,
> Always a Patriot, and sometimes a Placeman.
>
> (XIII. 20-1)

Again the ambivalences may be tipped *pro* or *contra*. Lord Henry is not as good as he thinks himself: he is complacent; a bore with his long speeches; not sufficiently aware of the slippery slope from patriot to placeman.[29] Yet he is far less of an Ultra than the Ministers of Oldborough's government. The palladium of British liberty remains the free press. A constitutional monarchy requires ministers who know how to behave at court. If he profits from office, this is not necessarily rampant corruption. It is proper to 'distinguish himself, advance his family . . . and serve his country'. It is mere sentimentalism to see politics *tamquam in republica Platonis* (Cicero's criticism of Cato). He has his 'foible', the poet

189

writes, 'but by no means sinister'. Is that not about right as a description of things?

The finest, and longest, of these part comic, part sympathetic political passages is Lord Henry's apologia in Canto XVI (72 f.), in which the poet's voice and that of the speaker intertwine in an extraordinary catena of the commonplaces of the age. It is worth full quotation.

–72–

A friend to freedom and freeholders—yet
No less a friend to government—he held,
That he exactly the just medium hit
'Twixt place and patriotism—albeit compelled,
Such was his Sovereign's pleasure (though unfit,
He added modestly, when rebels railed)
To hold some sinecures he wished abolished,
But that with them all law would be demolished.

–73–

He was 'free to confess'—(whence comes this phrase?
Is't English? No—'tis only parliamentary)
That innovation's spirit now-a-days
Had made more progress than for the last century.
He would not tread a factious path to praise,
Though for the public weal disposed to venture high;
As for his place, he could but say this of it,
That the fatigue was greater than the profit.

–74–

Heaven, and his friends, knew that a private life
Had ever been his sole and whole ambition;
But could he quit his king in times of strife
Which threatened the whole country with perdition?
When demagogues would with a butcher's knife
Cut through and through (oh! damnable incision!)
The Gordian or the Geordian knot, whose strings
Have tied together Commons, Lords, and Kings.

–75–

Sooner 'come place into the civil list
And champion him to the utmost'—he would keep it,
Till duly disappointed or dismissed:
Profit he cared not for, let others reap it;
But should the day come when place ceased to exist,
The country would have far more cause to weep it;

> For how could it go on? Explain who can!
> *He* gloried in the name of Englishman.

Chaucer might have enjoyed this. Lord Henry, glorying in his independence, yet justifies the profits of 'place' in an exercise to his landholding audience in which he seeks to be 'all things to all men' (XVI. 71)—or, at least, Tories call him Whig and Whigs a Tory. It is like Pitt's advice to Canning in Landor's Dialogue:

> appeal to immortal God that you desire to remain in office so long only as you can be beneficial to your King and country: that however, at such a time as the present, you should be reluctant to leave the most flourishing of nations a prey to the wild passions of insatiate demagogues; and that nothing but the commands of your venerable sovran, and the unequivocal voice of the people that recommended you to his notice, shall ever make you desert the station to which the hand of Providence conducted you.

Pitt, like Lord Henry, is talking 'cant political'. Yet many of the motifs of *Patronage* are gathered here. There are the attractions of domestic liberty on a country estate: 'Heaven, and his friends, knew that a private life/ Had ever been his sole and whole ambition.' Like Oldborough, there is a judicious retention of the middle ground between the Crown and the people: 'he exactly the just medium hit/ 'Twixt place and patriotism'. The loyalty of the commitment to the sovereign is unquestionable, and equally the opposition to 'rebels' ('demagogues' as Landor—and Byron—would say). There is a cautious hesitation before 'innovation', a declared commitment to the balance of the free Constitution—'Commons, Lords and Kings', the usual Whig declaration of friendship 'to freedom and freeholders', and thus a passsionate love of country: '*He* gloried in the name of Englishman.'

Lord Henry is not going to do anything very much, except keep the present system in place. On the other hand, the poet has described him as good and honourable. Many of the sentiments he utters are the proper ones. If that was not so, he would not utter them. In technique the satiric strategy is similar to that employed with 'The Isles of Greece' lyric. There is a gap between the ideal vocabulary men use and the dramatic situation in which imperfect humanity acts. Both the Southey figure (who speaks for Byron) and Lord Henry (who owns Norman/Newstead Abbey) have a shrewd eye on their audience. Both are on the make. But both need to express their commitment to freedom. Freedom of speech, freedom from the mob, the rule of law, the need to justify policies to the people, gradual not radical reform, loyalty to the national interest, respect for the Crown—if these things have become 'cant political' so much the worse for the nation, for what other 'cant', or what other political discourse, is credibly on offer?

It would be false to the skill of the poet to remove the ambivalences which the comic irony creates. One might alternatively seek to construct by extrapolation Byron as a Victorian liberal whose political creed, freed from the contamination of Lord Henry's self-interest, emerges as something like Lord John Russell's. Or turn the thing round, and handy dandy, here is a potentially radical critique of hypocritical greed. 'The rich man . . . look [s] after his rents . . ..What does he want with innovation?', *The Examiner* asked.[30] One thinks of the vituperation of the rentier class in *The Age of Bronze*. Either reading is simplistic. The multivalency of possible interpretation suggests Swift. Compare *An Argument Against Abolishing Christianity*. It is better that men should be hypocritical Christians than atheists, the voice of the proposer argues; if they repeat ideas in which they do not believe this will at least have some good effect on their conduct. Of course, it would be better to live like Christ one understands, *sotto voce*. That, unfortunately, is not possible in this world.

So the retention in *Don Juan,* however vestigially, of the ideals of the Whig Constitution and the great country house indicates that their influence has not yet been displaced. The tension between the ideal of a country '*really* free' and the 'cant political' of a luxurious society is intrinsic. There is no alternative to the Janus-faced discourse because the ambivalence is in the nature of things. However you describe it, the political fact is that Lord Henry, his kind of Parliament, his great house are the system now, in 1820 as in 1780. They are the representation of what Englishmen of Byron's class called freedom and are manifestations of how corrupt that notion of freedom might be.

There is no other society, no other political discourse available to the poet. Go to the Jacobins, and they guillotine the aristocratic would-be radical. Go to the radicals and they would obliterate Byron's class. To be free with them would be as if in jail. Go to Italy, as Byron did, and one belongs to no society and has no influence. To succeed within the British political system would be to resemble Lord Henry. The critic of rentiers in *The Age of Bronze* had been a rentier, was a fund-holder. The Whig, in office, is indistinguishable from a Tory. Out of office he has only a rhetoric of opposition. It is continually ineffective. It always had been in Byron's lifetime. That was the condition of being 'born for opposition'.

Epilogue

In the spring of 1821 the Christian inhabitants of the Peloponnese murdered a large part of the Moslem population. Some twenty thousand men, women and children were exterminated in an act of religious genocide. The insurrection against the Ottoman administration rapidly spread and the Turks retaliated in kind. The barbarous atrocities of the Moslems were graphically reported in Western Europe. It was written of the Christians that the Greek people had risen in a movement of national liberation against their oppressors. Philhellenes flocked to Greece to fight for freedom, a Constitution, and the regeneration of an ancient people. Meantime the Peloponnese and territories to the north degenerated into anarchic tribalism. With war came disease and starvation.

The arrival of Byron on this scene is of no intrinsic importance. He approached cautiously, and with an alert cynicism. The poet of the siege of Ismail had conceived, at least imaginatively, something of the horrors of war; the inventor of Lambro would have understood warlords such as Odysseus and Colocotrones. As a Whig he preferred the constitutionalist Mavrocordato.

Many of the Philhellenes returned to Western Europe disenchanted by terrible experiences. Others, less fortunate, were killed by the Turks. The Homeric custom of stripping the dead continued. Decapitation was a less classic humiliation. Many died of disease—Byron's fate. The Greek war demonstrates how much words deceive by submitting the show of things to the desires of the mind.

Had Byron lived there is no reason why he should have succeeded where others failed. His presence at Missolonghi publicised a cause not lacking in that verbal commodity. As an agent for the London loan his funds might have given him some influence until peculation had run its course. He thought of military glory. Greece was a graveyard for professional soldiers. Byron was an amateur. Ibrahim Pasha had no cause for concern on that account.

Since Byron wrote no significant literature in Greece, the tragic adventure is of little concern for this study. His Philhellenism, one merely notes, derives from a patrician education which saw events in the Peloponnese as if they were a continuation of classical antiquity, and from the usual Whig support for national liberation movements whether in the American colonies, Italy or Gréece. One wonders what he might have thought of the choice by the Treaty powers of Otho of Bavaria as the monarch of Europe's most recently invented nation.

His magnificently generous but Quixotic act of derring-do may also derive from the deep frustration engendered by the success of the Congress system in blocking liberal movements in Europe. If the British government apparently sat in powerless contemplation on the sidelines, here was an opportunity for the heroic individual to act. The end was similar to that of his youthful hero Lord Edward Fitzgerald. He died without acting, but left a name to fame. The aristocratic Whig revolutionary is often a calamitous figure of the times. Byron said he understood La Fayette. He might have thought too of the rootless vagabondism of de Staël. Byron belonged to an endangered species. His party, however, had time to adapt. The poet did not. The voyage to Greece was the last act of resistance to the detested memory of Castlereagh. Canning had learnt the lessons of that master, and modulated what he had learnt. He succeeded. Byron died.

He left the legend; and he left the poetry.

> But I have lived, and have not lived in vain:
> My mind may lose its force, my blood its fire,
> And my frame perish even in conquering pain,
> But there is that within me which shall tire
> Torture and Time, and breathe when I expire . . .

Notes

Chapter One

1. *The Gentleman's Magazine,* CXXXV (1824), 565, cited by Wilfred S. Dowden, 'The Consistency in Byron's Social Doctrine', *Rice Institute Pamphlet,* XXXVII (1950), 18-44.
2. *TLS,* 13 May 1949, p. 1, cited by Dowden, *op. cit.*
3. Journal, 17 November 1813: 'He has been a ''Héros de Roman'' of mine—on the continent; I don't want him here'; to Lady Melbourne, 8 April 1814.
4. *An Essay on the History of the English Government and Constitution* (2nd edn, Longman, London, 1823), ch. XXXVI.
5. G.M. Trevelyan, *Lord Grey of the Reform Bill* (Longmans, Green, London, 1920; new edn, 1952).
6. To John Hanson, 2 April 1807.
7. Journal, 16 January 1814.
8. Dedication, 17.
9. 'Lord Byron and the Genteel Reformers', *PMLA,* LVI (1941), 1065-94; 'Lord Byron as Rinaldo', *PMLA,* LVII (1942), 189-231; 'Byron and Revolt in England', *Science and Society,* XI (1947), 234-48; 'Byron and the New Force of the People', *KSJ* (1962), 47-64; '''Fare Thee Well''—Byron's Last Days in England', *Shelley and his Circle,* ed. Kenneth Neill Cameron, IV (Harvard University Press, Cambridge, Mass., and London, 1970), 638-53.
10. Leslie A, Marchand, *Byron: A Biography* (3 vols, Murray, London, Knopf, New York, 1957), and ed. *Byron's Letters and Journals* (12 vols, Murray, London, 1973–82).
11. *Politics in English Romantic Poetry* (Harvard University Press, Cambridge, Mass., 1970), ch. V which (for Byron) largely replaces earlier studies; Dora Neil Raymond, *The Political Career of Lord Byron* (Allen, London, 1924); Crane Brinton, *The Political Ideas of the English Romanticists* (Russell and Russell, New York, 1962).
12. *The Whig Party: 1807–1812* (Macmillan, London, 1939); *The Whigs in Opposition 1815–1830* (Clarendon Press, Oxford, 1967); also P.M.S. Dawson, *The Unacknowledged Legislator: Shelley and Politics* (Clarendon

Press, Oxford, 1980); Leslie Mitchell, *Holland House* (Duckworth, London, 1980); J. Michael Robertson, 'The Byron of "Don Juan" as Whig Aristocrat', *TSLL* (1976), 709-24; and 'Aristocratic Individualism in Byron's *Don Juan*', *SEL,* XVII (1977) 636-55.

13. *A Defence of the People* (Stodart, London, 1819). The issue is discussed in my edition of Hobhouse's *A Trifling Mistake* (University College Cardiff Press, Cardiff, 1984).

14. *Don Juan,* XV. 22.

15. 'Liberty and Whiggery in Early Nineteenth-Century England', *JMH,* LII (1980), 253-78.

16. *A History of the Early Part of the Reign of James the Second,* in Armand Carrel, *History of the Counter-Revolution in England* (Bell, London, 1857), p. 318.

17. Ed. cit., pp. 293-4, 338, 362-3, 377, 381, 406-7.

18. The commonplace nature of the claim is shown by the assertion being recorded in the *Oxford Dictionary of Quotations.*

19. *The Speeches of . . . Fox* (6 vols, Longman . . ., Ridgway, London, 1815), VI. 16-74 passim.

20. See below p. 19.

21. *Memoirs of the Whig Party During my Time* (2 vols, London, 1852– 54), I.8.

22. *Speeches,* ed. cit., V. 172.

23. *The Speeches of . . . Erskine* (3 vols, Ridgway, London, 1810), I. 263.

24. pp. 267-8.

25. *A History of England in the Eighteenth Century* (Longmans, Green, London, 1892 edn), IV. 311.

26. Kriegel, op. cit.

27. *A Trifling Mistake,* ed. cit., pp. 49-50.

28. Trevelyan, ed. cit., p. 52.

29. Idem, p. 48.

30. Russell, op. cit., p. xi.

31. *The Substance of Some Letters . . . During the last Reign of the Emperor Napoleon* (2 vols, Ridgway, London, 1816).

32. *Memorials and Correspondence of . . . Fox,* ed. Lord John Russell (4 vols, Bentley, London, 1853– 57), II. 361. Subsequent quotation from pp. 372, 368-9, 374.

33. *Memoirs of . . . Sheridan* (2nd edn, 2 vols, Longman . . ., London, 1825), I. 301 f.

34. Trevelyan, op. cit., p. 60.

35. *English Constitution,* ed. cit., p. 318.

36. Notes to *Corruption.*

37. Chs. 14 and 25.

38. Austin Mitchell, op. cit., p. 24.

39. *Parliamentary Debates,* XXX. 896.

40. Earl of Ilchester, *The Home of the Hollands 1605– 1820* (Murray, London, 1937), p. 180.

Chapter Two

1. Byron, *Works* (17 vols, Murray, London, 1832–33), II. 148.
2. See *The Life and Correspondence of Major Cartwright,* ed. F.D. Cartwright (2 vols, Colburn, London, 1826), II. 47 f.
3. *Memoirs of Sheridan,* ed. cit., II. 352. See also J. Landfield, 'Sheridan's maiden speech: indictment by anecdote', *Quarterly Journal of Speech* (1957), 137-42.
4. *Further Memoirs of the Whig Party 1807–1821* (Murray, London, 1905), p. 123.
5. Byron, *Works,* ed. cit., II. 207.
6. House of Commons, 17 February 1812.
7. Samuel Bamford, *Passages in the Life of a Radical* (2 vols, Simpkin, Marshall, London, 1844), I. 148.
8. Coldham to Newcastle, H.O. 42. 119. Sec. H.O. 42. 118-20; Malcolm I. Thomis, *Luddism in Nottinghamshire* (Thornton Soc. Record Series xxvi, Phillimore, London and Chichester, 1972): F.O. Darvall, *Popular Disturbances and Public Order in Regency England* (Oxford University Press, London, 1934).
9. E.P. Thompson, *The Making of the English Working Class* (Gollancz, London, 1963); Malcolm I. Thomis, *The Luddites* (David & Charles, Newton Abbot, 1970).
10. Frank Peel, *The Risings of the Luddites, Chartists & Plugdrawers* (Senior, Heckmondwike, 1880). See also, *The Life of Thomas Cooper, Written by Himself.* (Hodder and Stoughton, London, 1872).
11. *Parliamentary Debates,* XXIII (1812), 951-5 and 1029-39.
12. 24 July 1812.
13. Byron, letter to Hodgson, 5 March 1812.
14. Cf. Blackstone, *Commentaries,* II. 27; Scott, *Ivanhoe.*
15. *The Journal of Thomas Moore,* ed. Wilfred S. Dowden, vol.I. (University of Delaware Press, Newark, 1983).
16. *Letters and Journals,* ed. cit., vol. 3 (1974), pp. 204, 242, 253.
17. Ibid., pp. 215, 213, 228.
18. J.G. Lockhart, *Life of . . . Scott* (Cadell, Edinburgh, 1892 edn), p. 311.
19. 'Sonnet to George the Fourth, on the Repeal of Lord Edward Fitzgerald's Forfeiture', 12 August 1819: '*This* is to be a monarch, and repress/ Envy into unutterable praise . . .'.

Chapter Three

1. P.M.S. Dawson, *The Unacknowledged Legislator: Shelley and Politics* (Clarendon Press, Oxford, 1980), p. 169.
2. 2nd edn, 1818, p. 49.
3. Howard Weinbrot, *Augustus Caesar in 'Augustan' England* (Princeton University Press, New Jersey, 1978); Howard Erskine-Hill, *The Augustan Idea in English Literature* (Arnold, London, 1983). On p. 235 of the latter generous reference is made to my own works on this subject.

4. Among many: C.P. Brand, *Italy and the English Romantics* (Cambridge University Press, Cambridge, 1957); Kenneth Churchill, *Italy and English Literature 1764–1930* (Macmillan, London, 1980); Laurence Goldstein, *Ruins and Empire* (Pittsburg University Press, Pittsburg, 1977); Roderick Marshall, *Italy in English Literature 1755–1815* (Columbia University Press, New York, 1934); Paul Zucker, *Fascination of Decay* (Gregg, New Jersey, 1968). Quotations are from Roscoe in Marshall, p. 275, Boswell in Marshall, p. 87, Sismondi, 1832 abridgement of the *History,* penultimate paragraph.

5. *The Florence Miscellany* (1785) is important, but belongs to a later phase.

6. I. 113-4, III. 329, II. 150, III. 340, 404-5, 352, 87.

7. IV. 783-4, II. 11, IV. 815.

8. Letter to W.S. Smith, 13 November 1787.

9. 'Thanksgiving'Ode, 1816, st. viii. For the issue 'Can tyrants but by tyrants conquer'd be?', see Casti (pessimistically), *Animali Parlanti* XIV. 44, and Volney (optimistically), *The Ruins* (English trans., 4th edn, Johnson, London, 1801), p. 83.

10. XII. August 1818, p. 7.

11. IV. 90 f. See also III. 19-20.

12. *The Yellow Dwarf,* 2 May 1818, p. 142.

13. 1815 Ode, st. i and ii, sonnets I, xiv, xv, xxi.

14. *Hellas,* 72, *Hellas,* Preface, *Ode to Liberty,* 171-8. I suggest only *some* of the complexities.

15. E.g. 310, p. 771 on the 'repeated disappointments' of the liberals; editorial, 376 'still more at a loss than before to chuse between evils' in the 'stagnant corruption of Courts', and the 'ambition' of Bonaparte, 378.

16. Byron, Note to *The Two Foscari.*

17. *Italy* (3 vols, Galignani, Paris, 1821), II. 459, 206, III. 163 f., 305. See also the conclusion of Sismondi's abridgement.

18. Habeas Corpus was temporarily suspended in 1817. In Italy Lord William Bentinck's promise of a constitutional government in Genoa in 1814 was disowned by Castlereagh as 'Whiggish and revolutionary politics'. Charles Kelsall's and Lord Holland's Constitutions remained paper schemes. See Marshall and C.J. Bartlett, *Castlereagh* (Macmillan, London, 1966), also Hazlitt's 'On Modern Apostates', and editorials *Examiner,* 384 and 385.

19. *Historical Illustrations* (2nd edn, Murray, London, 1818), pp. 196-7.

20. 'Safety sits not on a throne,/ With CAPET or NAPOLEON!/ But in equal rights and laws . . .'. *Ode (From the French)* published by Byron in *The Morning Chronicle.*

21. *Monthly Review,* LXXXVII, November 1818, p. 301, *British Review,* XII, August 1818, p. 5 f., *Quarterly Review,* XIX, April 1818, pp. 231-2.

22. *British Review,* no. cit., p. 15, *Quarterly Review,* no. cit., p. 232, *Monthly Review,* no. cit., p. 295-6.

23. Part 2. III. 17; II. 7 and 21.

24. 514n, 484n; *Historical Illustrations* ed. cit., pp. 424, 466, 468. See Giovanni Foà, *Lord Byron, poeta e carbonaro* (Florence, 1935); E.R. Vincent, *Byron, Hobhouse and Foscolo* (Cambridge University Press, Cambridge, 1949); Andrew Rutherford, 'The Influence of Hobhouse on *Childe Harold's*

Pilgrimage Canto IV', *RES*, n.s. 12 (1961), 391-7.
24. *Historical Illustrations*, 20 f.
26. pp. 322 and 326.

Chapter Four

1. K.G. Feiling, *The Second Tory Party 1714–1832* (Macmillan, London, 1938).
2. Ravenna Journal, 13 January 1821. See also *The Revolt of Islam*, IX. xxvi.
3. Letters to Murray, 31 August and 29 September 1820. For *specific* relation between contemporary events and the plays see Thomas L. Ashton, 'The Censorship of Byron's *Marino Faliero*', *HLQ*, XXXVI (1972), 27-44; E.D.H. Johnson, 'A Political Interpretation of Byron's *Marino Faliero*', *MLQ*, III (1942), 417-25; Daniel P. Watkins, 'Violence, Class Consciousness, and Ideology in Byron's History Plays', *ELH*, XLVIII (1981), 799-816.
4. Raymond Postgate, *That Devil Wilkes* (Dobson, London, 1956), p. 208.
5. To Kinnaird, *c.* 27 August 1819, discussed by Erdman, 'Byron and Revolt in England'.
6. Byron hoped for a Constitution on the American model; Ravenna Journal, 9 January 1821.
7. October 1820; to Hobhouse, 22 April 1820. See also to Hobhouse, 29 March 1820; the radicals should be 'dealt with' like Jack Cade or Wat Tyler.
8. To Murray, 21 February 1820; 'My Dictionary': Augustus; to Augusta Leigh, 15 October 1819. Burke is discussed by Madame de Staël, *Considerations on the French Revolution* (3 vols, Baldwin . . . , London, 1818), II.36.
9. To Hobhouse, 29 March 1820.
10. To Hobhouse, 22 April 1820, and 12 October 1821. Cf. Montesquieu in de Staël, to 'cut up the tree by its roots to obtain its fruit', op. cit., II. 383.
11. To Murray, 21 February 1820; to Hobhouse, 22 April 1820.
12. *Life of William Lord Russell* (4th edn, Longman, London, 1853), p. xiii.
13. See Bamford, op. cit., II. 79 and 96.
14. Op. cit., I. 269-72.
15. I adopt Carlyle's portrait from *The French Revolution*.
16. Marchand analyses the issue admirably in his *Life*, p. 841. Also relevant is John Barrell's *English Literature in History 1730–80: An Equal Wide Survey* (Hutchinson, London, 1983)—a Marxist view of the role of the gentry.
17. My account is derived from Thomas W. Laqueur, 'The Queen Caroline Affair: Politics as Art in the Reign of George IV', *JMH*, LIV (1982), 417-66. See also Roger Sales, *English Literature in History 1780–1830, Pastoral and Politics* (Hutchinson, London, 1983).
18. To Murray, 17 August 1820; to Count Alborghetti, 23 November 1820.
19. To Hobhouse, 8 August 1820.
20. Brand, op. cit., p. 192, who discusses numerous Italian patriotic tragedies, including Mary Russell Mitford's *Rienzi* (1828) and Bulwer Lytton's *Rienzi*

(1835). Miss Russell also wrote *Foscari* (1826).

21. Chester W. New, *Life of Brougham* (Clarendon Press, Oxford, 1961), p. 3.
22. Byron, *Works,* ed. cit., XIII. 234.
23. New, op. cit., p. 113.
24. Kriegel, op. cit., p. 269.
25. *Faliero,* I. ii. 64; III. i. 32-3, 43; *Foscari,* I. i. 240 f.; II. i. 149 f.
26. Cited by Charles Chenevix Trench, *Portrait of a Patriot* (Blackwood, Edinburgh, 1962), p. 311.
27. James T. Boulton, *The Language of Politics* (RKP, London, 1963), pp. 226-32.
28. Marshal, op. cit., p. 354.
29. Maria Edgeworth, *Patronage,* ch. xxiii.
30. 37 and 41. See also de Staël, op. cit., I. 367: 'equality . . . can never signify . . . equality of rank or property'.
31. 'the populace are not interested—only the higher and middle orders', Ravenna Journal, 24 January 1821.
32. I. ii. 301 f., 461 f.
33. Byron, *Works,* ed. cit., XIII. 126.
34. 3rd edn (1823), I. 486 and 467.
35. *Byron's Poetry* (Murray, London, 1965), p. 102.
36. Programme of the 1985 Cheltenham Festival of Literature.
37. Brand, op. cit., 198 f.; Byron to Hobhouse, 26 April 1821. See Iris Origo, *The Last Attachment* (Cape and Murray, London, 1949).

Chapter Five

1. To Moore, 1 October 1821.
2. Byron, *Vision,* st. 86; *Examiner,* editorials, 695, 768; *The Times* in Galignani's *Messenger,* 28 July 1821. The trial is reported by William H. Marshall, *Byron, Shelley, Hunt, and 'The Liberal'* (University of Pennsylvania Press, Philadelphia, 1960).
3. Trench, op. cit., p. 163.
4. Wordsworth, cited Marshall, op. cit., p. 48. The charge was commonplace.
5. 'The Rise and Progress of Popular Disaffection', XXXII (1816–17), 511-52.
6. Ferdinand of Spain, *Examiner,* 639.
7. Junius, *Letter* 41.
8. The speech is recorded in *The North Briton, 46 Numbers Complete* (4 vols, London, 1772), III. 186-91.
9. *Boswell on the Grand Tour: Italy, Corsica, and France 1765–66,* ed. Frank Brady and Frederick A. Pottle (Heinemann, London, 1955), p. 53.
10. 632.
11. *War and Peace,* ch. 1; de Staël, *Considerations on the French Revolution,* ed. cit., II. 340, 379-80, part of her long attack on the 'unlimited despotism and the shameless corruption of the civil government under Bonaparte', II. 362.
12. As he admits in the next stanza.
13. *The Letters of Junius,* ed. John Cannon (Clarendon Press, Oxford, 1978), Dedication, p. 9.

14. *North Briton*, ed. cit., III. 21-2.
15. *The Infamous Essay on Woman*, ed. Adrian Hamilton (Deutsch, London, 1972), p. 71. I am also indebted to Trench, Raymond Postgate, and George Rudé, *Wilkes and Liberty* (Clarendon Press, Oxford, 1962).
16. Trench, pp. 312-3.
17. Anon., 'A Letter to J. Kidgell'.
18. *North Briton,* 19.
19. The close relationship of the poem to contemporary parliamentary debates is explored by Stuart Peterfreund, 'The Politics of ''Neutral Space'' in Byron's *Vision of Judgment'*, *MLQ,* XL (1979), 275-91.
20. 'Notwithstanding all the strong articles in our last Liberal Magazine, neither Government nor people has made a stir; England is still a monarchy, and not even a single change in the ministry has been effected!' *John Bull,* in Marshall, op. cit., p. 202. The ineffectuality of the magazine (and the low company Lord Byron was keeping) were common criticisms, Marshall shows.

Chapter Six

1. To Murray, 16 February 1821—a hypothetical political plan, but cf. Medwin, *Conversations of Lord Byron,* ed. Ernest J. Lovell, Jr (Princeton University Press, New Jersey, 1966), pp. 164-5.
2. *Epilogue to the Satires,* II. 251.
3. Hazlitt, *Preface* to *Political Essays,* discusses at length the apostasy of the Whigs; Cobbett, *Rural Rides,* ed. George Woodcock (Penguin Books, Harmondsworth, 1967), p. 178.
4. Milton, Sonnet 22.
5. *Imitations of Horace, Sat.* I. i. 116 and 121.
6. *Epilogue to the Satires,* I. 8, adapted.
7. *Life of Sheridan,* ed. cit., I. 344-5. I note Byron's positive reference to Grey, XII. 82.
8. Anti-union speech, 26 May 1800.
9. *Quarterly Review,* April 1823, quoted by Steffan and Pratt, 61. 4n.
10. Voltaire, *Dictionnaire Philosophique,* 'Guerre' and 'Tyrannie'; Peter Vassallo, 'Casti's *Animali Parlanti,* the Italian Epic and *Don Juan*: the Poetry of Politics', first published in *Byron: Poetry and Politics,* ed. Erwin A. Stürzl and James Hogg (Institut Für Anglistik und Amerikanstik, Universität Salzburg, Salzburg, 1981), pp. 166-203.
11. *Conversations of Lord Byron,* ed. cit., p. 205.
12. E Tangye Lean, *The Napoleonists, A Study in Political Disaffection 1760–1960* (Oxford University Press, London, 1970).
13. Byron attended the debates in the Lords on French affairs, 12 April, 23 May 1815, 19 February 1816, on which I draw passim.
14. *Animali parlanti,* XIV. 62.
15. 1878 edn, p. 117.
16. Possibly an allusion, via *Hamlet,* V. i. 314, to 'The Isle of Dogs' in *The Liberal,* and to Byron's more radical associates.
17. Quoted by John Cannon, *Aristocratic Century* (Cambridge University Press,

Cambridge, 1984), p. 155.

18. *Journeys to England and Ireland,* ed. J.P. Mayer (Doubleday, New York, 1968), pp. 42-5.
19. De Lolme, 'Liberty, has at last disclosed her secret and secured an asylum to herself', quoted by Cannon, op. cit., p. 157.
20. Hazlitt, 'What is the People?'. The entire essay is pertinent.
21. Godwin in Cannon, op. cit., p. 164; Landor, *Dialogues,* Romilly to Wilberforce.
22. Cp. also the highwayman in *Caleb Williams.*
23. C.J. Bartlett, *Castlereagh,* ed. cit., p. 185.
24. Ed. Peter Garside (University College Cardiff Press, Cardiff, 1984), p. 20.
25. *The Ruins,* ed. cit., pp. 388-90.
26. 44. 6, 8.
27. References are to the Aldine edn, (2 vols, Dent, London, 1893). For Boyd, see *Byron's 'Don Juan'* (New Brunswick, 1945), p. 167.
28. *Histoire des Républiques Italiennes* (16 vols, Nicolle . . ., Paris, 1809–18), XVI. 358: 'la constitution britannique . . . nous a appriser à considerer la liberté comme une protection du repos, du bonheur, et de l'indépendence domestique.'
29. Cannon's description of the ambivalence of the system provides historical evidence of the tensions Byron depicts. Profits from place were uncertain in relation to the costs of office. Op. cit., p. 140.
30. Editorial, 605.

Index

205

Index

207

Index

209

Index